Domesday Book

Alterations & Emendations.   p. 325—

Proper names p. 49

Domesday Book.

Domesday Book:

A POPULAR ACCOUNT

OF THE

EXCHEQUER MANUSCRIPT SO CALLED,

WITH

Notices of the Principal Points of General Interest which it contains.

BY

WALTER DE GRAY BIRCH, F.S.A.

ETC.   ETC.

PUBLISHED UNDER THE DIRECTION OF
THE COMMITTEE OF GENERAL LITERATURE AND EDUCATION
APPOINTED BY THE SOCIETY FOR PROMOTING
CHRISTIAN KNOWLEDGE.

LONDON:
SOCIETY FOR PROMOTING CHRISTIAN KNOWLEDGE
NORTHUMBERLAND AVENUE, CHARING CROSS, W.C.;
43, QUEEN VICTORIA STREET, E.C.
BRIGHTON: 135, NORTH STREET.
NEW YORK: E. & J. B. YOUNG & CO.
1887.

CONTENTS.

CHAPTER I.

CHAPTER II.

CHAPTER III.

CHAPTER IV.

CHAPTER IX.

CHAPTER X.

CHAPTER XI.

CHAPTER XII.

CHAPTER XIII.

CHAPTER XIV.

CHAPTER XV.

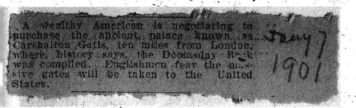
DOMESDAY BOOK.

CHAPTER I.

INTRODUCTORY NOTICE OF DIVISION OF LAND IN
ENGLAND.

THE division of land into allotments or districts, the
profits and produce of which were recognised as
proper to individuals subject to the paramount rights
of the sovereign, undoubtedly reaches back into
remote antiquity, and it is probable that, at first,
very similar conditions existed over the whole civil-
ised world. The title to the land lay solely in the
fact of the presence of the occupier by whose
prowess inimical entry was resisted. Reprisals,
probably common enough at first, soon taught
mutual forbearance, and thus was started the ground-
work of a system which has been elaborated without
ceasing until the present day.

Of the laws, written or unwritten, which affected
the occupation of land in England much is known,
either positively or by induction, from an examination
of the phraseology of Charters conveying land from
the king, or the governing body, to private individuals
or corporations; and much may be gathered from

B

the writings of those who have made Anglo-Saxon
history an especial object of research. In the
seventh century grants relating to the transfer of
land were vague, irregular, and often ambiguous or
apparently inconsistent.[1]

The person to whom the drawing up of the
deed was entrusted, appears to have considered
his duty well performed if he succeeded in string-
ing together foreign words with little apparent
utility, and in many instances producing a text
which it would be difficult to translate according
to the recognised rules of grammar and syntax.
Gradually, to this epoch of vagueness succeeded that
of order and method ; the eighth and ninth centuries
are found to be periods of transition, when the
archaic form, derived from types of transfer deeds
current at a more remote period in southern and
central Europe, exists side by side with the conventional form adopted, built up on models almost
classical in their antiquity, and systematised for local
requirements by Anglo-Saxon notaries. In the tenth
century we find that the form has become with few
exceptions fixed, and after a preamble or proem of
greater or less length, as the caprice of the scribe or
draughtsman inclined, the employment of the important terms in which the legal transfer was contained
follows with certain unimportant variations. This
was the usual form of title-deed carrying with it the
possession of landed property, which obtained in

---

[1] Texts of these may be consulted in the first volume of my
"Cartularium Saxonicum," which embraces all known from
the earliest times to A.D. 837.

England at the close of the tenth and beginning of
the eleventh century; and those who held the land,
whether king, religious or secular corporation, or
private individual, and whether the land so held was
by a lease for life, or for a series of lives, or for ever,
"imperpetuum," held it by virtue of a *boc* or "charter,"
setting forth the manner in which they had become
so possessed and the terms under which it was
henceforth to be held.

It would be, probably, impossible to state the
proportion of lands falling into the four classes of
(1) folk or peoples' common lands, (2) king's or
crown lands, (3) monastic and religious holdings,
(4) private owners' lands. The second of these
roughly divided classes grew out of the first (but yet
in some cases it would seem that the whole domain
belonged to the king, a principle which is commonly
found current among savage tribes of the present
day); and the third and fourth were in the main
derived from the second. Nevertheless the Church
owed much to the munificence of private owners,
who not unfrequently bequeathed land in reversion
to ecclesiastical and religious bodies in return for the
expressly stipulated support of those on whose inter-
cession they looked with so much confidence. Actual
extent or area was apparently secondary to productive
capability; every foot of arable or pasture required
to be reclaimed from forest and woodland; and
from the fact that in the earliest cases the grant
usually sets forth the number of families settled on
the estate it is tolerably evident that land considered
merely as land, without resident husbandmen or

agricultural occupiers, was a worthless and undesirable possession.

Simple and unassuming as they doubtless were in the earliest days of Christianity in England, episcopal and monastic institutions gradually acquired vast landed possessions in proportion as their moral influence, teaching, and example made themselves felt and respected. It was but natural, after all, that to the Church, to which, as to a central point of light, religion, science, literature, education, sanctuary, hospital, and many other humanising elements naturally and necessarily gravitated, a gradual control over the lands in the vicinity of her precincts should accrue, whether as the result of gratitude for spiritual ministrations and moral elevation, and for services growing out of the superior opportunities they possessed (which none but the Church could so aptly confer on those who sought her assistance), or as the result of a dread and awful veneration of the unseen power which she claimed to wield at will.

The terrible denunciations and imprecations which form the customary exordium of the Anglo-Saxon Charter, directed against those who interfere with the provisions expressed in the grant were, undoubtedly, sufficiently powerful to deter any one from endeavouring to annul or divert the possession of the property thereby conveyed.

In another place[1] I have recorded a list of no less than two hundred and forty religious establishments

[1] "Fasti Monastici Aevi Saxonici, or a List of Heads of Religious Houses in England previous to the Norman Conquest." 1872.

which originated in England before the coming of
the Normans. Several of these institutions were,
it is true, poor and insignificant, but the greater
number grew apace, and if we may take the extant
Chartularies of Worcester,[1] Bath,[2] Glastonbury,[3]
Canterbury,[4] and Winchester,[5] or the Inquest of
Ely,[6] as fairly indicating the extent of land in the
power of these respective foundations at the close of
the Saxon and Danish dynasties, it will be obvious
that a very large proportion indeed of the area of
the realm was thus bestowed.

It has been shown by a learned writer[7] on Saxon
history, how the early Church was planted and
propagated in England. One great cause of the
multiplication of the sacred edifices lay in the fact
that in all likelihood, every *mark*, or district, had its
religious establishment, its *fanum, delubrum, sacellum*,
or *templum* (according to the copious phraseology of
the Latin authors), or its *hearh*, as the Anglo-Saxons
in one instance quoted [8] designated it ; and that the
priest, or body of priests, serving these ancient centres
of local divine worship, had lands which had been
gradually acquired by purchase, gift, or bequest, and
perhaps also drew support from the freewill obla-

---

[1] Cotton MS., Tiberius, A. XIII.
[2] Corpus Christi Coll., Cambr., No. CXI.
[3] Bodley Libr., Oxford, Wood MS. 1.
[4] Cotton MS., Claudius, D. X.
[5] Add. MS., 15,350.
[6] Cotton MS., Tiberius, A. VI.
[7] J. M. Kemble, " Saxons in England," vol. ii., chap. ix.
[8] Kemble, " *Codex Diplom.*" No. DCCCCXCIV. A.D.

tions of their congregations. A well-grounded plan,
according to this writer, of turning the *religio loci,* or
local religious bias, to account was acted on by all
ancient missionaries, and wherever a substantial
building was found to be in existence, as at St.
Pancras Church, Canterbury, for example, it was
taken possession of for the benefit of the new religion.
This subject will be found treated with greater detail
in a subsequent part of this work.

As for the land held by private owners, however
absolutely it was held in the first case, when paramount power fell into the hands of a ruler who had
sufficient support to enable him to enforce obedience
in his own locality, the private owner would only
have held peaceable possession of his fields on
condition of giving something in return for guaranteed
security. This, in the days of old, days of unrest
and constant watchfulness at best, days of anxious
dread and unceasing precaution, of sudden invasion,
of cruel and overpowering incursion, of merciless
extermination, rapine, and massacre, could but be a
military service, that is a compact of mutual assistance,
defence, and protection, which, however rude, irregular, and uncertain at the beginning, was not long
in developing into a more regular system in England,
long before the coming of the Normans.

CHAPTER II.

THE MANUSCRIPT SURVEY OF ANCIENT TERRITORIES.

THE BEADDINCTUN CHARTER.

THE division of England into counties and hundreds, as we know them to-day, or even as they
were known in the eleventh century,[1] has been attributed by many archæologists to King Alfred. For
example, it has been recently shown by Mr. H. E.
Malden that there was no southern boundary of
Surrey except the undefined track of the virgin forest
of the vast Andredes weald. In the same way, the
contiguous county of Sussex had but a doubtful boundary on the north, and these facts led to some curious
results in the work of the commissioners. Dr. Pauli,
the author of the excellent " Life of Alfred the Great,"
however, considerably qualifies the general idea in
stating that " it may be supposed that Alfred, after
the spoliation of public and private property, during
the Danish incursions, re-arranged the boundaries,
although the assertion that he caused a formal survey
and measurement of the lands to be made, seems to
have been taken from the History of the Domesday
Book.[2]" Kemble, in like manner, in his masterly

---

[1] Not quite the same thing, for boundaries in many instances
could not have been so well defined as they now are.

[2] Translation by Thorpe (Bohn's Series), p. 120.

work on the "Saxons in England," in a chapter
which treats of the territorial organisation in *marks*,
and in the *ga* or *scir*, based upon the natural con-
formation of the country, of the soil and usufruct of
its produce, with their separate jurisdictions and
executive officers, shows the gradual development of
areal distinction to have been of far higher antiquity.
He says,[1] "Looking to the permanent character of
land divisions, and assuming that our present hundreds nearly represent the original in number and
extent, we might conclude that if in the year 400
Kent was first divided, Thanet then contained only
one hundred heads of houses, or *hydes*, upon three
thousand acres of cultivated land, while in the time
of Beda, three centuries later, it comprised six hundred families or *hides*, upon eighteen thousand acres.
It is a common saying that we owe the institution of
shire, tithing, and hundred divisions, to Ælfred. Stated
in so broad a manner as this, I am compelled to deny
the assertion. . . . . Not one word in corroboration of it is to be found in Asser or any other contem-
poraneous authority, and there is abundant evidence
that the system existed long before he was born, not
only in other German lands, but even among our-
selves." Kemble continues, however, to show that
he is unwilling to declare the tradition to be absolutely without foundation, and thinks it probable that,
after the confusion and devastation which were the
natural outcome of the Danish wars, the king was
compelled to make a new muster or regulation of

[1] Birch's Edit., vol. i., p. 247.

the tithings, and even in some cases to cause a fresh
territorial division to be established on the new
principle. But the strongest argument against all
this, is the total silence of all contemporary writers.
It has, however, been long well known[1] that previous
to the erection of counties, or even of conglomera-
tions of contiguous hundreds, there were territorial
divisions of large or small areas, within the great
kingdoms, neither well known by name nor well
defined by strict boundaries, and probably for the
most part isolated from each other by the neutral
forest lands which allowed them thereafter that elas-
ticity which enabled them to subsist, for a time at
least, unaltered. These were, so to speak, *oases* of
primæval civilisation and human habitation, under
the shadow of the almost universal forest with which
pre-historic England was clad. How these territories
first sprang into being it is difficult at this distant
period to decide. Nor is it necessary for the scope
of the present work to enquire too deeply:

No doubt various causes operated in many ways
towards the clustering of individual families. Inter-
marriages, the attraction of a heroic name, the
subjugation of the weak by the strong, and many
other ways readily suggest themselves to our consideration as anciently operating in this way. To
them succeeds the transitional or secondary period,
when the groups of homesteads and villages, thus
united each to other by friendship, kinship, or accident

[1] *Journal of the British Archæological Association,* vol. xl.,
1884. "An Unpublished MS. List of some early Territorial
Names in England," by W. de G. Birch.

of locality, made themselves feared and recognised abroad, and for convenience's sake, received peculiar and appropriate designations by which each group thus constituted was known to those who had need of its intercourse, availed themselves of its protection, or dreaded its ravages. We may, by means of a record which was accidently discovered only two years ago, trace even in present names the echoes of the early names of some at least of these primæval areas. The manuscript to which I refer is of the late tenth or early eleventh century, written on a fly leaf in a copy of Ælfric's "Latin Grammar," for the use of Anglo-Saxon students. Spelman, Kemble, Gale, Pearson, and other writers, have printed somewhat similar lists of territorial names from late and faulty Latin translations of this Anglo-Saxon text, but of all the manuscripts which I have been able to trace, the one here referred to in the British Museum Harley MS. 3,271, folio 6 *b*, is the oldest and best text, and indeed the only Anglo-Saxon copy. From certain indications, which tell their own tale, such as, for example, the division of words at the wrong place, there can be little doubt that this MS. is a copy of an older one now lost. It appears to represent, in its first place, a memorandum written down, about the seventh or eighth century, by an early surveyor or commissioner, of those tribes and their territorial or political areas, by no means all in existence in his day, with which he was more or less personally acquainted. In the Venedotian Code (printed among the ancient laws of Wales, in the Record Commission, 1841, p. 185, 8vo edit.), a manuscript written after the year 1080, but containing the ancient laws of Wales, said to have been collected by Howel Dda, or Howel the Good, in or about the year 743, a date which would correspond with the origin of this MS. of ancient territories, Mr. O. C. Pell, in a paper recently read before the Royal Historical Society, finds it recorded that " Dyvnwal, son of Clydno," *measured the whole of Great Britain* "before the Crown of London and Supremacy of this Island were seized by the Saxons." This present MS. may therefore be founded on a copy of Dyvnwal's Measurement, with some additional paragraphs introduced at the end referring to the Saxon kingdoms. The list of territories is not complete. Those who are familiar with the History of England previous to the coming of the Normans, will not fail to observe the omission of some of the well-known historical tribes and districts, as the Magesætæ, the Meonwaras, and so forth. Nevertheless, as it stands, and as a transcript of an older document, it is a valuable record of Saxon history, and, as a forerunner of the Domesday survey, claims considerable attention at our hands.

The contents are as follows, when reduced to a table :—

1.	Myrcna landes	... ...	30,000 hides.
2.	Wocen sætna	... ...	7,000 ,,
3.	Westerna ...	... ...	7,000 ,,
4.	Pecsætna ...	... ...	1,200 ,,
5.	Elmed sætna	... ...	600 ,,
6.	Lindes farona, with Hæth-feldland ...	... ...	7,000 ,,
7.	Suth Gyrwa	... ...	600 ,,

Table continued —

8.	North Gyrwa	...	...	600 hides.
9.	East Wixna...	...	...	300 ,,
10.	West Wixna	...	...	300 ,,
11.	Spalda	...	...	600 ,,
12.	Wigesta	...	...	900 ,,
13.	Herefinna ...	...	...	1,200 ,,
14.	Sweordora ...	...	...	300 ,,
15.	Gifla	...	...	300 ,,
16.	Hicca	...	...	300 ,,
17.	Wiht gara ...	...	...	600 ,,
18.	Nox gaga ...	...	...	5,000 ,,
19.	Oht gaga ...	...	...	2,000 ,,
20.	Hwinca	...	...	7,000 ,,
21.	Ciltern sætna	...	...	4,000 ,,
22.	Hendrica ...	...	...	3,500 ,,
23.	Unecung ga	...	...	1,200 ,,
24.	Aro sætna ...	...	...	600 ,,
25.	Færpinga ...	...	...	300 ,,
26.	Bilmiga	...	...	600 ,,
27.	Widerigga ...	...	...	600 ,,
28.	East willa ...	...	...	600 ,,
29.	West willa ...	...	...	600 ,,
30.	East Engle...	...	...	30,000 ,,
31.	East Sexena	...	...	7,000 ,,
32.	Cantwarena	...	...	15,000 ,,
33.	Suth Sexena	...	...	7,000 ,,
34.	West Sexena	...	...	10,000 ,,

Of these we may fairly conjecture the following localities:—

1. Mercia, or the eight counties of Gloucester,

Worcester, Hereford, Warwick, Oxford, Cheshire, Stafford, and Salop.

2. The Hundred of Woking. The parish of Woking, the principal and eponymic place, was in Saxon times part of the royal demesne.

3. Westerna I cannot localise.

4. The Settlers, in the Peak land of Derbyshire.

5. The region of Elmett, near Leeds. There is still a village of " Barwick in Elmett."

6. Lindsey, or the " Parts of Lindsey," the "Lindo " of the Antonine Itinerary, with Hatfield, in the West Riding of Yorkshire.

7, 8. The Fen districts of Lincolnshire, Cambridgeshire, and Huntingdonshire.

9, 10. The "Weeks," now scattered throughout Hants and Somerset, or—if one may follow the late Mr. J. B. Davidson—Week St. Germans, and Week St. Pancras, in Devonshire.

11. Spalding, and its neighbourhood.

12. Wigesta I cannot localise.

13. Perhaps the district of Harvington, in Worcestershire, a place signalised by the recent discovery of Celtic and Anglo-Saxon remains.

14. Perhaps Swerford in Oxfordshire.

15. The Yeovil district in Dorsetshire.

16. Worcestershire, the territory of the Huuiccas or Huiccii.

17. The Isle of Wight.

18. Knook in Wiltshire. " Knook Castle," the centre of the area, is an ancient and very extensive earthwork of great military strength and importance.

19. Ot Moor, a marshy tract of considerable extent in Oxfordshire.

20. Wincanton, in Somersetshire, with Roman remains and the British fort of "Kennewilkins Castle." The first part of this word is apparently connected with the "*Cuno-*" of British names; the latter, with the territorial name of Hwinca.

21. The Chiltern range of chalk hills, extending across England from Wiltshire, through the counties of Berkshire, Oxfordshire, and Buckinghamshire, to Suffolk, is probably too extensive a tract for these settlers; but there are two parishes of Chiltern or Chittern, in Wiltshire, which may be identical with it. That of Chiltern All Saints is situated near the River Wiley, and in the vicinity of Knook Castle, referred to at No. 18 above.

22. Hendrica is of difficult identification, but if it may be referred to "Hendre," that form enters into the composition of many places in the West. On the other hand, Henbury, near Bristol, may satisfy the conditions. The union of the British *hen* or *hean* (old), with the Saxon *burg* or *byrig*, is analogous to that found in other names, as, for example, in Glastonbury.

23. Unecung-ga may be the *ga*, or district, about the River Onny, which is a small stream in Shropshire, running into the River Teme.

24. The Aro-sætna point to the lands on the confines of the River Arrow in Warwick.

25. For Færpinga I cannot suggest any explanation.

26. Bilmiga, of which a variant Birminga is found

in the British Museum, Hargrave MS., 313, f. 15 b.
(a late copy of this early list of territories), may
possibly refer to Birmingham, the oldest seat of the
iron manufacture in England although unnoticed in
our ancient records, but I am unwilling to speak
positively as to its identity. The " Billings," on the
other hand, like the " Weeks," now represent a dis-
integrated, or never unified, clan, who have left
traces of their eponymic hero among the place names
of many midland towns and villages scattered over
the realm, from Yorkshire and Lincolnshire to Sussex,
from Salop to Kent. · Far away to the north the
parish of Bellingham, in Northumberland, of the
enormous extent of upwards of twenty thousand two
hundred acres, chiefly moorland, on the River Tyne,
with numerous remains of ancient circular earth-
works and fortifications in its vicinage, offers itself to
reasonable consideration in respect of this ancient
place name.

27. Witheridge Hundred in Devonshire, full of
ancient vestiges, may be conjectured.

28, 29. The neighbourhood of the River Wylye,
or Wily, an affluent of the great River Avon, and
eponymic of the county of Wilts, is probably that
here indicated by East and West Willa. The extensive district watered by this ancient river glitters with
diverse evidences of early settlement.

30. The remaining territories of the East Saxons;
31. The East Saxons; 32. The men of Kent; 33.
The South Saxon; and 34, The West Saxons, present no difficulty; but we cannot say that their early
extent, given in the manuscript, is in agreement with

the sites ascribed in later times to these respective designations. It is not unlikely that these entries have been interpolated by the scribe who copied the original list into the blank page of Ælfric's Grammar, with a view of bringing a list, which he knew to be antiquated, up to the standard of his own times.

Among the earliest forms of survey of individual holdings, which appear to foreshadow the comprehensive work of the Domesday, is that of the land of Beaddinctun (which Kemble and Thorpe, following him, identify with Bedhampton, in Hampshire, called Betametone in Domesday, but I see no reason why it should not be Beddington in Surrey),[1] contained in a letter of Denewulf, Bishop of Winchester, to King Edward, about A.D. 901-908. The Latin text is a faulty translation of the Anglo-Saxon original: both copied into the celebrated. "Codex Wintoniensis," or Anglo-Saxon chartulary of· Winchester Cathedral, British Museum, additional MS. 15,350, f. 96 b. The Anglo-Saxon text is as follows :—

"Ic DENEWULF bisceop kyðæ EADWARDE kyninge minum hlafurdæ ymb þæt land on BEADDINCTUNE þæ ðu mæ firmdig to pæræ ðæt íc þæ lendæ. þonnæ min leof hæbbe ic nú æt ðam hipum fundæn on Wintæ ceastræ gæ æt gieldran gæ æt .giengran þæt híe mæ mid ealræ æstæ unnun his mæ ðæt to bociunnæ þinnæ deg spuðæ to brucannæ spuðum to lænannæ ðæ þæ leofust bið.

Þonne his þæs lonðæs hund seofontig hida . and is

---

[1] Both these sites are in the diocese of Winchester.
[2] "Cartularium Saxonicum," No. 618, 619.

nu eall ge þæred and ðu hit æst min laford mæ to læt.
þu þæs hit ierfælæas and mið æðnum folce aburod.
And ic ðu sælf þæt ierfæ to ge strindæ. þæt ðær mon
siððun bi þæs. And þæ his þæ nú spyðæ eadmod-
licæ unnon. Þonnæ min leóf siondon hipun nu firm-
díge þet hit æfter þínum degæ to þæræ stopæ æft
agyfæn síe. Ðonnæ ís þær nú irfæs þæs þæs stranga
pintær læfæd hæfð. nigon ealð hriðru. and feoper. and
hund ændlæftig ealdra spina. and fiftig pæþæra
butan þam scipæ and spinum þæ ða hirdas habban
sculon. ðara ís tpæntig ealdra. And þær is hund
endlæftig ealdra sceapa. ꝺ seofæn þeopæ mæn. And
tpæntig flicca. and næs þær cornæs mare þonne
þær þæs bisceopæs færm gæ gearpodu. and þær
hund niogontig gæ sapenra æcæra.

Þonne biddæð þæ bisceop ꝺ þa hipan on Wintan
ceastræ ðæt to ælmæssan for Godæs lufan and for
ðæræ haligan círícean, þæt ðu þære stopæ londæs
maræn ne pillnſe. for ðam þe hím ðyncð ynbæ dune
hæs. Þæt naðær ne þæ ne ús God ne þurfa on cunnan
for þæræ paniungæ on urum dæge for þam þe ðæræ þæs
spiðæ micel Godes bæbodd þa mæn þa lond to þære
stoðæ ge sealdæ."

. Thorpe's translation is as follows :—"I [1] bishop
Denewulf announce to King Eadward my Lord concerning the land at Bedhampton, which thou wast
desirous that I should lease to thee. Now then,
my beloved, I have settled with the convent at Winchester, both with old and with young, that they, with
all good-will, have granted me to charter it to thee,
for thy day, whether to enjoy it or to lease it as to

---

[1] "Diplomatarium," p. 162.

thee shall be most desirable. Now of this land there
are seventy hides, and it is now all stocked ; and
when my lord first let it to me, it was unprovided
with cattle and laid waste by heathen folk; and I
myself then provided the cattle, and there people
were afterwards. And we now very humbly grant it
to thee. Now my beloved, the convent are desirous
that after thy day it be again given up to the place.
Now of cattle, which the severe winter has left, there
are nine old oxen, and a hundred and fourteen old
swine, and fifty wethers, besides the sheep and swine
which the herds are to have, of which there are
twenty old, and there are a hundred and ten old
sheep, and seven serf men, and twenty flitches : and
there was no more corn there than was provided.
for the bishop's sustenance. And there are ninety
sown acres. Now the bishop and the convent at
Winchester pray thee in charity, for love of God, and
for the holy church, that thou wilt not desire more
land of that place, because it seems to them, with
reference to thy behest, that God should have no
need to accuse either thee or us for its diminution
in our day; because of that the command of God
was very strong when those lands were given to the
place."

CHAPTER III.

DESCRIPTION OF THE MANUSCRIPTS OF THE DOMES-
DAY BOOK AT THE EXCHEQUER.

THIS remarkable record, we are told,[1] the oldest and most valuable survey among the national archives, was formerly kept by the side of the Tally Court, in the receipt of the Exchequer, under three locks and keys, and in the charge of the Auditor, the Chamberlains, and the Deputy Chamberlains of the Exchequer, until, in the year 1696, it was deposited with the other records in the Chapter House at Westminster.

The " Book " consists of two volumes of different sizes and appearance.

The first volume is the larger of the two. It contains three hundred and eighty-two leaves of parchment, with five old fly leaves at the beginning, and four at the end of the book. Facsimile pages from each of the volumes have been published by the Palæographical Society in autotype photography. A good example of a page of the first volume very slightly reduced may be seen in the *Athenæum*, No. 3,079, Oct. 30, 1886, and in the *Journal* of the British Archæological Association, 1886.

The leaves measure $14\frac{1}{2}$ in. by $9\frac{3}{4}$ in., and are for

[1] "Domesday Commemoration," Royal Historical Society. 1886.

the most part arranged in quaternions of four double,
or eight, leaves, although this arrangement is not
invariable. The rubbed and worn look of the first
and last leaves of the portion containing each county
appears to indicate that the returns for the several
counties were kept separate for some time before
being bound together in a volume as they are now.
All the counties, however, do not begin a separate
sheet, Cheshire for example affording an instance to
the contrary. There are three leaves smaller than
the others, viz. : folios 42, 76, and 81. There are
also pieces of parchment added to complete an entry
which could not be contained in the space allowed
for it. One is a scrap cut off a page already used
and ruled with the lines vertical. Another folio, 81,
has been inserted in the wrong place, for it should
come between folios 82 and 83.

The lines are ruled on the pages with what is
called a dry point, and on the margin, as in many
other manuscripts of this and other periods, may be
observed minute holes made by a little prickwheel,
or other instrument, which was used as a guide to
the ruler. The number óf lines to the pages is not
uniform, but varies from fifty to fifty-nine, but the
writing does not always correspond with the line, and
sometimes exceeds the number of the lines ruled, a
practice which has been thought to have been
followed in order to rectify any miscalculation of the
space allotted for the entries.

The pages of the manuscript are divided into two
columns, and perpendicular lines are ruled to mark
the margins and central space between the columns,

Blank pages, such as folio 126, clearly show the method of ruling, which follows the usual style employed by writers for a double-column manuscript. In volume II., which is of smaller dimensions, the dry point used for the ruling has sometimes cut through the vellum, or caused it to crack.

The writing is very clear and beautiful, the letters being all distinctly and separately formed, the only difficulty which is experienced in reading would arise from the continual abbreviations which, although very numerous indeed, are very simple in character, and, except in rare instances, no ambiguity could arise even on this score. In another place[1] will be found a list of the principal abbreviations and contractions.

There is no ornamentation or ornamental initial letter, and in this respect the Domesday Book differs from the great majority of manuscripts; but the name of the county under description is written at the head of each page in red ink, and a dash or stroke of the same coloured ink is employed to distinguish capital letters in the text. The names of places are also distinguished by a red line running through the middle of the letters, which must not be considered as cancelling these words.

In several places additions have been written on the side and bottom margins, the place at which they are to be inserted being indicated by marks, and there are erasions and alterations, as for example at folios 63, 64, 67, 91.

The account of Domesday Book issued by the Royal Historical Society, from which the foregoing

[1] See p. 323.

remarks are mainly derived, states that the same scribe was not employed throughout the surveys of Derbyshire and Yorkshire, and the "Feodum Rotberti de Bruis," in folio 332*b*, being noticeably in a different handwriting. At the County of Lincoln, however, the original hand recurs.

The very character of the handwriting, which is technically called "set minuscules," has been said to bear but little resemblance to either the bookhand or the chancery charter hand of the period, and may with great probability have been introduced by some of the foreign ecclesiastics, for writing was like other acquirements, almost exclusively confined to the churchmen who figured in the court of William the Conqueror. Some have thought that the handwriting resembles an Italian hand; and if this conjecture be correct, that the scribes were, indeed, of that country, it is quite possible that Lanfranc, the Lombard Archbishop of Canterbury, whom William of Malmesbury designated with the compliment of "literatura perinsignis," had supervision of the work of transcription, and employed scribes of his own country to execute it.

The fly-leaves of the volume contain memoranda of various kinds and dates, made by the officers of the Exchequer; and an extent of lands, and an inquisition (both original documents of the thirteenth century), have been inlaid on one leaf.

The second volume of the Domesday Book is of smaller size, and contains full reports for the three extensive counties of Essex, Norfolk, and Suffolk. This contains four hundred and fifty leaves of vellum, measuring between $10\frac{1}{2}$ and $10\frac{5}{8}$ inches one way, and $7\frac{5}{8}$ to $6\frac{1}{2}$ inches the other.   The parchment is mostly of a coarser character, and the writing, which is by several hands and more cursive, is generally larger than that of volume I.   The lines are marked in the same way, but are farther apart; the number in a page varying from twenty to twenty-eight, except in the case of two leaves (folios 229, 230) inserted in the middle of the Norfolk survey which have forty lines.   In this volume the double column has been abandoned for the single column.   The varying quality of the parchment and the frequent changes of the hand-writing suggest to the describer of the book for the commemoration, that the volume is composed by binding together a quantity of separately prepared returns, rather than transcribing them.   Just such a method would seem to have been acted upon in the case of the " Exon Domesday " which will be described further on.[1]   The red coloured ink employed is of a different kind from that in the first volume, and is much more sparingly used.   There are also one or two clumsy attempts at ornamental capitals, but they are of no artistic value.

The date of the completion of the survey is given in the colophon to this volume as follows :—

" Anno millesimo octogesimo sexto ab incarnatione domini vicesimo vero regni Willelmi facta est ista descriptio non solum per hos tres comitatus sed etiam per alios."

That is :—

" In the one thousand and eighty-sixth year from our Lord's Incarnation, but the twentieth of the

[1] See p. 54.

reign of King William, this description was made, not only throughout the three counties but also throughout the others."

The survey was probably commenced in the year 1085, and completed in 1086.

The whole,[1] that is, the original work on the survey, the transcription or fair copy, and the codification, were completed in less than eight months, and three of these eight were winter months.

The commissioners appointed to make the survey were to inquire the following points :—

The name of each place?

Who held it in the time of King Edward the Confessor?

The present possessor?

How many hides were in the manor?

How many ploughs were in the demesne?

How many homagers?

How many villeins?

How many cottars?

How many free tenants?

How many tenants in socage?

How much wood, meadow, and pasture?

The number of mills and fishponds?

What had been added or taken away from the place?

What was the gross value in the time of King Edward the Confessor?

The present value?

---

[1] Eyton, referred to by the Record Office desciber of the Domesday Book for the Royal Historical Society's commemoration.

And how much each freeman or socman had, and
whether any advance could be made in the
value?

All this was to be triply estimated—First, as the
estate was held in the time of Edward the Confessor.
Secondly, as it was bestowed by King William.
Thirdly, as its value stood at the formation of the
survey, and it was to be stated if any increase could
be made in the value.

The inquisitions of each county having been
severally taken, they were sent to Winchester, then
the capital city of the realm, and were there method-
ised and enrolled as we now see them. The
codification of the original returns resulted in the
formation of the two volumes.

The first volume in folio contains the following
counties :—

1. Kent.	16. Worcestershire.
2. Sussex.	17. Herefordshire.
3. Surrey.	18. Cambridgeshire.
4. Hampshire.	19. Huntingdonshire.
5. Berkshire.	20. Bedfordshire.
6. Wiltshire.	21. Northamptonshire.
7. Dorsetshire.	22. Leicestershire.
8. Somersetshire.	23. Warwickshire.
9. Devonshire.	24. Staffordshire.
10. Cornwall.	25. Shropshire.
11. Middlesex.	26. Cheshire.
12. Hertfordshire.	27. Derbyshire.
13. Buckinghamshire.	28. Nottinghamshire.
14. Oxfordshire.	29. Yorkshire.
15. Gloucestershire.	30. Lincolnshire.

In the second volume :—

Essex ; Norfolk ; Suffolk.

The book[1] covers, in which the Domesday was bound when it was deposited at the Chapter House, Westminster, are still in existence, and are carefully preserved. In that depository Russian leather covers were recently (perhaps it may be said ill advisedly, because the old covers are part of the life and history of the book) substituted for the old ones. After the transfer to the Public Record Office the two volumes were taken to pieces for the purpose of facilitating the photographer who had been entrusted with the facsimile reproduction of the text by the photozincographic process ; a process recommended only for its cheapness, but completely unsuited for the accurate reproduction of such a manuscript, as indeed all processes must be which require subsequent manual assistance by way of finishing and correcting failures in the action of the chemicals employed during the progress of reproduction.

The celebrated " Codex Alexandrinus," in the old royal collection of MSS., in the British Museum, No. 1 D.V.—VIII., a copy of the fifth century of the Old and New Testaments in Greek, presented by Cyril, the patriarch of Constantinople, as a right royal gift to King Charles I., in 1628, was in like manner taken to pieces by the order of the keeper of the manuscripts, when that precious work was photographed throughout under the direction of the trustees of the British Museum.

[1] " Roy. Hist. Soc. Commemoration."

On the return of the Domesday Volumes from Southampton, where the photography was carried out, they were placed in the present bindings by Rivière, in 1869.

The issue[1] of the Exchequer contains, under the date of Michaelmas, 14 Edward III., A.D. 1340, the following interesting entry relating to the binding of the second or quarto volume :—

"To William, the bookbinder of London, for binding and newly repairing the Book of Domesday, in which is contained the counties of Essex, Norfolk, and Suffolk, and for his stipend, costs, and labour: received the money the fifth day of December by his own hands—3sh. 4d."

It has been thought that this entry may possibly refer to the old cover of the smaller volume, which was, as already stated, removed to the Chapter House.

Nothing is known precisely as to the date of the so-called Domesday Chest, a curious specimen of early iron-work, later by many centuries than the book whose name is attached to it. An illustration of this chest is given in the Facsimile Edition of the book.

In Sir Francis Palgrave's "*Introduction to the Kalendars and Inventories of the Exchequer,*"[2] a "large chest" is described, which bears a strong resemblance to this particular coffer, in an entry on 16th January, 2 Henry VI., or A.D. 1424, ". . . . a coffer of leather, bound with iron, secured by three

---

[1] Devon.
[2] Vol. i. p. 118 (Roy. Hist. Soc. Comm.).

locks . . . . which . . . was placed in a large chest in the Great Treasury at Westminster, also locked with three locks. . . . "

The external measurement of the "Domesday Chest" are, length 3 ft. $2\frac{1}{2}$ in., breadth 2 ft. 1 in., height 2 ft. 3 in. The massive lid measures 3 ft. $7\frac{1}{2}$ in. by 2 ft. 3 in. It was formerly secured by three locks, and a small compartment inside has an additional lock. This chest was brought from the Chapter House with Domesday Book itself to the Public Record Office.

CHAPTER IV.

DESCRIPTION OF THE MANUSCRIPT KNOWN AS THE ABBREVIATIO AND THE BREVIATE IN THE RECORD OFFICE.

THE ABBREVIATIO.

THE *Abbreviatio*,[1] as it is styled, of Domesday Book is also preserved among the Treasury MSS., in the Record Office. It is, as its name implies, an abridgment, apparently compiled early in the reign of Edward I.

The handwriting of this manuscript is a fine example of native caligraphy. The capital letters are illuminated. In the margins of some of the pages are circlets of gold, in which are contained heads, or half-length conventional portraits, and busts, of the chief tenants whose lands form the subject of the pages thus illustrated. Prefixed to the text are leaves of vellum with six illuminations, or pictures, of incidents which occur in the legendary life of Edward the Confessor. These have been executed in a somewhat rude but singularly attractive style of art, possibly, we are told, not later than the reign of Henry I.[2]

---

[1] "Roy. Hist. Soc. Comm."   [2] Ib.

The six illuminations represent the following incidents in the life of the Sainted Edward, king and confessor :

1. Edward the Confessor charging Earl Godwine with causing the death of Alfred, the king's brother.[1]

2. Earl Godwine offers to prove his innocence by ordeal of eating a piece of bread which has been blessed by the king.[2]

3. The vision of the King of the Danes drowned while passing from a boat on board a ship.[3]

4. The vision of the Seven Sleepers of Ephesus turning from their right to their left sides, thereby portending war, famine, and pestilence.[4]

5. The miracle of the Eucharist.[5]

6. The legend of the ring given by Edward the Confessor to St. John the Evangelist.[6]

The reproduction of these illustrations would be interesting not only for the history of the Saint as depicted in mediæval *cultus*, but also as a valuable contribution to the art work of the period, of which there is yet much to learn.

---

[1] "Lives of Edward the Confessor," Ed. H. R. Luard, Rolls Series, p. 271.

[2] Ib., p. 272.   [3] Ib., p. 215.   [4] Ib., p. 273.   [5] Ib., p. 250.

[6] Ib., p. 276.   In the manuscript marginal references have been added, by a nearly modern hand, to the pages of the "Historiæ Anglicanæ Decem Scriptores." Ed. Twysden, London, folio, 1652, where some of the incidents depicted are alluded to.

·THE BREVIATE.

THE so called *Breviate*,[1] another abridged copy of the Domesday Book, originally was in the office of the Remembrancer of the Exchequer. This, the earliest record, we are told, as regards subject-matter, though perhaps not compilation, was removed from this office to the Record Office at the time of the reconstruction of the latter, and is the subject of the present notice. It is in the form of a small folio volume, and still retains its original oaken binding with metal bosses. A careful comparison of this text with the printed copy of the Exchequer Domesday Book in the Public Record Office, and the Exon Domesday, reveals the fact that this is a very partial abridgment. In it, we are told, the *villani*, the *bordarii*, and the stock of *animals*, etc., are omitted. The object for which it was compiled for the use of the treasury of the Exchequer is not very apparent, and it cannot be stated with certainty to what extent this reduction of the text has been carried until a precise investigation has been made between the several records. Some idea, however, of the extensive abridgments and variations may be gathered from extracts of the beginning parts of each

---

[1] Description in an unpublished "Catalogue of Records remaining in the Office of the King's Remembrancer of the Exchequer," printed uniform with other Record Commission publications, but withdrawn. A copy is preserved in the MS. department of the British Museum.

volume, which have been published in the *Journal* of the British Archæological Association, for the year 1885.

The manuscript under our notice appears, from the character of the handwriting, to have been made about the twelfth century; but there is not sufficient internal evidence to determine the actual period of the preparation of the volume. It does not appear that either the *Abbreviatio* or the *Breviate*, were noticed by Sir Henry Ellis when he wrote his "Introduction to Domesday Book," in 1833. The volume probably, at some early period of its fortunes, formed one of the literary treasures of a Welsh religious establishment, and we have been told in official places that there are reasons which satisfactorily account for its appearance in its present place of deposit. It is curious to notice that another Domesday manuscript, the Arundel MS., which is described in a subsequent part of this work, comes from the celebrated Cistercian Abbey of Margam, in South Wales.

A miscellaneous collection of other subjects in handwritings of various dates is scattered throughout the volume. Among others the following :—

1. On the fly-leaf attached to the cover are two short prophecies by Merlin, the far-famed Arthurian Wizard, to whom, as is only natural, a vast number of pseudo-prophecies have been improperly attributed.

2. A chronicle, in twenty-five pages, especially treating of Wales and Welshmen. It begins, *secundum artem*, with the creation, after the manner of a great

many medical histories, and concludes with these notices of the year 1283 :—

"David Walensis cum duobus filiis uxore et filiabus capti sunt fraude nepotum," and 1286 "Combustio domorum apud Stratam-Floridam," or Stratfleur in Glamorganshire.

3. Prognostications dependent upon the day of the week on which the 1st of January falls in any year—a favourite augury in England.

4. A prophecy for the year 1302.

5. A chronicle in seven pages, embracing the period between A.D. 600 and 1298. There are entries relating also to Wales—as for example, the building of Cardiff under William the First, under A.D. 1181. "Edificata est Kerdivia (Cardiff) sub rege Willelmo primo." A.D. 1298, " Desponsata fuit dompna Alina filia Willelmi de Brewes Johanni de Moubray in villa de Sweynese; etas pueri viii annorum." The lady Alina, daughter of William de Brewes, was betrothed to John de Moubray, at Swansea, his age being eight years.

6. On the fly-leaf, before the text of the Domesday, a pedigree of the Duchy of Normandy, from Richard "sanz peur," to William the Conqueror, and other notes. This appears to be in the handwriting of the scribe who has written the body of the abridged Domesday, which follows :—

7. Then follows the abridged Domesday, which is comprised in two hundred and fifteen leaves, or four hundred and twenty-nine pages. The size of the page is twelve inches and a half, by eight inches and a half; and the text occupies eight inches by four and a half

D

The returns, or surveys, are made in the following order of counties (which may be compared with the order exhibited by the Exchequer Domesday) :—

Kent.
Sudsexe.
Sudereiæ.
Hanteschire.
Bercshire.
Wilteshire.
Dorsete.
Sumersete.
Deveneschire.
Cornwaille.
Middelsexe.
Hertfordschire.
Buckingehamschire,
    vel Bokingehamschire.
Oxenefordschire.
Gloucestreschire.
Wirecestreschire.
Herefordshire.
Grentebrigeshire, *vel*
    Grantebrigeshire.

Huntindonshire, *vel*
    Huntedoneshire.
Bedefordshire.
Northamptonshire.
Ledecestreshire, *vel*
    Leicestreshire.
Warewicshire.
Stadfordscire.
Sciropescire.
Cestrescire.
Derbyscire.
Snotingehascire.
Roteland.
Eorewicscire.
Lincolescire et Lindeseie.
Clamores de Everwicshire.
    in Nortreding.
Essexe.
Nordfolke, *vel* Nortfolc.
Sudfolke, *vel* Sudfolc.

8. To this Domesday succeed sundry abridged memoranda[1] of the pedigree and possessions of the powerful family of Breuse, or Braose, and of the

---

[1] These miscellaneous memoranda are well worthy of publication ; they would probably throw some new gleams of light upon the history of South Wales, of which this period requires all the enlightenment that can be brought to bear on it.

Lordship of Gower; as well as charters and other documents relating to the Earls of Warwick in the time of Edward I.

9. Charter of King John to William de Braosa, granting to him the whole land of Gower. To this are added "the boundaries of the same land."

10. The charter of William de Beauchamp, Earl of Warwick, to the "burgeys de Sweynesse," the burgesses of Swansea.

11. A note concerning the descent of the land of Gower. "Sciendum quod primi conquestores terræ Gower fuerunt comites Warrewickiæ, unde primus vocabatur Roger comes, cui successit Margeria soror ejus, quâ mortuâ, successit ei Henricus de Novo-Burgo, filius ejusdem Margeriæ post vero mortem Henrici successit Willillmus de Bello Campo de quo in hâc parte folii fit mencio, etc." These entries sufficiently show that the volume has a close connexion with the family of Beauchamp, Earls of Warwick, and it may be reasonably conjectured that at one time it belonged to the celebrated William de Beauchamp, Earl of Warwick.

13. The last of the miscellaneous matter is a poem in three pages, on the sepultures of saints, commencing thus :—

> " I sunt les mervailes dites
> Come par ordre sunt escrites
> Ore parlerat cest escrit
> Des seyns ou sunt enseveliz
> En Engleterre par parties
> Par les Engleis establies
> Saint Alban fust li premir martir."

The burial-places of the celebrated saints in England have frequently formed the subject of early and mediæval tracts. There is an interesting tract of this nature in the Waltham Abbey manuscript in the British Museum, Harley, 3,776, with which this may be compared.

CHAPTER V.

DESCRIPTION OF THE ARUNDEL AND COTTONIAN MANUSCRIPTS IN THE BRITISH MUSEUM.

THE ARUNDEL MS.

THE Arundel Domesday Manuscript in the British Museum, Manuscript Department, follows, in order of classification, after the *Abbreviatio* and the *Breviate*. Like these, this copy is abbreviated, but not in the same way. It is a folio volume (No. 153), of the beginning of the twelfth century, consisting of eighty-five leaves of vellum, nicely written in an elegant style of native handwriting. It contains the returns for only twenty-four counties, and is otherwise imperfect, the abbreviation consisting in the main of the omission of notices of payments due to the king. But it has great value as an ancient text, and should be carefully collated with the Exchequer Domesday in any future edition of that book. It has never been printed. The order of the counties here is the same as that of the *Breviate*, but the following counties are wanting :—

Kent, Sussex, Surrey, Hampshire, Berkshire, Derbyshire : and after Rutlandshire follows only the *Civitas et Comitatus Eboraci*. A leaf is wanting between folios 47 and 48, and another between folios 77 and

78. The illustrious editor, Gale, has written some memoranda concerning the survey at the beginning of the volume. He considers the manuscript is a copy of the *Abbreviatio*, or abridged Domesday Book of the Exchequer. This Arundel Manuscript formerly belonged to the Cistercian Abbey of Margam in Glamorganshire, a monastery which has, by its enforced dissolution, unwillingly contributed many other valuable historical manuscripts and charters to our national collections in the Museum. It is curious to remember that the *Breviate*, as is mentioned in the account of that book, also comes apparently from the southern part of Wales. A parallel edition of the texts of the *Abbreviatio*, *Breviate*, and this Manuscript would be a valuable appendix to the Record Commission Edition of the Domesday Book.

THE COTTONIAN MS.

There is a very nicely-written, and nearly contemporary, abridged copy of the Domesday Survey of the County of Kent in the British Museum, Cottonian MS., Vitellius C. VIII., folios 143–156. The volume contains, as well, a number of miscellaneous historical and literary pieces, bound up in the same covers, but having little or no connexion with one another. It was exhibited to the members of the Domesday Commemoration, and has been described in the *Journal*[1] of the British Archæological Association.

[1] Vol. xli. p. 259.

This small and handy roll was probably carried about
in the pocket of an early possessor, for it is much
worn at the beginning, and has a few deficiencies.
At first it was in form of a roll, but when it passed
into the hands of the collector of the Cottonian
Library it was cut up into leaves or pages, and is now
inlaid into fourteen leaves, of which the second page
or *verso* in each leaf is blank, as would naturally be the
case with a roll. The handwriting appears to be of
the early part of the twelfth century, and not very
unlike the small neat hand of the scribes who wrote
the Exchequer Domesday. The text agrees pretty
closely with that of the Domesday Book, but is
deserving hereafter of a careful collation, if ever the
Domesday Book is published with variorum notes.

Of the late paper copies, manuscript extracts, and
fragmentary portions of Domesday, which occur in
manuscripts such as chartularies, registers, and cowcher
books of religious houses, it is not necessary here to
say anything; but there are several unpublished
documents of the highest importance in connexion
with the Domesday Book, and contemporary with its
era, among the manuscripts in the British Museum.
This is rendered abundantly evident from the fact
that within a very short time an original record has
been found of the famous Plea or Lawsuit which was
tried at Penenden Heath in Kent, wherein is given a
summary of the evidence taken in the year 1072, referred to in the Domesday Book, concerning the lands
reclaimed from Odo, the powerful bishop of Bayeux,
by Lanfranc, Archbishop of Canterbury, on behalf
of his see and of the monasteries of St. Augustine

and Christchurch. The early chronicler, Eadmer of Canterbury, and other historians, down to and including the Rev. Mr. L. B. Larking,[1] the latest expounder of Kentish Domesday history, have given notices of this great suit, which also attracted the attention of Spelman and Wilkins; and William of Malmesbury[2] points out the beneficial effects of the decision arrived at on that occasion upon the English Church. But to one and all of these writers this document, now preserved among the Cottonian Manuscripts in the British Museum, was unknown. The text, and some further remarks on this relic, will be found in a subsequent chapter[3] which deals with the historical points illustrated by the Domesday Book. Other similar documents doubtless will hereafter come to light to reward patient searches now that public attention has been so strongly directed to the Domesday Book, and these records, when recovered and arranged in proper order, will form new and peculiarly valuable illustrations of the Domesday in the hands of future editors.

[1] "The Domesday Book of Kent" (a facsimile), with translation, notes, and appendix. London, 1869, folio.

[2] "Gesta Pontificum" (Roll's series), p. 70.

[3] See p. 293.

CHAPTER VI.

DESCRIPTION OF THE "INQUEST OF THE COUNTY OF CAMBRIDGE," OR THE "INQUISITIO COMITATUS CANTABRIGIENSIS," IN THE BRITISH MUSEUM.

FIRST among the few manuscripts which belong to the class of pre-Domesday surveys, we must take cognizance of the " Inquisitio Comitatus Cantabrigiensis," or " Inquest of the County of Cambridge," which was published by Mr. N. E. S. A. Hamilton, of the British Museum, in the year 1876, and under the auspices of the Royal Society of Literature, who generously found the means for defraying the cost of its publication. This is the original return made by the *juratores*, or *sworn surveyors*, of the county of Cambridge, in obedience to the king's mandate, from which the Exchequer Domesday Book for that county was afterwards compiled by the royal secretaries. It is much to be regretted, as Hamilton states, that the only manuscript[1] (British Museum, Cotton. MS. Tiberius, A. vi.) in which this important document is known to exist, has been injured by time and neglect, and, above all, has lost several

---

[1] Exhibited in the King's Library on the occasion of the Domesday Commemoration.

of its leaves. The return is consequently defective
at its end. The greater part, however, has fortunately
come down to us, and the text, printed by the above-
mentioned editor with great care, for the first time,
and in parallel columns with the corresponding
entries extracted from the Exchequer Domesday
Book, contains abundant evidence that we have
in this very precious Cottonian MS. *the original
source* from which the Exchequer Domesday of
Cambridgeshire was compiled. "It is singular,"
writes Hamilton, "that so important a document
should have been extant only in a solitary manuscript
unpublished, and exposed in consequence to many
risks of being lost or destroyed. Doubtless, numerous
historical and literary treasures still exist among our
ancient manuscripts which are unknown to students
and antiquaries. But in regard to this particular
manuscript, the strange part is, that from the days
of Selden to those of Ellis—that is, for a period of
about two hundred and fifty years—its existence had
been known, and its importance as elucidating Domesday history understood, and in part, at least, acknow-
ledged." Even the indefatigable Sir Thomas Duffus
Hardy, late deputy-keeper of the public records,
has omitted all notice of this manuscript from his
account of the Exchequer Domesday Book, the
"Inquisitio Eliensis," and the Exon Domesday
Book which will be presently described, in his
"Descriptive Catalogue of Manuscripts Relating to
the History of Great Britain and Ireland," Vol. II.
Thus Mr. Hamilton, although by no means pretending
to have discovered this important fragment, was the

first to bring its importance to light, and to give it to the learned world.

It is doubtful if any previous student of the Domesday Book had ever distinguished the essential difference between the "Inquisitio Comitatus Cantabrigiensis," or "Inquest of the County of Cambridge," and the comparatively far less important, but yet highly interesting, "Inquisitio Eliensis," or "Inquest of the Lands of the Monastery at Ely," a mere record of the landed property belonging to the monks of Ely Abbey, therein described as the lands of St. Ædeldryd, the founder of the nunnery of Ely in the seventh century. This inquest had been quoted over and over again, and was printed by Sir Henry Ellis in the folio edition[1] issued by the Commissioners of Public Records in the year 1816; while the still more valuable portion of the manuscript, containing the survey of the lay as well as the ecclesiastical lands, in the shape of a copy of the original Domesday returns made by the jurymen, or *juratores*, in obedience to the orders of William the Conqueror, had been overlooked by every one, although it occupies the folios adjacent to the "Inquisitio Eliensis" in the same volume. Among other literary celebrities, Selden in 1596, Gale in 1722, Philip Carteret Webb,[2]

---

[1] Vol. iv. pp. 397 *et seqq.*

[2] "A short account of some Particulars concerning Domesday Book, with a view to its being published. By a member of the Society of Antiquaries" (P. C. Webb). Read at a meeting of the Society, 1755. London, 1756, 4to. This contains, among other things, a list of the parts of the Domesday Book printed up to that time, and of transcripts of parts of it in public or

who collected useful materials for a bibliography of
the " Domesday Book," in 1756, and R. Kelham[1] in
1788, all well known and conscientious writers on
the Domesday Book, appear to have been strangely
ignorant of the true and important nature of this
manuscript. Even the illustrious author and antiquary,
Sir Henry Ellis, whose indispensable " Introduction
to Domesday Book," in two volumes, 8vo, 1833
(now ripe for revision and republication, notwithstanding the unwillingness of Canon Isaac Taylor
to accept some portions of it), and folio edition
of "Indices" and "Additamenta," 1816, forming
Vols. III. and IV. of the Record Commissioners'
edition of Exchequer Domesday Book, connect
his name for ever with the great survey, simply
prints, incredible as it may seem, that portion of the
Cottonian Manuscript which relates to the monastic
lands of Ely, and omits, without even reference or
mention, the more valuable portion, which Mr.
Hamilton detected and first gave to the world.
Even among modern and more critically-disposed
writers, Mr. Stuart A. Moore,[2] who has worked at
the Domesday Book of Northamptonshire, has failed
to distinguish these differences.

private hands. Webb was also the author of "A Short Account
of Danegeld, with some further particulars relating to William
the Conqueror's Survey," 1756.

[1] "Domesday Book, illustrated, containing an account of that
ancient record, as also of the tenants in capite or serjeantry
therein mentioned ; and a translation of the difficult passages,
with occasional notes." By R. Kelham. London, 1788, 8vo.

[2] In *Athenæum*, 25th April, 1885.

The manuscript from which Hamilton's text is taken, and which, so far as is still known, is the only remaining exemplar, is numbered Tiberius A. VI., among the Cottonian Manuscripts in the British Museum. Its contents are:—1. An early copy of the "Anglo-Saxon Chronicle" down to the year 977. 2. A memorandum, entitled "De portione crucis reperta a Sergio Papa," etc., "Notice of a portion of the Cross found by Pope Sergius." 3. "Names of the Popes who sent the pall to the Archbishops of Canterbury, from Augustine to Anselm." 4. The "Inquisitio Eliensis." 5. The "Inquisitio Comitatus Cantabrigiensis," which forms the subject of these present remarks. 6. A valuable collection of copies of charters and early documents relating to the monastery at Ely, and a later chronicle of England from the reign of Hardacnut to the twentieth year of King Edward III., A.D. 1346, written in French. This "Inquest of the County of Cambridge" is contained between folios 76 and 113, one leaf being lost between folios 111 and 112. It is written on vellum, in double columns, about thirty-one lines to a page, and in a fine bold book-hand of the concluding years of the twelfth century, about the year 1180. Its pages are embellished with elegant capital letters in blue and red colours, and some of the initials have been occasionally ornamented with the incipient floriation which is a characteristic of the manuscripts of that period. The "Ely Inquest," or "Inquisitio Eliensis," is in the same manuscript and in the same handwriting, but it has been placed before the "Inquest of the County of Cambridge,"

and thus out of its true chronological order, by
those who arranged the MS. for binding, probably
when it first passed into the possession of the noble
founder of the Cottonian Library. This now occupies
folios 38–70 of the manuscript volume.

This "Inquest" is indispensable for the study of
the Cambridgeshire Domesday, and its publication
constitutes, as Hamilton truly states, a real contribution to historical knowledge.   He gives numerous
examples, showing how far the facts recorded in
the Domesday Book at the Exchequer have been
therein abridged or extended, sometimes imperfectly,
from the original return.

We may here conveniently give a few examples
from the parallel columns of the book, to explain the
value of the "Inquest" more clearly :—

/ / 32 𝖘 mſ̄ꝛ [STAPLEHOM HUNDRED.]

MS. Cotton. Tiberius A. VI. cf. 79.	*Domesday Book,* vol. I., p. 195a, col. 2.
"In hoc hunɗr . Enisam mu-sardus ī caueleio de comite alano unam .h̄. 7 dimi. 7 .xx. ac̄ tenet .III.ᵇ³ .c̄. ibi ē. P̄ra .7. II. c̄. ibi. sūt in dominio .I.Ꝯ uillanꝰ .IIII. bor. unus . ser. Silua .XII. por. Pastura ad pecuñ . uille .LX. o. .III. minꝰ .XL. por . unꝰ runcꝰ . Inꝶ totum ual .XL. sol. 7 qñ receꝑ ·XL. sol. T.R.E. .XL. sol . Hanc P̄ram tenuit herulꝶꝰ homo ædiue pulcre . potuit dare & uenɗe cui voluit."[1]	"In Chauelai teñ Enisant de com̃ . I . hiɗ 7 dim̃ . 7 xx. ac*s. P̄ra . ē .III. car̄ . 7 ibi sunt in dñio .II. 7 .IIII. borɗ cū .I. car̄. Ibi .I. seruꝰ . Silua .XII. porc̄. Pasīa ad pec̄ uillæ. Val 7 ualuit sēp .XL. sol. Hanc 'trā tenuit Herulꝶꝰ hō Eddeue . dare 7 uenɗe potuit."

[1] Hamilton, p. II.

It will be seen that the Domesday Book in this passage leaves out the interesting names and the quantities of sheep, pigs, and the horse (*runcinus*). Throughout the manuscript, names, appellations, and quasi-surnames are frequently found, which have been omitted by the compilers of the Exchequer Domesday Book, either for the sake of brevity, or because they were indifferent to recording them, not having been enjoined to do so.

The following shows that the vaguely-mentioned six *sochemanni*, and one of them a *homo regis*, of the Exchequer Domesday Book, were entered in the original return as belonging to their respective lords, the Queen Ediva "the fair," Archbishop Stigand, Robert filius Wimarci, King Edward the Confessor, and Earl Algar. The curious error in the Domesday value T.R.E., viz., I. for L, is also worthy of notice.

[WERLEIA, *or* WEDERLAI HUNDRED.]

Ib., fol. 108 *a*.

"In h·hundr Oreuuella. p IIII. ñ . se de . t.r.e. 7 m°. Et de his .IIII. ñ. tenet comes Rog. unam . ñ . 7 . i. uir . 7 ¶ciam partem unius uirge .i. carr . 7 dim . ē ibi ¶ra. Dimid . č . 7 dimidia . ñ . in dominio .I. carr. uillanis .II. uillani , III. bor. q'sq de . v. ac's. unus ser . Pratum .I. carr Silua ad sepes refici. In¶ totum ual .xx. sol . 7 qñ recep xxx. sol . t.r.e. 1 . sol. Hanc . ¶ . tenerunt .vi. sochemanni . 7 . 11°. istorum fuer̃t homines ediue.

Ib., p. 193 *b*.

"In Orduuelle teñ . R. comes .I. hid . 7 I. uirg . 7 IIIᶜˡᵃ . par̃t uni⁹ uirg̃. T̃ra . ē . I . car̃ 7 dim. In dñio dim̃ hida 7 ibi dim̃ car̃ . 7 II. uilti 7 III. bord cū . I. car̃. Ibi un⁹ seruus . 7 p̃tu . I. car̃ . 7 nem⁹ ad sepes reficiendas. Val .xx. sol. Qdo recep ; xxx. sol . T.R.E ; I. solid. Hanc ¶ra tenuer̃ .vi. sochi . 7 dare 7 uende ¶ra suā potuer̃. Vn⁹ eo₃ hō

Habuerunt .ıı. partes uirge. Et .ııı.⁹ soche. homo stigandi archiepi. Habuit unā uir. 7 ıııᵃ. par. unius uirge. Et ıııı⁹; homo Robti filii Wimarci. tenuit .ı. uir 7 ꝑciam par. uni⁹ uirge. Et q'nꝑ homo. r.e. tenuit .ıı. partes uni⁹ uirge. 7 unam inuuardum inuenit iste. Et .vı.⁹ homo comitis algari tenuit unam uir. 7 ꝑciā par. unius uirge. Et oms̄ isti potuer̄t recedě. Tres istorum sochemannoꝣ ꝑdıctorū acomodauit picotus uic̄ecom̄ Rogerio com̄. ppꝇ placita sua tenenda - Post occupauerunt seruientes euis ita. atꝗ retinuerunt eos sine libatore cum ꝑris suis qᵒd rex inde nicħ habuit.⁹neꝗ habet. sicut ıp̄e picot⁹ testatur."[1]

regis. E. fuit. 7 inuuardū inuenit uicecomiti."

"Tr̄es istoꝣ socħoꝣ accōmodauit picot⁹ Rogerio comiti. ppꞇ placita sua tenenda. sꝗ postea occupauer̄ eos hōēs comitis 7 retinuer̄ cū ꝑris suis; sine libatore. 7 rex inde seruitiū ñ habuit nec hꞇ. sic̄ ipse uicecomes dicit."

In this extract the concluding paragraph is a good example of the reduction of words and conversion of phrases employed by the drafters of the final form of the survey, as seen in the Exchequer Domesday Book.

In the spelling of the names of persons and places there is a remarkable difference between the Inquest of the County of Cambridge and the Exchequer Domesday Book of the same county. This is shown more at length in the following list. The reference

---

[1] Hamilton, p. 77.

numbers correspond with the pages of Hamilton's. edition :—

INQUISITION OF THE COUNTY OF CAMBRIDGE.	EXCHEQUER DOMESDAY BOOK.
Abbericus, 15, 16.	Albericus.
Achillus, 74, 79.	Achi.
Ædiua, 2, 4, &c. ; Eadiua, 14; Ediua, 27, 34, 37, &c.	Eddeua : Æideua.
Aibricus, 16.	Abricus.
Aldredus, 73.	Eldredus.
Algarus, 59.	Algar.
Algarus Cappe, 88.	Cabe.
Almarus, 32.	Elmarus.
Alsi squitrebil, 41.	Alsi.
Alstanus, 7.	Adestanus.
Aluredus, 55.	Alucradus.
Aluricus Campe, 39, 43.	Aluric.
Aluricus Cemp, 37.	Aluric.
Anschillus, 57.	Anschil.
Ascelina, 53.	Azelina.
Bondus, 47.	Bundi.
Brient, 35.	Brien.
Colsuenus, 63, 67 ; Colsueinus, 63.	Colsuan.
Edricus, 37.	Edericus.
Enisam Musardus, 11.	Enisant.
Erchingarus, 87.	Erchenger.
Esgarus Stalrus, 26, 72.	Asgarus.
Ethsi, 75.	Ezi.
Euerardus, 9, 10.	Eurardus.
Fredebertus, 46.	Fridebertus.
Fulco, 83 ; Fulcuinus, 82.	Fulcuius.
Galfridus, 8.	Gaufridus.
Galterus, 14.	Walterus.
Gaufridus, 5, 13, &c.	Goisfridus.
Gerardus, 39.	Girardus.

E

Godlamb, 51, 71.   Gollam, Gollan.
Godwinus Wambestrang, 54.   Goduin.
Gold, 93.   Goldus.
Gurd, 55, 58; Gurdus, 48, 37.   Guerd, Guert.
Halardus, 48.   Heraldus.
Haraldus, 22, 19; Haroldus, 11.   Haroldus, Heraldus.
Horulfus, 50.   Orulfus.
Hugo de Bolebec, 12, 14.   Hugo.
Hugo Pedeuolt, 66, 77.   Hugo.
Hugo Pincerna, 60.   Hugo.
Lefsi, 29.   Lepsi.
Leoffled, 25.   Leflet.
Leshusa, 83.   Leuene.
Limarus, 30.   Ledmarus.
Nicholaus, 1.   Nicol.
Oto, 59.   Otho.
Picotus, 1, 36, &c.   Picot, Pirotus.
Sania, 62.   Sagena.
Segarus, 25; Sigarus, 44.   Sigar.
Snellingus, 38.   Snellinc.
Thobillus, 1.   Tochil.
Thocus, 22, 24.   Tochi.
Thurgarus, 22.   Turgar.
Tochillus, 50; Tokillus, 32.   Tochi.
Turbertus, 78.   Turburnus.
Turbertus, 86.   Turbertus Godingus.
Turkillus, 53.   Torchil.
Vlfus, 42; Vlfus fenesce, 90.   Vlf.
Unfridus, 56.   Hunfridus.
Waldeuus, 58; Walleuus, 51.   Wallef.
Walleuus, 83.   Walleter.
Wichomarus, 21; Wihemarus, 22.   Wihomarc.
Wigonus de Mara, 10.   Wighen.
Withgari, 23.   Wigar.

This list shows caprice and inattention which is not easily to be explained. All the variations are of

gréat·interest.¨ Many· go far· to bear··out· what· has
been; suggested more than · once, and with · good
reason, that to some ¨ extent. at¸ least the·scribes .
óf the fair copy or Exchequer Domesday Book were
guided by phonetics rather than strict adherénce to
their original manuscript.

The variations in the place-names are ˙ equally
numérous. ˙ A few are subjoined :—

INQUISITION OF THE COUNTY OF CAMBRIDGE. · ·	EXCHEQUER·DOMESDAY · BOOK.
Bathburgeham, 35 36, 37.	Badburgh, Badburham.
Carletona, 20, 21.	Carletone, Carlentone.
Catareio, Cetereio, 75, 76.	Cietriz.
Caneleio, 11.	Chanelai.
Ceterio, 75, 82 ; Chatriz, 44.	Cetriz, Cietriz.
Choeie, 15.	Coeia.
Erlingetona, 83.	Erningtune, Erningtone.
Fordam, 3, 7.	· Forham.
Fulemere, 44, 45.	Fuglemære, Fugelesmara.
Hateleia, 56.	Atelai.
Scenegeia, 54 ; Sceningeie, 59.	Scelgei.
Stapelfo . . . . 2.	Staplehor.
Tosta, 87.	Tosth.
Tripelâue, Trippelâue, 43, 44, &c.	Trepeslav.
Wendeie, 58, 59.	Wandreie Wandei.
Werleia, 68.	Wederlai.
Wrattinga, 23, 24.·	Waratinge.
Wurteuuella, 81, 82.	Witeuuella, Witeuuelle.

In several of these names the etymologically correct spelling which is found in the *Inquisitio* has
undergone corruption in passing through the pen of

the foreign scribe of the Exchequer MS., who depended, evidently to some measurable extent, upon his own peculiar phonetic differentiation. It would almost seem as if he had written from dictation, and not from actual inspection of the material which he was condensing. This phonetic factor seriously interferes in many instances with the true etymology of place-names; and this to so great an extent that we cannot accept Domesday forms of names of places as evidence of the ancient form of the words; unless they are supported by other contemporary examples of use.

CHAPTER VII.

DESCRIPTION OF THE "EXETER BOOK" OR "EXON DOMESDAY," IN POSSESSION OF THE DEAN AND CHAPTER OF EXETER.

THIS magnificent manuscript, which approaches very nearly to the Domesday Book itself in the palæography which its pages exhibit, and which, next to the Domesday Book, is the most comprehensive of all the supplementary records, is called the "Exon Domesday," because it is preserved among the muniments, charters, and other manuscripts belonging to the Dean and Chapter of Exeter Cathedral. It was exhibited by their permission in the King's Library at the British Museum, during the recent Domesday Commemoration, and the peculiarly free, bold, Italian character of the handwriting, shows a considerable resemblance to the writing of the Domesday Book in the Exchequer. Sir Henry Ellis, who printed the whole text as an appendix to the Domesday Book, has given[1] a very exhaustive notice of this manuscript, and evidently examined it with the greatest attention. It has also formed the subject of much careful investigation at the hands of the late

---

[1] Introduction to vol. iv. *Liber Censualis* (Record Commission).

Rev. Robert W. Eyton, M.A., Rector of Ryton,
Salop, one of the most profound Domesday scholars
of this century. In the main body, the manuscript
presents a survey of the five south-western counties
of Wiltshire, Dorsetshire, Somersetshire, Devonshire,
and Cornwall. It is supposed to contain, so far as
it extends, an exact transcript of the *original returns*
made by the commissioners at the time of preparing
the general survey, from which the Exchequer Domesday itself was afterwards digested and compiled. It
is curious that the arrangement of the counties in
Domesday Book appears to be significant. The
finished work begins at the south-eastern corner of
England, and works along towards the south-western
corner, in a line of what may be termed the south
coast counties. Thus we have 1, Kent ; 2, Sussex ;
3, Surrey ; 4, Hampshire ; 5, Berkshire. These five
counties, we may fairly surmise, had a book re-
sembling, in some general characteristics, the Exon
Domesday, which represented their group. The next
five counties follow in the order which they exhibit
as above in this Exeter manuscript. The Exchequer
Domesday arrangement then goes back to the east
and commences a fresh belt or zone, beginning with
Middlesex and Hertfordshire, and embracing seven
counties as it runs along the map to Herefordshire
on the west. The remaining counties carry on the
system of arrangement as will be shown in the list of
counties mentioned further on in the chapter devoted
to the history and description of the Domesday
Book.

The Exon Domesday is a vellum manuscript of

small folio size, and contains five, hundred and thirty-
two folio leaves or double pages.. The skins of which·
it is composed vary in the number of leaves from one'.
to twenty. The landed property of each of the more
considerable tenants begins a new sheet, and those of
almost every tenant a new page.   Ellis finds that the
lands held by the same tenant in·the three·most
westerly counties of these five are grouped. together,
the counties following·each other generally, but· not
always in.the same order.   In like. manner the sum-
maries of landed property in the two .contiguous
counties of Wilts and Dorset are classed together. ·

. As in the Exchequer Domesday Book, and indeed
in. most manuscripts of any great dimensions of. a,
character such as the Domesday, so also. in this .
instance, different transcribers have evidently been
employed in the execution of the different parts of
which it consists.   Ellis found·a proof of this in .the
mode .of writing the marks and abbreviations, and
more particularly in the contraction used for .*et*,
which distinguishes two, if not three, hands in a
remarkable manner.   There is, also, occasional
evidence·in the manuscript itself that different persons were at work on the copying.   For example, at
the bottom of folio 316 are the words *hoc. scripsit
Ricardus* ;. in folio 414 an interpolation into ·the
text, of the words *usque. huc scripsit R.* The hand-
writing·and the colour of the ink on folios 153 *b*, and
436 *b*, are different from the rest of the manuscript.
Three leaves which contain entries relating to Wiltshire hundreds are written upon vellum of a much
smaller size than the other leaves of·the work, and in

a handwriting proportionately smaller. When the text of the Exon Domesday was so opportunely printed by Ellis in 1816, folio 347 was missing, and there was little expectation of ever recovering the leaf which had evidently been cut out of the book. The recovery of it is due to Mr. W. C. Trevelyan, who, on the occasion of arranging some ancient documents among the archives belonging to his grandfather, Sir John Trevelyan, Baronet, fortunately came upon the missing leaf,[1] and promptly transmitted it to Mr. R. Barnes, Chapter Clerk of Exeter, who thus was as fortunately as unexpectedly enabled to restore it to its proper place in the manuscript. From circumstances (communicated at the time by Mr. Trevelyan), which attended the discovery, there is reason to believe that the leaf had been in possession of his family at least as far back as the year 1656, but no reason is assigned for the removal of the leaf in the first instance.

The sheets or quires of which the Exon Domesday Book consists were bound up in two volumes, about the end of the fourteenth or beginning of the fifteenth century and numbered, but apparently without any particular system of arrangement, and in so careless a manner, we are told, that the leaves containing the description of lands of the same tenants were frequently placed in different parts of the work. This defect was, however, remedied before the printing of the Record Commission edition, by Ellis, by separating the quires, and re-arranging the contents in the order as they are now printed, follow-

---

[1] Record Edition, p. 327*.

ing, as near as the matter would permit, the plan of the Exchequer Domesday Book, and the whole was re-bound in one volume, as it now stands.

From the exhaustive description to which we have referred, many important facts may be gathered. The contents include no less than three copies of the "Inquisitio Geldi, or Taxation of the Hundreds for the Danegeld," a tax originally instituted with a view of buying off the Danes, and not, as Kelham[1] declares, to defray the expenses the king had been at in compiling the survey. This idea is sufficiently refuted by the amount which the tax produced, any one county yielding more than sufficient to meet the entire costs of the survey. Yet it is clear that the tax was raised at the time of the survey, and connected with it, and that, at least in these five counties of the south-west, it was collected by the same commissioners.

Of the three copies of this taxation, the last two exhibit occasional variations in substance, in mode of expression, in the names, and order of the hundreds. The second copy, which we may call B, contains nearly all the matter of the first, or A, with some marginal or interlinear additions. These additions are incorporated into the text of the third, or C copy, which in this respect appears to be a corrected edition of the other two. The subjoined is a specimen of this part of the work, the parts in square brackets being additions :—

[1] "Domesday Book Illustrated," p. 6.

A, fol. 1.

In hunđ calne sŧ .LXXX. & .XI. hiđ. Inde hŧ rex de ŧra Eddide regine.I. bru'hã.xx. hiđ. i' đnio Eduuarđ⁹ uiĉ .v. hiđ. Abb'a uuiltone .I. hiđ. Ricarđ⁹ puignant.II. hiđ. & đ. Alueređ⁹ de ispania.III. hiđ. & đ. & .I. u'g'. vxor Edricii.I. hiđ. & .I. u'g'. Gunfrid⁹ maledoct⁹ . II. pb'r hiđ. & .VII. agros Nigellus .I. hiđ. & p.L. hiđ. & .III. u'g' & .III. agris reddite s't regi.xv. lib. & .v. soŧ. In hunđ cepehã reddite sŧ regi celwiæ socii ei⁹ p .III. hiđ. & đ que adia- cent hunđ calne .xxI. soŧ.

B, fol. 7 b.

In hundrets de calne sŧ. LXXXX. et .I. hiđ de his hŧ Rex de ŧra regine edit .x. hiđ i' đnio. [Barones .xxvI. hiđ et điñ, et. duas parŧ.I. uirg]' Eduuarđ⁹ uiĉ .v. hiđ. Abba- tissa de Wiltonia .I. hiđ Ricarđ⁹ puinant .II. hiđ et đim. Aluerđ⁹ de ispania .III. hiđ et đim et .I. uirga. Vxor Edrici .I. hiđ et .I. uirga. Gunfrid⁹ maledoct⁹ .II. hiđ. et .vII. acros. Nigell⁹ pbr .I. hiđ. et p.l. hiđ. et.III.uirgiset.III. acris st redditæ regi .xv. lib et .v. soŧ. [& p .x. hiđ . de ŧra heraldi quas uillani regis tenent ñ hŧ rex ghildu'.]'in hundreto de cepehã re- cepunt collectores geldi .xxI. soŧ. p .III. hidis et điñ. De hundreto de calna q's retinueŧ.

C, fol. 13.

In hunđ de calna sŧ. LXXXI. hiđ. De his hŧ Barones i' đñio .xxvI. hiđ et điñ et .II. partes .I. uirgæ. Inde hŧ rex de ŧra reginæ Edit .x. hiđ i' đnio . Edward⁹ uiceĉ .v. hiđ . Abba de Wiltona .I. hiđ. Ricarđ⁹ puinant .II. hiđ et điñ. Aluered⁹ de ispania .III. hiđ et .III. uirg'Vxor Edrici.I.hiđ et.I. uirg'. Gunfrid⁹ maledoct⁹ .II. hiđ et .II. partes .I. uirge. Nigell⁹ pbr .I. hiđ. Et p .l. hiđ et .III. uirgis et ŧŧia parte .I. uirge. redditæ sŧ regi.xv. lib et. v. soŧ. De .x. hiđ q"s tenent uillani regis de ŧra heraldi ñ hŧ rex geldv'. Collectores geldi de cepehã recepunt i' hoc hundreto geldv .III. hidarv' et điñ. et hoc retinueŧ.

¹Interleaved. ²On margin.

At the end of the second copy of the "Inquisitio Geldi" for Wiltshire is the account for Shaftesbury, Dorchester, Bridport, and Wareham in Dorsetshire, exactly as in the "Exchequer Domesday." The Gheld-inquest for Dorsetshire is entered subsequently, and after it; the few manors of that county contained in the manuscript are introduced before those of Devonshire, Cornwall, and Somersetshire. At a later part comes the Gheld-inquest for the two Somersetshire hundreds which had not been before noticed, with other matter of a similar nature.

The inquisition of each hundred gives the following details :—

1. The total number of hides.

2. The number held by the king and barons in demesne, together with an enumeration of those exempted from the tax.

3. The number of hides for which the tax was paid, and the amount.

4. The arrears of taxes, and the reason for the arrear.

In some cases the third head is placed after the first. Ellis gives a collection of instances showing conclusively that throughout the survey the Gheld, or tax, is computed at the rate of six shillings for each hide. The few examples of variation being trifling, and probably, even then, owing to the mistakes of the copyist.

The table, which now forms folio 532 of this

volume, indicates the order in which the contents
were arranged at the time of making :—

l. 65   "Dominicatus S.[1] Regis.

Terræ Reginæ Mathildis.[2]

Terra Boloniensis comitissæ.[3]

Hugonis Comitis.[4]

Comitis de Moritonio.[5]

Terræ æcclesiarum in Cornubia.

Terræ episcopi Constantiensis.

Terræ Osmundi[6] episcopi.   In Sommerseta.

Terra Abbatissæ Sancti Eduuardi.[7]   In Sommerseta.

Terra Gisonis[8] episcopi.

Terra Walchelini[9] episcopi.   In Sommerseta.

Terra Exoniensis episcopi.

Inquisitio Gheldi.   In Deuenesira.

In Cornubia.   In Sommerseta.

In Dorseta.

Terræ elemosinarum.   In Deuenesira . et Sommerseta.

Terra Abbatis Hortonensis.

Terræ Cerneliensis Abbatiæ.

[1] ? Scilicet.

[2] Maud, wife of King William I.

[3] Ida, the wife of Eustace, E. of Bologne, who died about
A.D. 1080.

[4] Hugh E. of Chester, A.D. 1070—1101.

[5] ? Robert, E, of Moretaine, in Normandy, half-brother of
William I.

[6] Osmund, Bishop of Salisbury, A.D. 1078—1099.

[7] Shaftesbury, Dorset.

[8] Giso, Bishop of Wells, A.D. 1061—1088.

[9] Walcheline, Bishop of Winchester, A.D. 1070—1098.

Terræ Mideltonensis Abbatiæ.
Terræ Abbodesberiensis Abbatiæ.
Adeliniensis[1] Abbatiæ. In Dorseta . et Somerseta.
Terra Abbatiæ de Bada.[2]
Tauestochensis[3] Abbatiæ.
Bulfestrensis[4] Abbatiæ.
Glastiniensis[5] Abbatiæ.
Micheleniensis[6] Abbatiæ.

Among the interesting peculiarities of this text must be noticed the frequent mention of the money which was retained by the collectors (*Collectores*, or *Congregatores*) in Wiltshire for their own use. These sums vary in amount; such as, for example, ten shillings, "twopence less than twelve shillings," fourpence, etc., but the scale upon which the remuneration was calculated is not recorded. In the Dorsetshire inquest these officers are mentioned three times, twice in cases of overcharge, and once as improperly retaining the proceeds of the tax, as much as forty pounds out of a total county result of £415. 8s. 9½d. In Devonshire, the money which the collectors retained or received for emolument is more systematically noticed. Here the collectors, styled *Fegadri*, or *Hundremanni*, seem, in twenty-four out of thirty-one hundreds, to have retained by custom the tax of one hide respectively to their own use. At the end of the Devonshire Inquest, the names of the

---

[1] Athelney, Somers.   [2] Bath, Somers.
[3] Tavistock, Dev.
[4] ? Buckfastleigh, or Bucfestre, Dev.
[5] Glastonbury, Somers.   [6] Muchelney, Somers.

persons who transmitted the sums which the tax
realised to the royal treasury at Winchester are mentioned. They were William Hostius and Ralph
de Pomario. In Cornwall, on the other hand, there
is no mention of the tax-collectors; and in Somersetshire two entries relate to these officers.

The Gheld inquest for Somersetshire is of interest
for the details which it contains respecting the expenses of collecting and transporting the total sum
of £509 : viz., 40s. for the carriers ; 9s. 8d. for hire
of animals, the writer, mending the bags, and wax ;
51s. 3d. not accounted for by the carriers.

At the end of the account, says Ellis, is an abstract
of the landed property of the powerful Benedictine
abbey of Glastonbury in the four counties of Wilts,
Dorset, Devon, and Somerset ; a summary of the
property of St. Petrock's Abbey, in the county of
Cornwall ; an enumeration of the lands of Ralph de
Mortuo-mari and Milo Crispin, in Wilts ; a twice-
repeated account of the lands of Robert filius Giroldi,
in Wilts, Dorset, and Somerset ; and the Norman
Earl of Moretaine's land in Wilts, Dorset, Devon,
and Cornwall.

It is satisfactory for the accuracy of this manuscript
to notice that, upon collation of the returns of the
lands which form the great bulk of the Exon survey
with the corresponding entries in the Exchequer
Domesday Book, Ellis found that, with a few trifling
variations, they coincided. He found, indeed, one
entry only in the Exon manuscript which has been
omitted in the Exchequer Book ; this relates to
the manor of Sotrebroc in Devonshire. The Exeter

book, however, does not prove to be complete in its contents; only one manor in Wiltshire, a very imperfect series of manors in Dorsetshire, one omission in Somersetshire, numerous omissions in Devonshire, are pointed out by that indefatigable scholar. In Cornwall, however, every manor mentioned in the Exchequer Domesday Book finds a corresponding entry in the Exon Domesday.

The names of the tenants in the time of King Edward the Confessor are far more frequently preserved in the Exon than in the Domesday Book. But, in the systematic arrangement of the subjects, the Exchequer Book indicates a decided preference over the Domesday Book of Exeter which gives many proofs of its being the original from which the former was compiled.

Two remarkable features of the manuscript still remain to be described. They are the live stock and the names. The Exon Book uniformly supplies us with additional knowledge to that given in the Exchequer Book. In this respect it resembles the "Inquest of the County of Cambridge," described already in another part of the work. Thus both the Exon and the Cambridge County Domesdays bear independent testimony as to the proper interpretation to be placed on the statement (in the Anglo-Saxon Chronicle in the Bodleian Library at Oxford, but not in any other copy of the Chronicle), that there was not "an ox, nor a cow, nor a swine" left that was not "set down in his writing."[1] This was only true

---

[1] "Anglo-Saxon Chronicle," A.D. 1085.

of the manors, but incorrect of the property of the
peasantry, with whom, of course, the king had no
immediate concern, they being directly responsible
only to their superior lords.   The Exon manuscript,
then, enumerates the live stock upon every estate. .
An account is rendered, more or less accurately, of
the number of oxen, sheep, goats, horses, and pigs, exactly in the same manner as it is given in the second
volume of the Exchequer Domesday, which contains
only the surveys of the three important and extensive
counties of Essex, Norfolk, and Suffolk.   The reason
for omitting this enumeration in the shortened entries
of the first volume of the Exchequer Domesday
Book is considered by Ellis to be, that the live stock
was constantly liable to fluctuation day by day and
year by year, and, therefore, an enumeration would
be practically useless very soon after the time when
the survey was made.   Incidentally, these facts tend
to show that the surveys of the three eastern counties
above mentioned (which show also a marked variation in diction from that of the first volume) were
transcribed *in full* from the original returns, and thus
the second volume of the Exchequer Domesday
represents the unabridged condition of the first state
of the commissioners' work.

Ellis, with that accustomed indefatigable spirit
which characterises his works, has tabulated a series
of variant synonymous expressions in the Exon and
Exchequer Domesdays, of which the following are
the most important :—

EXON DOMESDAY BOOK.	EXCHEQUER DOMESDAY BOOK.
Agia.	Acra.
Gablatores.	Censores.
Sacerdotes.	Clerici.
reddidit Gildum.	geldabat.
Leuga.	Leuca.
Mansio.	Manerium.
Molinus.	Molendinum.
Denarii.	Nummi.
Pascua.	Pastura.
Nemusculum.	Sylva.
Die qua rex Edwardus fuit vivus et mortuus.	T. R. E. (tempore regis Edwardi).
Tagnus.	Tainus.
Dominicatus Regis.	Terra Regis.

The second important peculiarity of the Exon Domesday is in the spelling of the proper names of persons and places. Such, for example, are :—

EXON DOMESDAY BOOK.	EXCHEQUER DOMESDAY BOOK.

Persons.

Ulwardus Wite.	Vlwardus Albus.
Abbas de Prelio.	Abbas de Labatailge.
Abbas de Alienna.	Abbatia de Adelingi.
Adret.	Eldred, Edred.
Bristecus.	Brictric.
Willielmus Capra.	Willielmus Chievre.

Places.

Rilchetona.	Chilchetone.
Pillanda.[1]	Welland.[1]
Pediccheswella.	Wedicheswelle.
Illebera.	Lilebere.
Padenab'ia.	Wadenebene.
Gluinanuit.	Clunewic.

[1] This and the following word are examples of the confusion of the Anglo Saxon þ and P, by scribes.

F

Exon Domesday Book.	Exchequer Domesday Book.
	Places.
Dueltona.	Oveltone.
Lidefort.	Tideford.
Wirlbesliga.	Wasberlege.

In the last folio of the Exon Domesday Book are titles of lands similar to those which in most of the counties in the Exchequer Domesday Book precede the text of the Survey.

CHAPTER VIII.

THE DOMESDAY BOOK: ITS ORIGIN, DATE, OBJECT, FORMATION, AND MODE OF EXECUTION, AUTHORITY AND CUSTODY IN EARLY TIMES.

HAVING now taken a rapid survey of the antiquity of land division in England, the surveys connected with it, and the various manuscripts in which the notice of these matters is comprised, we may return to the consideration of the contents of the Domesday Book in the Exchequer, which forms, as it were, the centre around which these records revolve, shedding their lights upon from several points of view, and illustrating the numerous points which demand and require investigation. The perfect study of Domesday is a science which, like other sciences of the present day, would claim the attention of a lifetime—aye, more than a lifetime, to be strictly and exclusively devoted to an unceasing inquiry into the matters of which it bears evidence. But although we cannot give that exclusive attention to all its details, we may, as I shall show, obtain an intelligent appreciation of at least some of the many salient features of the work if we devote a little time and attention to the evidence which its text either actually affords, or fairly permits to be deduced from the entries contained therein.

The term *Domesday* has been of some difficulty in respect of its signification.[1] The Anglo-Saxon *Domas* were *laws*, or *dooms*, and the *Domboc*[2] of King Alfred was, if it actually existed, a code of laws. It has been already shown that a Survey of the eighth century exists, rude and incomplete as it was. According to Ingulph, Alfred had an Inquisition and Register made at the time of his division[3] of the kingdom into county hundreds and tithings, which was called, from its place of deposit, the "Roll of Winchester." The term "*Domesday*" may, no doubt, owe something to the *Domboc* for the construction of the name, but we must remember that it bears in its colophon the title of *Descriptio*. I have found[4] among the original charters of William the Conqueror, in possession of the dean and chapter of Westminster, one with a fragmentary seal (No. xxiv. 3), granting to the abbot of St. Peter's, Westminster, eight hides of the manor of Piriford, in the Crown demesne of the Forest of Windsor, free from *scot*, and *custom*, and the "*census pecuniæ, quæ geld vocatur anglice*," attested by William, bishop of Durham (A.D. 1086-1096), "post *descriptionem* totius

---

[1] The Anglo-Saxon Gospels use the words *domes dæg*, "judgment day," in Matt. x. 15, xi. 22, 24. C. *dom-dæg*, in the Ecclesiastical Laws of Canute, cap. 25, and in Cædmon, 10412.

[2] *Dom-boc* occurs in the laws of King Æthelstan, cap. 5, and the Ecclesiastic Laws of King Edgar, cap. 9.

[3] But really long anterior to Alfred.

[4] Birch, "Seals of William the Conqueror," in Trans. Roy. Soc. Literature, vol. x. (new series).

Angliæ." Other names by which the book appears
to have been known are recorded by Ellis, such
as :—"Rotulus Wintonie," or "the Winchester Roll" ;
"Scriptura Thesauri Regis," or the "Writing of the
king's Treasury"; "Liber de Wintonia," the "Book
of Winchester"; "Liber Regis," the "king's book,"
and so on. Some see in the word *Domesday* a
metaphorical *Dies Judicii*, or *Judgment Day;* others,
a *liber judiciarius*, or *Book of Judgments*, because
it spares no one, as the great day of judgment, and its
decision must be final and without controversy.

The term is not, moreover, restricted to this manuscript alone. There were local surveys and records,
known in the early mediæval days as the "Domesdays" of Chester, York, Norwich, Ipswich, Evesham ;
Winchester, between. A.D. 1107 and 1128; the
"Domesday " of the nuns of Haliwell ; the "Domesday" of Ralph de Diceto, dean of St. Paul's, otherwise called the Domesday of St. Paul's, A.D. 1181;
and the Boldon Book of Survey of the Palatinate of
the Bishops of Durham, A.D. 1183.

It has not been ascertained at what period the
term "Domesday" was first applied to the survey,
which is now universally known by that name. I
have, however, found among the manuscripts in the
British Museum an early notice of the MS. under
that identical designation, and possibly there may be
other notices even older than this in which this title
is used, but they have escaped the close scrutiny of
Ellis and other writers on the Domesday Book.
Ellis, indeed, declares that the book was always
distinguished by this name.

In the Royal Library of Manuscripts in the British Museum, the folio MS. 6 c. xi. a copy of the *Epistolæ* of St. Jerome, which at one time belonged to Thomas Wolsey, the unfortunate archbishop of Canterbury, as is attested by his signature on the first page, I find a letter written by a certain William de Poterna, or William of Pottern, a village near Devizes, in Wiltshire, to R. (probably Robert), Prior of Bath, sending him an extract from the "*Liber de domesdai*," relating to Bath. The date of this is about A.D. 1198. Perhaps the writer, following the pernicious practice of his times, had intended to cut the part containing the letter, only five lines, out of the leaf, for vellum was scarce in some places in the twelfth century, and MSS., as we know from many instances, were often mutilated for the sake of blank pieces of vellum for their leaves. If he had done so, he would have mutilated that part of the text of the manuscript which is contained on the other side. It is to this compunction of the writer, who intended to write lower down where the leaf is blank on both sides, but did not cut the letter out when he saw his mistake, that we owe the preservation of this interesting and early specimen of private correspondence.

The text of this letter is worthy of reproduction :—
"Kmo Dño. R. Priori Bath. Witt de Pot⁹na salt. Inueni in libro de domesdai ; qd villa de Bath cum estona solebat geldare cum Sira de Sumersett' p. x.x. hidis. Sunt 7' in eadē uilla xl. mesuagia q̃ reddunt p annū. iiij. libr̃. sunt ibidē vij dom⁹ vacue. 7' vna dom⁵ qᵃm quidā int⁹pres tenet p duobȝ solt. Barones 7' puincie hnt in ead villa. L. solt. valt̃.

The passage referred to here by William de Poterne is that which is found on folio 87 a. col. 2 of Domesday Book.

Rex teñ ESTONE. Ibi ·sī. ii. hidæ. 7 gelđ p una hida. T⁹ra. ē. x. caī. In dñio. ē. i. caī. 7 ii. serui. 7 vii. colibti. 7 xiii. uilli. 7 iii. borđ 7 iii. cotaī cū v. caī. Ibi. ii. molini redđ. c. denaī 7. L. ac pᵃti. 7 ii. leū. siluæ minutæ. in lḡ 7 laī. Hæ. ii. hidæ fueī 7 sī de dñica firma burgi BADE. REX teñ BADE. T. R. E. geldb p xx. hiđ. q̨do scira geldb. Ibi hī. rex. lxiiii. burḡses. redđtes. iiii. lib. 7 qᵃꝓ xxᵗⁱ 7 x. burḡses aliog hõum redđt ibi. lx. soliđ. Ibi hī rex. vi. uastas domˢ. Istud burgū cū p̃dicta ESTONE. redđ. lx. lib ad numerū. 7 unā marḱ auri. Ꝑter hoc redđt moneta ..c. soliđ. Eduuard⁹ redđ. xi. lib de Ꝑcio denario huj⁹ burgi. De ipso burgo . ē una domˢ ablata. Hugo inīpres teñ. 7 uał. ii. soliđ.

It is curious, too, that the precise time of making the survey has been the subject of great diversity of opinion. Some have quoted the " Red Book of the Exchequer," in support of the date of A.D. 1080, whereas this valuable manuscript merely states[1] that the work of the Domesday was undertaken at a time subsequent to the total reduction of this island to the Norman authority. Matthew Paris, Robert of Gloucester, the annals of Waverley, and the chronicle of Bermondsey, date the record in A.D. 1083 ; Henry of Huntingdon, in A.D. 1084. The " Anglo-Saxon Chronicle," in a passage which has been quoted in another place, attributes the order to commence the

[1] A. C. Ewald, s. v. "Domesday Book," in Encyclop. Britannica, new edit. vol. vii. p. 350.

survey in A.D. 1085; Simeon of Durham, Florence of
Worcester, Roger de Hoveden, and Hemingford, in A.D.
1086. This year 1086 tallies with the memorandum
of the completion of the survey at the end of the
second volume : "*Anno millesimo octogesimo sexto.*
ab incarnatione domini vigesimo vero regni Willelmi
facta est ista descriptio non solus per hos tres comitatus sed etiam per alios." The "Ypodigma Neus-
triæ" and Ralph de Diceto give the date of A.D.
1087. It is unfortunate that William of Malmesbury
omitted to give a precise date to his otherwise valuable and critical account of the taking of the survey :
"Provinciales[1] adeo nutui suo substraverat, ut sine
ulla contradictione primus censum omnium capitum
ageret, omnium prædiorum redditus in tota Anglia
notitiæ suæ *per scriptum* adjiceret, omnes liberos
homines, cujuscunque essent, suæ fidelitati sacra-
mento adigeret."

Ellis has arrayed several proofs that the years
1085-6 have been correctly chronicled as the time
when the work was carried out, and we cannot but
believe that by the multiplication of subordinate
inquests, taken, perhaps, by the sheriffs of counties or
other local officers previous to and in anticipation of
the coming of the Royal Commissioners, the work
must have been completed in a remarkably short
space of time; and that from a transcript or abridge-
ment of the returns sent in from the different
counties, the great register was afterwards formed
which has so long been known by the name of
Domesday.

[1] "Gesta Regum," ed. Hardy, vol. ii. p. 434.

As for the origin and object of the Domesday, it is not at all unlikely that William the Conqueror and his advisers had in their minds some older principle of survey, although that ascribed to King Alfred was hypothetical, notwithstanding that one writer laments "that the Domebook of Alfred, so much respected in Westminster Hall to the time of Edward IV., has since been lost." The Anglo-Saxon Chronicle gives the fullest account of the proceedings of the king on the occasion at the commencement of the year 1085, when the formation of the survey assumed a practical commencement. The anonymous writer of that sole copy of the Chronicle which is preserved among the MSS. of Archbishop Laud in the Bodleian Library at Oxford, records in simple and vigorous language the plain facts, which have never been disproved ; and allowing something, perhaps, for the writer's evident disapprobation of the king's proceeding, we may take it as presenting a very faithful narrative of the way in which the work was first set on foot. He writes :—

"Ða[1] to þam midepintre þæs se cyng on Gleapeceastre mid his pitan. 7 heold þær his hired v. dagas. 7 siððan þe arcebiscop 7 gehadode men hæfden sinoð þreo dagas. Ðær þæs Mauricius gecoren to biscop on Lundene. 7 Willelm to Norðfolc. 7 Rodbeard to Ceasterscire. hi þæron ealle þæs cynges clerecas. After þisum hæfde se cyng mycel geðeaht

---

[1] "Anglo-Saxon Chronicle," ed. Thorpe (Rolls Ser.), vol. i. p. 353. From the Laud MS. in the Bodleian Library, No. 636.

and spiðe deope spæce þið his þitan ymbe þis land hu hit þære gesett. oðde mid hþilcon mannon. Sende þa ofer eall Englaland into ælcere scire his men. 7 lett agan ut hu fela hundred hyda þæron innon þære scire. oðde hþet se cyng him sylf hæfde landes 7 orfes innan þam lande. oðde hþilce gerihtæ he ahte to habbanne to xii monðum of þære scire. Eac he lett geþritan hu mycel landes his arcebiscopas hæfdon. 7 his leodbiscopas. 7 his abbotas. 7 his eorlas. 7 þeah ic hit lengre telle. hþæt oðde hu mycel ælc mann hæfde. þe landsittende þæs innan Englalande. on lande oðde on orfe. 7 hu mycel feos hit þære purð. Spa spyðe nearþelice he hit lett ut aspyrian. þ' næs an ælpig hide ne an gyrde landes. ne furðon. hit is sceame to tellanne. ac hit ne þuhte him nan sceame to donne. an oxe. ne án cú. ne án spin. næs belyfon. þ' næs gesæt on his geþrite. 7 ealle þa geþrita þæron gebroht to him syðdan."

In English this may be read as below :—

" An MLXXXV. . . . . . . Then[1] at mid-winter the king was at Gloucester with his *witan*, and there held his court five days ; and afterwards the archbishop and clergy hâd a synod three days. There were Maurice chosen Bishop of London, and William to Norfolk, and Robert to Cheshire. They were all the king's clerks. After this the king had a great council, and very deep speech with his *witan* about this land, how it was peopled, or by what mén ; then sent his men over all England, into every shire, and caused to be ascertained how many hundred

---

[1] B. Thorpe. (Rolls ser.), vol. ii. p. 186.

hides were in the shire, or what land the king himself had, and cattle within the land, or what dues he
ought to have in twelvemonths from the shire. Also[1].
he caused to be written how much land, his archbishops had, and his suffragan bishops, and abbots,
and his earls ; and, though I may narrate somewhat
prolixly, what or how much each man had who was a
holder of land in England, in land, or in cattle, and
how much money it might be worth. So very
narrowly he caused it to be traced out, that there
was not one single hide, nor one yard of land, nor
even, it is shame to tell, though it seemed to him no
shame to do, an ox, nor a cow, nor a swine was left,
that was not set down in his writ. And all the
writings were brought to him afterwards."

This minute inventory-taking of cattle has been,
in many cases, omitted[1] by the Commissioners in
drawing up the Exchequer Domesday Book, nor is
it made one of the questions at the commencement of the *Inquisitio Eliensis*, and, on this
account, some have seen a tendency to exaggera-
tion in the language of the author of this passage
in the Anglo-Saxon Chronicle. But the *Inquisitio
Comitatus Cantabrigiensis* shows clearly that the
original enquiry embraced a census of the stock.

---

[1] Perhaps it was omitted for the sake of brevity, and because
the estimated number must have been known to vary from time
to time, almost from day to day, and therefore could not well
be assessed. The same love of brevity may account for the
frequency of the contractions used by the scribes of the
Survey.

For example, in the Manor of Bercheham, the original Inquest-records "vi. animaŧ oci. xxxvi. o. LXIII. por. XL.VIII. capre," that is, six beasts un-employed, thirty sheep, sixty-four pigs, forty-eight she-goats, none of which find any mention in the corresponding passage.in the Exchequer Domesday. The original inquest and the Ely inquest contain, in like manner continually, entries purporting to show the number of *animalia ociosa; asina cum pullo,* a "she-ass with a foal;" *asini,* "asses;" *boves,* bullocks; *capræ,* she-goats ; *equæ,* mares, some *cum pullis,* with their colts; *equa clauda,* a lame mare ; *equi,* stallions ; *mulus,* a mule ; *oves,* sheep; *porca,* a sow; *runcinus*[1] a "rosin," a "rowney," or pack or draught horse ; *pulli,* foals or colts ; *vaccæ,* cows, some *cum vitulis,* with calves ; and so on.

Blackstone sees in this record the formal intro-duction of legal feudal tenures, a new policy, not as some would have it, imposed upon an unwilling nation by the harshness of the Conqueror's method of government, but nationally and freely adopted by the general assembly of the whole realm in the same manner as other nations of Europe had previously adopted it, upon the same principles of self-security. On the close of the survey, which was brought to.an end the following year, A.D. 1086, the king at Sarum received the submission of all the principal land-owners to the yoke of military tenure, thereby becoming the king's vassals and doing homage and

---

[1] Runcilus, in the Essex Domesday, quoted by Spelman, *gloss.* p. 493.

fealty to him,[1] affirming, as freemen, "liberi homines,"
" by compact and oath that they were willing to be
faithful to King William their lord, both within and
without the whole realm of England." Thus was
accomplished at once, all over England, by common
consent of the responsible persons of the kingdom, a
political change which had recently in France only
gradually been brought about by the surrender of
allodial or free lands to the king, who restored them
to their owners in fee, to be held by them and their
nominees as crown vassals. Some consider that the
almost general consensus of historians in unifying
the notices of the survey, and of the homage performed to the king, indicates the close relation which
the two facts bear to one another. While others, on
the other hand, are of opinion that tenures were in
use before the Norman advent, and that the evidence
afforded by the Domesday Book bears no reference
to any simultaneous surrender and feudal re-grant in
the manner already described.

The appointment of Commissioners (or *Legati*, as
the Domesday Book calls these officers) was the
natural sequence of the royal order to prepare the
surveys.

For the midland counties they were Remigius,
Bishop of Lincoln; Walter Giffard, Earl of Buckingham; Henry de Ferrers; and Adam, brother of
Eudo dapifer; these probably associated to their
side some principal person in each shire. Our

---

[1] This is borne out by the passage in the " Gesta Regum" of
William of Malmesbury, which has just been quoted.

acquaintance with this procedure rests upon the statement in the Cottonian Manuscript Tiberius A XIII. the chartulary of Worcester Monastery, compiled by Heming, the Worcester monk, in the twelfth century. The antiquary Hearne prints this passage, and also another from the same MS., containing the list of jurors—local personages for the most part—for the Hundred of Oswaldeslaw, in Worcestershire. The "Inquisitio Comitatus Cantabrigiensis," edited by Hamilton, from another Cottonian MS., to which we have already drawn attention in a previous chapter, in like manner records the names of the jurors for the following hundreds in Cambridgeshire: Stapleton, Caueleie, Stane, Radesfelda, Flamencdic, Childeforda, Witlesforda, Tripelaue, Herningeforda, Werleia, Stouue, and Nordstouua. The several juries consisted of about eight or nine prominent local tenants, mentioned by name, and included also, probably only as a matter of form, "omnes alii franci et angli." So, too, the *Inquisitio Eliensis*, after the preamble setting forth the object of the Inquest, tabulated the jurors according to the hundreds of:—Staplehou, Cauelai, Stanas, Erningeford, Trepeslau, Radefelde, Flammigedic, Witelesforda, Wederlai, Stouu, Pampeworda, Nordstouue, Cestretona, Ely (two hundreds), Wedwines-treu, and Bradeuuatre (two hundreds), and Odeseia in Hertfordshire.

The inquiries to which the Commissioners were ordered to direct their attention have been already mentioned in Chapter III., derived from the opening words of the *Inquisitio Eliensis*. *p. 24 John*

The object of this survey, ostensibly, was this:—

that every man should know, and be satisfied with, his rightful possessions, and not with impunity usurp the property of others. But, besides this, those who possessed lands had their exact political position and liabilities in the state more clearly defined. They became the king's subjects or vassals, paying a yearly tax by way of fee, homage, or land tax, in proportion to the amount and fertility of the lands they held. By means of this survey the king acquired an accurate, or tolerably accurate, knowledge of the possessions and revenues (as far as land went) of the Crown. He obtained also a very useful roll of the names of the responsible tenants; ample means of ascertaining the military strength and civil population of the country, a basis for readjusting the incidence of taxation, and a register to which those whose titles had been unjustly withheld, or might in future be called in question, could appeal without cavil at its testimony.

The schedule of inquiries which were to form the basis of the task set before the Commissioners was, on the whole, carefully adhered to by the persons, whoever they were, who actually prepared the rough materials. How these officers became possessed of the immense amount of information which is so closely digested in the Exchequer Domesday Book in so short a time as we know it was acquired it is impossible to conjecture, except on the supposition that they accepted written evidence prepared by the sheriffs, bailiffs, and other agents of the great tenants especially with a view to simplifying their labour. But it is curious that no evidence of this nature has come down to us. And, if this hypothesis be not accepted, the only one that remains is that a general convention of the tenants-in-chief, holding large or small areas of land, took place, at which they all rendered oral testimony, on oath, before the Commissioners, who could not have personally examined, even had they desired to do so, more than a very small proportion of the estates which they describe and estimate.

The arrangement of the contents of the book is, generally speaking, in this way. Each shire is treated separately, with the exception to be noticed presently. Before the text is placed a numbered list of the principal landowners in the county :—The king first in order; following him, the great church and lay tenants; these, in turn, followed in many cases by smaller proprietors, grouped in classes as "servientes regis," "taini regis, or "elemosynarii regis," *i.e.*, the King's serjeants, the King's Thegns, the King's almsmen, &c."

This tenant-roll is followed by the "*Clamores*" and "*Invasiones*," or accounts of lands alleged to be held unjustly and claimed by others. The manors and lands are arranged under the "hundreds," or corresponding county sub-divisions in which they lie, and the particulars in answer to the schedule of enquiries, of which the record was to be a reply, are set down under each manor.

We may take, for example, the preliminary list prefixed to the Domesday Book for Norfolk, as a very good illustration of the system followed in preparing the synopsis of the contents. It is as follows :—

I. Willelmus[1] Rex.

II. Episcopus baiocensis.

III. Comes de mauritonio.

IIII. Comes Alanus.

V. Comes Eustachius.

VI. Comes Hugo.

VII. Robertus Malet.

VIII. Willelmus de Warena.

VIIII. Roger bigot.

X. Willelmus Episcopus.

XI. Osbertus Episcopus.

XII. Godricus dapifer.

XIII. Hermerus de ferer̄.

XIIII. Abbas de Sancto Edmundo.

XV. Abbas de eli.

XVI. Abbas Sancti Benedicti de ramesio.

XVII. Abbas de Hulmo.

XVIII. Sanctus Stephanus de cadomo.

XVIIII. Willelmus de escois.

XX. Radulfus de bellofago.

XXI. Rainaldus filius Iuonis.

XXII. Radulfus de Toenio

XXIII. Hugo de monte forti.

XXIIII. Eudo dapifer.

XXV. Walterus Giffart.

XXVI. Roger pictauiensis.

XXVII. Iho Tallebosc.

XXVIII. Radulfus de Limesio.

XXVIIII. Eudo filius Spiruwic.

---

[1] The contractions are filled out *in extenso* in this list, for the sake of greater clearness.

G

XXX. Drogo debeuraria.

XXXI. Radulfus bainardus.

XXXII. Rannulfus piperellus.

XXXIII. Robertus grenon.

XXXIIII. Petrus Valoniensis.

XXXV. Robertus filius Corbutionis.

XXXVI. Rannulfus frater ilgeri

XXXVII. Tehellus britto.

XXXVIII. Robertus de uerli.

XXXVIIII. Hunfridus filius alberici.

XL. Hunfridus de bohun. *Humphrey de Boh*

XLI. Radulfus defelgeres.

XLII. Gislebertus filius Richeri.

XLIII. Rogerus de ramis.

XLIIII. Iuikellus presbiter.

XLV. Colebertus presbiter.

XLVI. Edmundus filius pagani.

XLVII. Isaac.

XLVIII. Touuus.

XLVIIII. Johannes nepos Walerani.

L. Rogerus filius renardi.

LI. Bernerus arbalistarius.

LII. Gislebertus arbalistarius.

LIII. Radulfus arbalistarius.

LIIII. Robertus arbalistarius.

LV. Radberellus[1] artifex.

LVI. Hago.

LVII. Radulfus filius Hagonis.

LVIII. Vlchetellus.

LVIIII. Aluredus.

---

[1] Rabellus, in the text.

It is curious that Kent, or Chenth as it is called, and the other counties in the first volume of the Domesday Book, commence with a survey of the chief town or towns of the shire, whereas the three counties in the second volume begin with the list of chief tenants.

The *Terra Regis* or King's Land is first noticed, then the hundred, the name of the tenant and of the place; afterwards, the detailed survey or description of the property condensed into a few lines, averaging from four to ten, but the diction, arrangement, and extent of the account is not the same in all counties, nor could this amount of uniformity be expected in treating so vast an area as that covered by the Domesday Book. Naturally some property was underrated by accident or fraud, some, on the other hand was overrated, but not with any design of oppression. Generally speaking, fairness and equity was maintained. Even the *Clamores* and *Invasiones*, claims between Norman and Norman on the king's gift, are stated without prejudice, the list which comes at the end of each county setting forth the lands held without a title from King William, by invaders or intruders.

The fact that the survey is neither quite complete in its notice of all tenures liable to the king's tax, nor correct in always omitting the lands which did not pay this geld, has been often mentioned. The names and extent of the hundreds have undergone some changes, which Ellis thinks great, but they are hardly greater than the place names of the parishes and manors themselves. The works of the late Rev. R. W. Eyton, relating to the Domesdays of Somersetshire, Dorsetshire, and Staffordshire; of the late Rev. W. H. R. Jones, for Wiltshire, not to mention others equally valuable as modern treatises on this Record, will be found to indicate changes in the names of places quite as remarkable for their variety, as are the names of the hundreds throughout the book. Some manors have been transferred from one hundred to another, or, at any rate, are now, and for long time past have been thus dislocated. Or, perhaps, the case may be stated differently thus, that the places are entered under a wrong hundred in the manuscript. A complete list of hundreds, wapentakes (which take the place of hundreds in Lincolnshire, Nottinghamshire and York, as local sub-divisions), rapes (in Sussex), and lasts (in Kent) would be a valuable and a welcome record of the political organisation of the land courts, but this is a work which still remains to be undertaken by a Domesday student. These areas take their name frequently from a tree, a thorn, a ford, a stone, a ditch or dyke, a *hlaw* or low, *i.e.*, a mound or tumulus, or some such natural feature, but not to the exclusion of other prominent or widely known spots, where the members of the hundred, the tax-paying tenants, could conveniently assemble to transact the matters which came within their duty to determine.

The omission of the four northernmost counties has been frequently noticed by writers. Northumberland, Cumberland, Westmoreland, and Durham have no survey recorded in the Domesday Book.

Lancashire does not appear under its proper name, but Furness and the northern part of this county, the south of Westmoreland and a part of Cumberland, appear in the West Riding of Yorkshire. The extensive part of Lancashire which is bounded between the rivers Ribble and Mersey, amounting to six hundred and eighty-eight manors, goes with the survey of Cheshire as "Terra inter Ripam et Mersham." Part of Rutland is described in the surveys of Northamptonshire and Lincolnshire. There are also other similar changes in Cheshire.

The reason for the omission of the northern counties is probably due to the fact that Durham and Northumberland had been laid waste, and offered little profitable attractions to the Royal Commissioners. The death in 1080, by murder, of Walchere, bishop of Durham, had been followed by an extensive vengeance taken for the king by Odo, the powerful brother of the Conqueror.[1] Lancashire was not a separate county in the Domesday period. Cumberland and Westmoreland were not as yet under

[1] "Occasionem dedit regi ut provintiæ illius reliquias, quæ aliquantulum respiraverant, funditus exterminaret." Will. Malm., "Gesta Regum," p. 271.

English rule; their southern parts then formed parts
of Yorkshire, and hence these parts are properly
included in that wide-reaching county. It was not
until the time of William II. that they became subject
to the English rule, for, according to Mr. Ewald,[1]
these were held by the Scottish kings as a fief on
the final overthrow of the old kingdom of Strathclyde.
The fact is, as we read in the "Introduction to the
Pipe Rolls of Cumberland, Westmoreland, and Durham," p. iv., that the undescribed district comprised
the earldoms of Northumberland and Cumberland,
both dependencies of the English Crown, but neither
of them merged in the general polity of England,
whose kings did not interfere with the internal con-
cerns of either province.

Notwithstanding these omissions, the survey was
carried out with as much care and exactness as the
times permitted, and hence the great value of the
record from topographical and territorial points of
view. Of manors mentioned in the Domesday, many
have since disappeared on account of depopulation
or absorption. Manors, we know, were created until
the statute of the eighteenth year of Edward I., known
as *Quia Emptores*, from the words with which it
commences. Sometimes new—that is, post-Domes-
day—manors were formed by being taken out of
others which were in existence in the Domesday
Book and still possess manorial character. Local
knowledge and inquiry will (as Ellis correctly shows)
frequently and materially assist research in this par-

[1] Encycl. Brit.

ticular. If the names of Roman cities in Britain (as, for example, Vinovium, or Vinovia, in the neighbourhood of Bishop Auckland, co. Durham, now Binchester Farm) are to be sought and found in the names of mere farms, it is not to be wondered at that the names of Domesday manors in some cases have shrunk down from human memory into the faintly recognisable names of very small and insignificant portions of land; and the clipped and disguised appellation of a country lane, a homestead, or a field, may not unfrequently perpetuate the forgotten nomenclature of a Domesday manor (itself in turn often named from a still more ancient property) now at length shorn, by the ruthless hand of time, of its pride, its power, and its political position.

The early custody of this manuscript has recently formed the subject of critical investigation by Mr. H. Hall, of the Record Office. He finds that the uncertainty which has always prevailed as to the matter is an excellent example of the almost insuperable difficulties encountered in pursuit of an apparently simple piece of information connected with the practice of antiquity. Ayloffe, Palgrave, and Madox were unable to form any definite opinion, and the evidence which they were in possession of has been merely repeated by later writers. Mr. Hall discusses three theories which he finds in vogue among modern scholars :—

1. That the manuscript was preserved in the Winchester treasury, from A.D. 1086, the completion of the survey, to an indefinite date not earlier than the close of the twelfth century, or even later.

2. The statements of Ingulph and the annalists of Burton-upon-Trent and Bermondsey tending to show that the book was preserved continuously at Westminster. And

3. That it was removed from Winchester to Westminster at a comparatively early date, probably about the beginning of the reign of Henry II.

Rejecting these in turn, Mr. Hall propounds a fourth theory, following the actual practice of the Exchequer of Receipt, as exemplified by existing contemporary records, as the only clue to the solution of the difficulty. The city of Winchester, as he justly observes, was the capital of the West Saxon kingdom and official seat of the Court. Here were deposited the king's "hoard," regalia, plate, and official records. Among the latter would be the standard work of Alfred, known as the "Dom-boc," and, perhaps, counterparts of certain charters (which are expressly stated[1] to have been made in duplicate). William the Conqueror's maintenance of Saxon laws and regal customs justifies us in believing that, at any rate during the early Norman period, while the Royal Treasury and official importance of Winchester continued, the Domesday Book was naturally deposited in the treasury there. This, however, involves con-

---

[1] For example, in Cotton Charter, ii. 21, a charter recording the acts of the Council at Kingston, A.D. 838, the following phrase occurs. "Duasque scripturas per omnia consimiles hujus reconciliationis conscribere statuimus, alteram habeat archiepiscopus cum telligraphis ecclesiæ Christi, *alteram Ecgberht et Aethelwulf reges cum hereditatis eorum scripturis.*" "Facsimiles of Ancient Charters in the British Museum," part ii., plate 26, and Augustus ii. 37, *ibid.* plate 27.

sideration of the following points which oppose it. Ingulph implies (1) that there was a Domesday of King Alfred preserved at Winchester, called Rotulus' "Wintoniæ"; (2) that the original of the survey of William the Conqueror was preserved in the same city and bore a similar designation; and (3) that he consulted the Register of Domesday in London. Mr. Hall believes that Ingulph saw the Domesday Register, as it now exists, at Westminster, whither it had migrated, not so much because Winchester had at that time been displaced as a financial centre in favour of the more convenient site at Westminster, but that the Domesday followed the peregrinations of the Court whenever important business was to be transacted, the original rotulets usually remaining in the Winchester treasury. Thus Winchester still remained the headquarters of the Treasury, and the normal depository of the three records mentioned by Ingulph. Thus, too, Domesday Book would be frequently found at Westminster, and on one of these occasions Ingulph consulted its pages, the book itself afterwards returning to its resting-place at Winchester. The Domesday MS. has travelled, Mr. Hall states, along with the Exchequer, through the eastern counties to York, where it rested for seven years.

Twenty years ago it was removed temporarily to Southampton for the purpose of being photographed, and on that occasion it suffered the incalculable injury of being taken out of its covers for convenience of a second-rate photographic process, and rebound in a new fangled style. The old binding is part of its life history, and certainly should

never have been permanently dissociated from the
text. If we may accept Mr. Hall's conclusions as to
the practice of the Exchequer chambers (viz., the
Exchequer proper, and the Exchequer of the Barons),
which was elaborated in its full perfection in the
reign of Henry I. at its new headquarters of West-
mister, and not Winchester (which, however, still was
used as a permanent place of deposit for treasure,
regalia, and records), the king's seal, the Domesday
Book (which was the constant companion of the
seal), and other records, passed from the latter city
to the former during the reign of Henry I. On the
authority of the "Dialogus de Scaccario," a nearly
contemporary official record, it appears that the Exchequer was revived at Westminster during the reign
of Henry II. (after suspension since 1139), under the
auspices of Nigel, bishop of Ely, the ex-treasurer
of King Henry I. The original Rolls of Domesday
were probably destroyed with other records when the
city was occupied and burned, and the royal treasury
doubtless sacked during the varying fortunes of the
civil war between the Empress Matilda and King
Stephen in the eventful year 1141. Mr. Hall would
submit that we may fairly accept the definite date
of A.D. 1108, or thereabouts, for the removal of the
Domesday Book to the Westminster Exchequer,
where, with probably rare exceptions, it passed an
uneventful career between the Thesaurus and the
Scriptorium from that early year in the twelfth century down to the time of Madox, "the first and last
historian of the Exchequer of the kings of England."

CHAPTER IX.

PERSONAGES—THE REMAINS OF THE SAXON FAMI-
LIES—REMARKABLE NAMES OF PERSONS—TITULAR
DESIGNATIONS.

THE remnants of the great families of the Saxon or
pre-Norman period are to be traced, in numerous
instances, throughout the Domesday. We cannot
show the exact manner in which the distribution of
the land in England was made among the companions of the Conqueror. No doubt, royal favour
or caprice in this respect was dispensed much in the
same way as it was with the high offices of the State,
the Army, and the Church. Twenty years had
elapsed since the battle of Hastings, and the land
had been probably apportioned very soon after the
establishment of the Norman power upon the wreck
of native institutions. The lands, therefore, had—at
least in the great majority of instances—been occupied for nearly twenty years by the grantees and reci-
pients of royal favour when the survey was made.
Add to this, many of the greater tenants had increased
their already extensive holdings by marriage with
heiresses.

Ellis cites two examples of this : Robert de Oili
married Aldith, the heiress of Wigod, lord of Wallingford, and Ivo Tailbois, the Conqueror's nephew,

married the countess of Chester, niece and heiress of Thorold of Bugenhale.[1] *p. 95 infra*

The forfeitures of a later day may be occasionally detected,—in the lands, for example,—taken from Gamelbar, Merlesuain, and other Saxon chieftains of the North, after their unsuccessful rising in A.D. 1069. The fate of Waltheof,[2] earl of Huntingdon and Northampton, is a well-known instance. Many representatives of the Saxon families took shelter— almost the only shelter available[3]—in the cloister, which was then, as in many succeeding centuries, the centre of all real progress and culture—the free library, the public hospital, the ever-open refuge and ready sanctuary, the school of art and design, the bank, the bazaar, the college, and the club.[4]

Some of these, doubtless, reappear as monks and heads of religious establishments; for example, Leuric, abbot of Peterborough, was the nephew of the benevolent and intelligent Leofric, earl of Mercia; Waltheof, son of Cospatric, earl of Northumberland, was abbot of the rich and famous abbey of St. Guthlac at Croyland, in the fen country; Elsi, abbot of the neighbouring monastery of Ramsey, had been a favourite in the courts of Edward the Confessor,

---

[1] See some account of this personage in Ingulph's "Chronicle," (Ed. Birch, Wisbech, 1883, *ad finem*, pp. 112, 152.

[2] "The Life and Times of Waltheof," by Edw. Levien, in "Journ. Brit. Arch. Assoc.," vol. xxx. p. 387.

[3] "Nec jam vix aliquis princeps de progenie Anglorum esset in Anglia, sed omnes ad servitutem et ad mortem essent redacti, ita etiam ut *Anglicus* vocari esset opprobrium," John of Oxenedes, p. 33. This is probably somewhat exaggerated.

[4] *Builder*, vol. li. p. 653.

King Harold, and King William; Ethelwold, abbot
of St. Benet's Hulme, in Norfolk, according to John
of Oxenedes,[1] had been King Harold's admiral.
Thus the monasteries became the refuge of those
who represented the intelligence, both political and
scientific, of the Saxons at the time of their fall, and
offered a congenial place of sanctuary to those who
carried with them the best remembrance and relics
of the history of their country.

Among the tenants in the time of William the
Conqueror who held their land immediately from the
king, and are ordinarily known as *tenants in capite,*
or chief tenants, there are many names of Saxons,
and perhaps in some cases Danes or Anglo-Danes,
who had managed to bear the brunt of the change
without total effacement. Such, for example, among
those who held T. R. E., *i.e.,* "in the time of Edward
the Confessor," are :—

Aiulf, the chamberlain, in Dorsetshire, who had
been *vicecomes,* or sheriff, in the time of Edward the
Confessor.

Ælldeua, a "free woman," in Berkshire, held in
the time of Edward the Confessor.

Agemund, in Hampshire, T. R. E.

Aldred, in Wiltshire, T. R. E.

Aldvi, in Somersetshire, T. R. E.

Alfhilla, in Devonshire, T. R. E.

Alfildis; her husband had held land in Wiltshire,
T. R. E.

Algar and Alric, in Devonshire, T. R. E.

Alric, in Staffordshire, T. R. E.

[1] "Chronicle," Ed. Ellis (Rolls), quoted in Ellis's *Introd.,*
p. xvii.

Alric, in Bedfordshire, T. R. E.

Alueua, in Devonshire, T. R. E.

Aluric, in Wiltshire, another Aluric in Dorsetshire, and a third in Devonshire, T. R. E., and so on through the alphabet. The total number of Saxons of high degree who are stated to have held land in the time of the survey and in the time of Edward the Confessor, either of themselves, by the husbands, or in descent from the fathers, or in some other manner is not very great, and probably falls far short of the very small number of five hundred. Among them are :—Cristina, one of the sisters of Edgar Atheling ; she held land in Oxfordshire, and occurs twice as a tenant *in capite* in Warwickshire. Cristina was the grandmother of Matilda, the queen of King Stephen. She built[1] a church in the town of Hertford, and eventually became a nun[2] in the famous Benedictine Abbey of Romsey, in Hants, in A.D. 1085. Derman Lundoniensis, who was tenant *in capite* in Middlesex, may have been a Saxon. William the Conqueror's charter, granting a hide of land at Gyddesdun, in Essex, to him, now preserved among, and as one of, the Corporation charters in the Guildhall, has been printed.[3] It is a curious example of a chief tenant's title to his land.

Edgar Adeling, or Atheling, held land also in Hertfordshire, but probably not earlier than the reign of William, as the holding is very small. Ellis thinks the Conqueror's forbearance towards this

[1] Chauncy, " History of Hertfordshire," p. 256.

[2] *Chron. Sax., ad an.* mlxxxv.

[3] "The Historical Charters of London," 4to., 1884, No. 2.

prince, called Edgar *Cilt*, or *Clito*,[1] grandson of
Edmund Ironside, and heir to the English crown by
descent upon the death of Edward the Confessor, is
to be ascribed partly to his feebleness of talent, and
partly to his alliance, through his sister Margaret,
with Malcolm, king of the Scots.

Godeva, the countess, widow of Leofric, earl of
Mercia, held lands in the counties of Leicester, Warwick, and Nottingham. She was sister of Thorold,
of Bugenhale, sheriff of Lincolnshire. This is the
lady who is connected in history with the freeing of
the inhabitants of Coventry from servile tenure by her
remarkable ride through the town. She was probably
dead when the survey was taken, but bestowed the
greater part of her possessions upon the priory of St.
Mary at Coventry. Dugdale, in his "Baronage," gives
an interesting account of this peeress, who has attracted no small share of romance around her name.

Godwin, a burgess of Bedford, possessed a hide and
the fourth part of a virgate of land in Bedford. He
held half the hide in the time of Edward the Confessor, the rest, which he had purchased after the
change of government, but a portion of it was claimed
and wrested from him by a Norman.

Cospatric was a tenant *in capite* of four entries in
Yorkshire, but Ellis quotes Kelham to show that it
is not certain that this is the celebrated earl of
Northumberland - of that name. The holdings of
Cospatric in the West Riding are, in many instances,
returned in the survey as "now waste." His son,
Waltheof, must not be confounded with the ill-fated

---

[1] A term indicative of Royal birth.

Waltheof, son of Siward, the earl, who had married
Judith, niece of William the Conqueror, and succeeded to the earldom of Northumberland.

Harold, son of Ralph, earl of Hereford, held lands
in chief in the counties of Gloucester, Worcester, and
Warwick. His father had married Goda, or Gethe,
the sister of Edward the Confessor.

Judith, the countess, wife of Waltheof, betrayed her
husband to the king in 1074. She held *in capite* many
lands in many counties, chiefly in the eastern midlands.

Osbern, bishop of Exeter, held lands as tenant
in capite in the counties of Sussex, Surrey, Hants,
Berks, Gloucester, and Norfolk. According to
Kelham, he was a kinsman of King Edward the Confessor, and related also to King William. He succeeded to the see of Exeter, March 28, 1074, and
died in A.D. 1103. It is interesting to note that
Bishop Osbern is stated, in the Domesday account
of Crediton, in Devonshire, to have produced before
the Commissioners certain charters to substantiate
the rights of the Church. Some early charters relating to this see have been published by the late
Mr. J. B. Davidson, from a Cottonian Roll in the
British Museum.

Osbern, son of Richard, who held lands *in capite*
in Herefordshire, Bedfordshire, Warwickshire, Salop,
and Nottinghamshire, was another of the important
surviving tenants of the Saxon days. He is identified
with Osbern, son of Richard Scrupe, and his principal seat was at Richards Castle, Herefordshire, a
stronghold named after his father, who had erected it.

Osward held lands in Wiltshire which his father

before him had held *in capite.* The same is entered among the chief tenants in Gloucestershire of the time of King Edward; and in Yorkshire he had held land previously to the taking of the Domesday Survey.

Oswold, a Surrey thegn, held *in capite* in the time of Edward the Confessor, and retained it.

Ravelin held one manor in the time of King Edward, in Yorkshire, which he retained at the time of the survey.

Saiet held one manor in the time of King Edward, in Bedfordshire, which he also retained.

Siward, the huntsman, held land in Oxfordshire, in the time of King Edward, which he is also credited with in Domesday Book.

Starcolf, a Dane, was a pre-Domesday tenant *in capite* in Norfolk, who maintained his position in the time of King William.

Svain, probably also a Dane, held lands in Wiltshire and Dorsetshire in the time of the Domesday, which is expressly stated to have been held by his father in the time of King Edward. He also held landed property in Northamptonshire for himself.

The Dane Sueno, also called Suanus, Suenus, and Svanus, held as tenant *in capite* in the counties of Essex and Suffolk. Morant[1] considers him (and is probably correct) to have been of Danish origin. Ellis records the name of his father Robert, which occurs in another place[2] of the Domesday Survey, and Morant gives[3] his grandfather's name Wimarc.[4]

---

[1] "History of Essex," vol. i. p. 273.
[2] Vol. f. 47*b.*   [3] Vol. i. p. 155.
[4] See index of Hamilton's "Inquis. Com. Cantabr.," p. 220.

H

Sueno had his castle at Rageneia, or Raylegh, in the hundred of Rochford, in the southern part of Essex. The lands which he held in the time of King Edward, and retained under the Norman government, passed to his son Robert of Essex, and afterwards to his grandson, Henry of Essex, hereditary standard-bearer to King Henry II. This tenant, in an expedition against the Welsh about A.D. 1163, abandoned his standard, and thereby contributed towards the defeat of the king, for which offence he was charged with treason, and being vanquished in a solemn trial by battle, had his life spared, but became a monk by royal command in the abbey of Reading.

Another son of Suein of Essex, called Edward, and his wife Edeua, both occur in another part of the Domesday Book.

Ivo Taillgebosc, or Tailbois, lord of Hoyland, or Holand, Lincolnshire, inherited the great possessions of the Saxon earls, Morcar of York and Edwin of Warwick, sons of Earl Algar, by his marriage with their sister Lucia. In the chronicle of Ingulph,[1] that chronicler gives a long and circumstantial account of his quarrels with the abbey of Croyland. Lucy, the countess, who had inherited the possessions of her brothers after their death, which had been compassed by the treachery of their own men, married, after the death of her first husband Ivo, Roger, son of Gerold Romara, in the time of Henry I., and had

---

[1] Ed. W. de G. Birch in 1883, from the Arundel MS. 178, in the British Museum ; the later part in the "Scriptores post Bedam," p. 513.

one son, William. She married a third time, Ralph, earl of Chester, in the reign of King Stephen, and by this marriage had a second son, Ranulf, afterwards earl of Chester.

Teodric, the goldsmith,—a useful occupation, which may, perhaps, in some degree account for his good fortune in avoiding the almost universal deprivation of landed possessions,—held land in Surrey, in chief under King Edward, which he still held under William in A.D. 1086. There is another goldsmith of the same name mentioned as holding in Oxfordshire; and Theodric, the goldsmith, held land in Berkshire in the time of the survey; but we cannot determine if these new tenants are identical with the pre-Domesday tenant of the same name in Surrey.

Turchil held in Wiltshire, in the Domesday period, the land which his father had previously held.

Turchil of Warwick held seventy-one manors in that county, four of which are mentioned as having been held by his father Alwine, who is called Vicecome, or Sheriff. Dugdale, the illustrious antiquary and author of the "Antiquities of Warwickshire," related that in the days of William Rufus, Turchil was known as Turchill of Arden, or Eardéne. His son, Siward, was not, however, able to obtain permission to hold any large proportion of his father's property, for William Rufus assigned the greater part of the lands to the earl of Warwick to augment the power and revenues of the earldom. Siward's holdings were held by military service rendered by him and his successors to the earls of Warwick.

Turchil's brother Gudmund, was under-tenant to him for four hides in Warwickshire.

Turgot and his mother held *in capite*, in Bedfordshire, the land of the father, who was a king's thegn.

Turstin held land *in capite* in Somersetshire which his father had held in the time of King Edward.

Siward, the huntsman (another important and useful occupation), retained in the Domesday Survey the land in Oxfordshire which he had held freely under King Edward.

Wlwi, the hunstman, did the same in Surrey.

Vlchetell of Norfolk, and Vlchil of Yorkshire, belong also to the class of survivor-tenants in chief. So also must be reckoned Vlf in Somersetshire ; and Vlf in Devonshire ; Vlgar in Hampshire ; Vlmar, a burgess of Bedford ; Ulsi in Hampshire ; Vluiet in Dorsetshire (perhaps two persons so named) ; Vluuard and Brictric in Somersetshire ; Wado in Wiltshire ; Alwine Wit in Hampshire ; Wluine in Staffordshire ; and others.

Among the tenants-in-chief who are mentioned in Domesday Book as having succeeded to property held by their fathers during the time of King Edward, notice must also be taken of Vluric of Hampshire ; Vluric of Wilts (a large proprietor) ; Vluric of Dorsetshire ; Vluric, the huntsman, of Hampshire, and another huntsman of the same name in Dorsetshire ; unless, indeed, some of these entries relate to the same person, which is difficult to be decided.

Having now gone summarily through the names of the proprietors of land in the time of the compilation of the Domesday Book, whose holdings can be shown to have been held by themselves or their families in the time of King Edward, we may conveniently examine the equally important index of persons[1] who are entered in the pages of the Domesday as holding lands in the time of King Edward the Confessor, and through later years anterior to the formation of the survey. This index is really a list of the Saxon landholders of England, for we may assume that few names, and those not important for their political position or for the extent of their tenures, have been omitted by the Commissioners, who had it specially in command from the king to declare, after stating the name of the place, " who held it in the time of Edward the Confessor." Ellis's exhaustive index occupies no less than two hundred and seventy-three octavo pages, and probably the total number of entries, allowing for the combining of different holders in the same or different counties but having the same name, and allowing also for the probable identity of persons entered under names of variant form, would not fall far short of eight thousand, whereas the same writer puts the total of Domesday tenants *in capite*, including ecclesiastical corporations, as amounting scarcely to 1,400.

Among the names which are conspicuous in this class of despoiled native landowners we may notice the following :—

Adelric, brother of Brictrec, the bishop of Worcester, A.D. 1033–1038. He held in Herefordshire.

Ærefastus, a Norfolk holder, better known as

---

[1] Ellis, Introduction, vol. ii.

Herfast or Arfast, bishop of Elmham, in A.D. 1070, from which place he removed the see to Thetford, in A.D. 1075, and died nine years afterwards in 1084.

Ailric, an Essex tenant, who gave his manor of Kelvedon to St. Peter's Abbey, Westminster. This Ailric went to sea to fight King William, and, on returning to his own place, fell ill, whereupon he made the best of his necessity, and granted his land to the abbey; and the Domesday expressly states that the representatives of the abbey have no charter to confirm their right to the property. Ellis, who finds King William's charter confirming the manor of Kelvedon to Westminster Abbey in the chartulary of that monastic institution, among the Cottonian manuscripts in the British Museum (Faustina, A. III., f. 60), wherein it is recited that Ailric's donation of the manor was confirmed by King Edward the Confessor, considers that the traditional evidence recorded by the Domesday Book is refuted in this particular as the chartulary goes. It is far more likely, however, that the charter in the Cottonian manuscript, like those of Edward the Confessor and William the Conqueror, still preserved[1] in charter-form among the archives of the abbey, is a forgery.

Aiulf, of Dorsetshire, held land in this manor in the time of King Edward, and continued to hold the same as under-tenant at the time of the survey.

---

[1] W. de G. Birch, "Seals of Edward the Confessor," in Transactions of the Royal Society, "Literature," vol. x. (second series), p. 141, and "Seals of William the Conqueror," *ibid*, vol. x., p. 161, *et seq.*

Albertus Lothariensis, who is found in the list of tenants *in capite* in the counties of Hereford and Bedford at the time of Domesday, held Celgrave, co. Bedford, before the survey was made. He was probably one of King Edward's foreign courtiers, and not of Saxon origin.

Aldeue, holder of land in Suffolk previous to the Domesday, was still the under-tenant in the time of the formation of the book.

Algar, earl of Mercia, occurs very frequently and over a large breadth of counties—from Cornwall to Lincoln, from Hants to Chester—as holding land previous to the Domesday Survey. He must not be confused, however, with another Algar, of Lincolnshire and other counties, who held land previous to the survey, and appears as sub-tenant of the Lincolnshire manor when the Domesday was compiled. Algar comes: this earl of Mercia was the son of Leofric, earl of Mercia, and the celebrated Lady Godiva. He succeeded to his father's dignities in A.D. 1057, having previously succeeded Harold in the earldom of the East Angles in A.D. 1053. King Edward banished him in A.D. 1055; and a second time in A.D. 1058; but, by the help of Grifin, prince of Wales, and the Norwegian fleet, he regained possession of his earldom of Mercia, and died in A.D. 1059, leaving two sons, Edwin and Morcar.[1]

Egelmar, Almar, Ethelmar, or Ailmar, bishop of Elmham, succeeded Stigand, his brother, in A.D. 1047, on the elevation of the latter to the Canterbury pri-

[1] See pages 107, 116, further on.

macy. Stigand was, however, deprived in A.D. 1070 by the synod held at Winchester. He held land previous to the survey. John of Oxenedes states that Stigand *invaded* successively the bishopric of Winchester and the archbishopric of Canterbury.

Alnod Cild, or Cilt, another holder of land before the survey, is identified with Ulnoth, fourth son of earl Godwine and younger brother to King Harold, whence the appellation of *Cilt*, an equivalent of *Clito*, a word indicating the royal blood of the personage who bore it.[1] Kelham[2] finds that he was sent into Normandy as a hostage upon Godwine's restoration from banishment. On the change in the government, Alnod was brought back to England, and kept in confinement at Salisbury until his death. His land at Alsistone, co. Sussex, was given by the king to Battle Abbey. He held lands before the Conquest in Buckingham, Kent, Sussex, Surrey, and Hants. The under-tenant, Alnod, of Kent, at the time of the survey, may perhaps be this Alnod cilt.

Alric, another Saxon holder of land previous to the survey, was a large proprietor in many counties. He was, in all probability, a tenant *in capite* of some portion of the land at the period of Domesday. Perhaps the Aluric and Aluricus, whom Ellis separates from this Alric, were really the same person.

---

[1] Among the names to whom this appellation Cilt is added are Brixe or Brixi, Eduuard, Eduin, Elmer, Goduinus; Leuric, Leuuin, or Leuuinus; Suein, Suan, or Suen; Vlfric, and Vluui. The word *Clito* is connected with the Lat. *inclytus*. · Spelman considers it to signify the eldest son, but Ducange any of the sons of a king. Cf. κλειτός, renowned.   [2] Page 174.

Aluuard and Aluuardus have their land separately scheduled by Ellis, but these two great proprietors of land before the Domesday Survey are probably identical. This separation of names forms one of the chief difficulties of studying the personal and biographical aspects of Domesday Book.

The same respective identity may be conjectured of Aluui, Aluuin, and Aluuinus, unless these properties are to be broken up into separate possessors of manors, who had the same name in each case.

Archil appears as the name of a large proprietor of land (or of several separate holders) in many counties, chiefly in Yorkshire, previous to the Domesday Survey.

Asgar or Esgar, the *Stalre* or *Stalrus, i.e.,* " Master of the Horse," or *Constabularius,* held lands in Buckinghamshire, Hertfordshire, Cambridgeshire, Warwickshire, Middlesex, and other counties. He was the son[1] of Adelstan, and grandson of Tovi, one of the founders and benefactors of the great abbey of Waltham, by Glitha, daughter of Osegod Scalp. The lands which he held by virtue of his office fell to the hands of Geoffrey de Mandeville, otherwise called " Goisfridus de Mannevile " in Domesday, and their descent is not infrequently recorded in the description of the manors in the book.

Azor, in the same way, was either the name of one large holder of lands in various counties previous to the taking of the survey, or there were many holders who possessed this peculiar name. From some of

---

[1] Harley MS. 3,776, f. 50 ("History of Waltham Abbey.")

the entries it is clear that it was not an uncommon one.....Brictric is another name which is credited with a large number of manors in various counties previous to the taking of the survey. It would be impossible to assign all the entries which Ellis has tabulated to the same personage. The Brictric who held in Gloucestershire had[1] the Honour of Gloucester, which was a noble lordship, and many other great estates by inheritance from his grandfather, Hailward Snow. He incurred the displeasure of Queen Maud (the Conqueror's consort, daughter of Baldwin, earl of Flanders), who in vain desired to marry him when he was ambassador at the court of her father. The lady probably only followed the example of her day when she took her revenge for the slight by procuring his imprisonment at Winchester and the confiscation of all his possessions. Some of Brictric's manors in Cornwall and Gloucestershire afterwards belonged to Queen Maud at the time of the survey; others went to Robert Fitz Haimon in the time of William II.

Brixi, the Saxon tenant of the manor of Hatcham, in Camberwell, co. Surrey, in the time of King Edward, is supposed to have given his name to the Hundred of Brixton, anciently called Brixistan. If this be so, it is a remarkable instance of the late formation of the nomenclature[2] of political subdivisions of counties, illustrated in a somewhat parallel manner

---

[1] Kelham, p. 165, from Rudder, "History of Gloucester," p. 739.

[2] The Norman personal surnames suffixed in many cases to Saxon place-names—as Stanton-Lacy, Stoke-Mandeville, and so forth, are, of course, still later. The transference of old English

in the present day by the formation of new districts, such as Saltaire, on the River Aire, in the parish of Bradford, West Riding of Yorkshire, established by, and named after, Sir Titus Salt; and Etruria, in Stoke-upon-Trent, Staffordshire, which takes its origin from the imitation of Etruscan pottery successfully carried on in that place by the Wedgwoods.

The creation of new Parliamentary boroughs endowed with names derived from parishes not conterminous with these boroughs is somewhat analogous to this.

Colgrim, Colegrim, Colgrin, is a Lincolnshire name, probably of Danish origin, and appertains to several holders before the Domesday period. The same name, Colgrin, is found in Thorold of Bugenhale's Charter,[1] A.D. 1051, to Croyland Abbey.

Copsi, the tenant of manors in Yorkshire and Lincolnshire before the survey, was vice-regent[2] to Tosti, the earl of Northumberland, and a considerable benefactor to the Church of Durham. He made submission to the Conqueror at the same time with Edwin and Morcar, and received the appointment of a procurator of the part of Northumbria beyond the River Tyne. He was assassinated[3]

place-names to Colonial sites, however well the practice may be defended on sentimental grounds, appears in many instances to be ill-advised and incongruous. It is, however, only the modern application of a classical and well known instance. Compare also Inkerman, co. Renfrew; Waterloo, cos. Hants, Lancaster, and York; Bethesda and Sebastopol, villages in Wales, &c.

[1] See Ingulph, Ed. Birch, p. 153.
[2] Ellis, Introduction, vol. ii., p. 72.
[3] Orderic Vitalis; Sim. Dunelm; Will. Pictav.

by his own people in consequence of his attachment to the new king.

Eddeua, called also Eddid, Eddida, and Eddied Regina, *i.e.*, the queen of King Edward the Confessor, held many manors, previous to the Domesday Survey, in the Counties of Kent, Sussex, Hants, Wilts, Devon, Cornwall, Bucks, Surrey, Berks, Dorset, Middlesex, Gloucester, Northampton, Rutland, Devon, Oxford, Hereford, Cambridge, Lincoln, Suffolk, Somerset, and others. She was the daughter of earl Godwine, and is called "the sister of Odo the Earl" in the Herefordshire Survey.[1] Her beauty is recorded in an epigram quoted by Ellis, from the Harley MS., 3,977, a *Consuetudinary*, or Customary of the Abbey of Bury St. Edmund's :—

"Sicut spina rosam genuit Godwynus Editham."

This beautiful lady must not be confused with Eddeua pulchra, or dives, the mistress of Harold, whose lands are distinguished throughout the Domesday Book with a care and accuracy which Ellis regards as evidently not unintentional. The personal charms of this Eddeua are indicated by her surname or appellation "Swannehals" or "Swan's-neck,"[2] quod gallicé sonat "*collum cigni*."

It is this personage who is alluded to in the Life of King Harold, found in the Cotton M.S., Julius D. vi., in which is narrated the account of two monks who watched the Battle of Hastings, and

---

[1] Fol. 186.

[2] "Edgyue Suanneshals," Cotton MS. Nero D 11, fol. 204.

obtained the permission of William the Conqueror to
bring away Harold's body, and afterwards carried the
mistress to aid their search.   The "Romance of the
Life of King Harold" in the Harley M.S. 3,776,[1]
however, relates the carrying away of Harold's body,
without any mention of this lady, and converts the
two monks into two hinds,[2] and speaks of his cure
by a certain woman, a Saracen,[3] who was very profi-
cient in the art of surgery.

Ellis, however, rejects this accepted notice of
Eddeua, and believes her to have been Editha,
daughter of earl Algar, the sister of earls Edwine
and Morcar, the widow of Griffin, or Grithfrid, prince
of the Welsh, and the queen of Harold.   He adduces
a passage in Duchesne's *Scriptores*, in support of
this view.   He considers Aldith, Editha, Algiva, or
Eddeua synonymous terms for the name of Harold's
second wife, who was not likely to be designated as a
queen in a Record which studiously avoided attaching,
even by implication, the dignity of King to Harold's
name.   Florence of Worcester[4] clearly states, that
"Algitha the Queen" was the sister of Edwine and
Morcar.   The lands of Eddeua pulchra were of very
great extent, amounting in the different counties to

---

[1] Edited by W. de G. Birch in 1885, p. 136.

[2] "Inde a duobus, ut fertur, mediocribus viris, quos franc-
alanos sive agricolas vocant, agnitus, et callide occultatus,
ad Wintoniensem deducitur civitatem." *Ibid.*, p. 34.

[3] " A quadam muliere, genere Saracena, artis cirurgice
peritissima," *ibid.*, p. 35, but compare chap. xvii., p. 187,
where she is named Edith, "a woman of shrewd intelligence,
"sagacis animi femina."   [4] Page 634.

two hundred and thirty hides, or perhaps about 27,600 acres, according to our system of comptutation. In Cambridgeshire alone, she held more than a hundred and fifty-eight hides, which subsequently formed part of the Conqueror's reward to Alan, earl of Bretagne. It is scarcely likely (as Ellis observes) that a mistress of Harold should have held such vast tracts of land; or that she should have held as an under-tenant who could not alienate himself for her service no less important a person than Goduinus cilt, whose appellation shows that he was a scion of the royal family, at Fulbourne, in Cambridgeshire.

Edmer atre is another Saxon tenant previous to the Domesday Survey. He, and Ordulf, another of more notable Saxons, are thought to have been partisans of Githa, the mother of Harold, when she instigated the people of Exeter in 1068 to break out into rebellion. The lands of these two holders were conferred upon the earl of Moretaine. His name has given rise to a strange error in the Exon Domesday, where it appears as Edmeratorius,[1] and in the same record at another place Ailmarus ater,[2] or Ailmer the Black.

Ednod, the dapifer, is perhaps the same as Ednod Stalre. He is called Eadnoth Stallere in the Anglo-Saxon Chronicle. Harold made him master of the horse or constable, as "Stallere" signifies; but he made peace with the Conqueror, and was killed in 1068 in opposing Harold's sons, Godwine

---

[1] Pages 190, 191.   [2] Page 487.

Eadmund, and Magnus, in their incursion into Somersetshire.

Edric or Edricus, is a name which cannot now be in all cases determined to represent one individual, but there are a great many entries under this name among the tenants previous to the change of Government. Among them is Edric Salvage, or Edrices Silvaticus,[1] "a very powerful thegn," "præpotens minister,"[2] the son of Alfric, brother of Edric Streone. This Edric was often attacked and despoiled by the chastellan of Hereford and Richard son of Scrob. He, however, retaliated and with the help of Blethgert and Ritwald, princes of Wales, devastated Herefordshire as far as the River Lugg, and captured an immense booty.

Eduinus, and Eduinus comes, Eduuardus, Eduui, Ednod, Elric, Elmar, Elsi, who became abbot of Romsey in 1080; Fregis or Fredgis, mentioned by Gaimar in his Metrical History, as joining with Copsi and Merlesuain against the Conqueror; Gamel, Gimelbar,—are all the names of large landowners, and probably important personages holding lands before the survey was made.

Gida, Gueda, Githe, Ghida, and Gisa, are synonyms of the mother of King Harold, sister of Sweyn,[3] King of Denmark, wife of earl Godwine. She escaped to Flanders from Exeter when William besieged that town, in A.D. 1068.

---

[1] Simeon Dunelm.   [2] Also, "Vir strenuissimus. '
[3] The "Romance of Harold" calls her the sister of *Canute*, "ex sorore *Cnutonis*,' *l. c.*, pp. 13, 113.

Godric, or Godricus, Goduin, and Goduinus, also are entered as great tenants, but it is impossible to attribute all the entries to the same personages. Goduinus, the son of King Harold, held land in Somersetshire. Gospatric of Yorkshire is another great name : he continued to hold lands, either *in capite* or as under-tenant of earl Alan, at the time of the survey.

Guert, Gurt, or Guerd, held land in Sussex, Cambridge, Bedford, Norfolk, and Suffolk. He was one of the brothers of Harold, and his death is depicted in the Bayeux Tapestry ;[1] and Ellis declares the death of this prince at the battle of Hastings to be one of the settled events of history. At the same time, the "Romance of the Life of Harold,"[2] which has been already alluded to more than once, contains an allusion to Gurth, which may be quoted here for what it is worth :—

"In the days of King Henry II. there was seen by that king himself, as well as the nobles and people of the land, a brother of Harold, named Gurth . . . . at the time of the arrival of the Norman little more than a boy, but in wisdom and uprightness of mind, almost a man. But he was at the period we speak of, of a great age, and, as we heard from many who saw him at that time, beautiful to look upon, noble in mien, and very tall in figure." Gurth, according to this manuscript, spoke myste-

---

[1] See the excellent description and facsimiles, in Mr. F. R. Fowke's work, published by the Arundel Society, 1875, 4to.

[2] Ed. Birch, p. 119.

riously respecting Harold, and declared that the body
of that prince was not at Waltham. No doubt a story
was prevalent, which supplied the material ground-
work for the "Romance of the Life of Harold,"
that he had escaped from Hastings. It is curious
that Giraldus Cambrensis, who wrote independently
of the fiction-loving Canon of Waltham Abbey, who
is accredited with the authorship of the Romance,
should also assert[1] that Harold fled from battle,
wounded, his left eye destroyed, and ended his days
in a holy and virtuous manner, as an anchoret, at
Chester, just as is set forth in the Romance,[2] on
which so much obloquy has been bestowed,

Gunnild, daughter of the powerful earl Godwine,
was another tenant of noble Saxon birth. Ellis gives
an interesting note of the discovery of her sepulchre
in the Church of St. Donat at Bruges, with the
inscription on a leaden plate recording her death
in 1087.

There was another Gunnilda, or Gunilda, half-
sister of King Edward the Confessor, and wife of
Henry the Black, Emperor of Germany, daughter of
Canute, King of England; she died in 1042, and
was buried in the same church. A third Gunnilda
is mentioned in the Anglo-Saxon Chronicle under
the year 1045. Ellis finds that she is a distinct
personage from the two above mentioned.

Harold, son of Ralph, earl of Hereford, and a
tenant in Warwickshire, was another noble Saxon, or

---

[1] "Itinerarium," ed. Francof., 1603, p. 874. See also Giraldi
Cambr. opera, ed. J. F. Dimock, vol. vi., p. 140 (Rolls Series.)

[2] Pages 96, 97.

Anglo-Dane, who held lands before the Domesday Survey. . . .

. .By Harold the Earl, as he is usually styled in the Survey, which would naturally withhold the title of king to one whom it considered an usurper, was held a vast territory in many counties. Ellis explains the "*invasions*," or "usurpations," of Harold, which are continually complained of in the Domesday Book, and his alleged violations of the property of the Church, as forcible entries upon lands or other possessions, made not only in Saxon but in Norman times, by the ministers or bailiffs of the great tenants, in the name, but without the knowledge, of their masters. This illustrious writer quotes in full a charter[1] among the Cottonian Collections in the British Museum, to show that this certainly was the case at Sandwich, where the toll of the port, belonging to Christchurch, Canterbury, had been invaded by Ælfstan, abbot of St. Augustine's, Canterbury, in the king's name, but against his wish or consent, in A.D. 1038, during the reign of Harold Harefoot.

The nobly-born Hereuuard[2] appears among the celebrated persons holding lands previous to the Domesday Survey. He is also called Heward and Herward. He was the younger son of Leofric, earl of Mercia, and was elected by the prelates and nobility who took refuge against the Norman rule

---

[1] Augustus ii. 90. See "Facsimiles of Ancient Charters," published under direction of the Trustees, part iv. plate 20.

[2] This man is the hero of many a tale. See "Camp of Refuge," by Ch. MacFarlane. Cf. also the account of Heward, or Hereward, in Ingulph's "Chronicle," pp. 116, 121, *et seq*.

in the Isle of Ely, a tract of land, at that time surrounded by marshes, to be the leader of William's opponents. Ingulph described Hereward as a very beautiful youth, tall, devoted to athletic sports, too fond of strife, complained of by those whom he surpassed to his father, and complained of in turn by his father to the King Edward, who outlawed him. His marriage with Turfrida, a noble maiden in Flanders, his deeds of daring sung of in the streets, his knighting by his uncle, Brand, the abbot of Peterborough, his successful opposition of Yvo Tailboys and Thorold, the Norman abbot of Peterborough, his death, and his sepulture at the famous Abbey of Croyland, are related in detail by Ingulph, according to whose testimony he left a daughter who took the name of Turfrida, after her mother. Ingulph says she was alive when he was writing his "Chronicle." She married Hugh of Evermont[1] or Evermure,[2] lord of the vill of Deeping.

Lefstanus, abbot of Bury St. Edmunds in Suffolk, is another of the great Saxon holders before the Domesday Survey. He became abbot of this great and rich abbey in A.D. 1044, and held the abbacy for twenty-one years.

Leuenot is a name frequently met with in many counties. Nothing is known of the person or persons who bore the name. The same may be said of Leueva, a name apparently borne by persons of either sex; Leuiet, Leuing, Leuuinus, and Leuric or Leuricus.

---

[1] Ellis, p. 146.   [2] Ingulph, p. 117.

The latter, however, included Leuric of Devonshire, who is said to have been nephew of Leofric, earl of Mercia, and related to the royal family, as the appellation *cilt* in the Lincoln Domesday testifies. He, too,[1] exchanged the ploughshare and the sword for the pastoral staff of an abbot, in the powerful Abbey of Peterborough in 1057. His proclivities, however, carried him into the army again in A.D. 1066.

Passing by without notice the names of many Saxon tenants of lands either in the time of King Edward or before the Domesday Book was compiled, mention may be made of Merlesuain, Merlesuan, or Merlosuen vicecomes, an illustrious tenant in Somersetshire, Devonshire, Cornwall, Yorkshire, and Lincolnshire. He attests charters[2] of King Edward the Confessor and William the Conqueror, which shows that for a time, at least, Ellis thinks, that it was in his capacity of *vicecomes*, or "sheriff," of Lincoln, that Wace sings of Merlesuain as one of those who had engaged to forward forces to the south in aid of Harold, when the ill-fated prince marched after the battle of Stamford Bridge against the Normans. In A.D. 1067, Merlesuan accompanied[3] Edgar the Atheling to the Scottish court.

Of Morcar, or Morcar the Earl, some particulars have already been given. He is recorded as an extensive holder in many counties before the survey.

---

[1] Cf. "Anglo-Saxon Chronicle," *ad annum*.

[2] In the *Liber Niger* of Peterborough, MS. 60, Society of Antiquaries, London.

[3] "Anglo-Saxon Chronicle," *ad annum*.

The name only occurs in Buckinghamshire as that of
an under-tenant of land at the time of the compilation
of Domesday Book, and does not find any place
among the tenants in capite under the new Government.

Osiet, a Bedfordshire landholder previous to the
coming of the Normans, continued to hold this and
other lands at the time of the survey. He is styled
præfectus regis.

R. the *Comes Vetus*, or the "Old Earl," a
pre-Domesday tenant in Norfolk, is identified by
Kelham in a note quoted by Ellis as "Old Earl
Ralph, the father of Ralph de Guader, earl of
Norfolk."

Robert, son of Wimarc, the *Stallere*, or Constable,
appears to have been one of the Kentish thegns of
Edward the Confessor. He was the father of Suein
of Essex.

Seman, a tenant in Surrey in the time of Edward
the Confessor, is noteworthy as being one of the few
who became under-tenants of their own lands on the
political change under William taking place. From
this time forward he became the *servus* of Oswold,
and paid a rent of twenty pence for his land, and he
lost the privilege of transferring himself to any other
lord.

Siuuard, or Siuuardus, is a name constantly occurring in the list of tenants before the survey. It is
difficult to say how many of these entries represent
the same person's land. But among the noble
Siwards is the earl of that name, who held estates in
Huntingdonshire and Yorkshire; another is the

thegn and kinsman of King Edward; a third is
Siuuard the priest, one of the "Lagemen of Lincoln
in the time of Edward the Confessor, who had been
succeeded in that office at the time the survey was
made by Leduuin, the son of Reuew. A fourth
Siuuard had the surname or appellation of Bar or
Barn. He appears among the pre-Domesday tenants
in Gloucestershire. This great chief took part in
the rebellion at Ely, described in the Anglo-Saxon
Chronicle under the year 1071. A fifth Siuuard is
designated as a rich Salopian Saxon, "dives homo de
Scropscyre," in the Worcester Chartulary compiled
by Heming, in the passage containing the *Comme-*
moratio Placiti, or record of the lawsuit between
Wulfstan, bishop of Worcester, and Walter, bishop
of Evesham.

Stanchil, a tenant in Berkshire before the Domesday Survey, is equated by Ellis with Turkill of the
Abingdon Chronicle,[1] where he, too, is called "a rich
man" (*dives*). He held Chingstune, or Kingston
Bagpuze, in the time of King Edward, but transferred
the superiority over his lands to the Abbey of
Abingdon, and this again at the time of the Survey
was held by Henry de Ferrariis.

Stigand, or Stigandus, the Archbishop, is another
tenant to whom a large estate belonged before the
Domesday period. Some facts relating to him have
been already mentioned. The names Tochi, or
Toche, Toli, Tor, Torchil, Toret, Tosti, Tovi, Turchil

---

[1] British Museum, Cotton. MS., Claudius C. ix. f. 133. See
the "Abingdon Chronicle," ed. Stevenson (Rolls Series).

or Turchillas, Turgot, Turold, Vctred, Vlf, Vlchel, Vlchil, Vlfac, Vlmar, Vlmer or Vlmarus, Ulsi, Vlueua, Vluiet, Vluric or Vluricus, Vluuard, Vluuinus, Wigot, Wluui, and many others, suggest for the most part Saxon, with, perhaps, a few Danish tenants before the Domesday Survey. How far the numerous entries under each name can be apportioned to the same person it is now impossible to declare. Several of these personages re-appear in the list of under-tenants, at the formation of the survey.

Some, as Tochi, Toui, Turchil, Turgot, were *hus-carles* and thegns of King Edward the Confessor. A Toli is designated *vicecomes* in Suffolk. Tosti may be the "Tosti comes," who appears as a tenant in several counties. Turold the Vicecomes is clearly Thorold of Bugenhale, or Bukenhale, Sheriff of Lincolnshire. He bestowed his Manor of Bokenhale[1] on the Abbey of St. Guthlac, Croyland. The text of his charter granting the Manor of Spalding to the same monastery in A.D. 1051 is still extant.[2] The names of some of the *nativi*, or those born of servile parentage, which occur in this charter, are of interest, but we must refer those who wish to examine them to the work in which the charter is printed.

Vchtred is a very old name. The person or persons under that name may, perhaps, have derived it from the sub-regulus of the Hwiccas, or Worcestershire Vhtred, who flourished three centuries before the Domesday Survey was commissioned.

[1] Ingulph's "Chronicle," ed. W. de G. Birch, p. 112.
[2] *Ib.* p. 153.

An Vlchel, called also Vlchetel or Wulketul, became abbot of Croyland at the appointment of Edward the Confessor in 1052. His unfortunate career is related at length by Ingulph, who succeeded him in the Abbacy[1] from which it appears that he gave great offence to Ivo Tailbois, Norman lord of. Holland in Lincolnshire, by publishing the miracles which were reported to have been performed at the tomb of earl Waltheof, in the Abbey. For this offence he was summoned to a Council at London, in A.D. 1075, deprived of his position, and committed to prison at Glastonbury, in Somersetshire, under charge of abbot Thurstan, whom Ingulph stigmatises as very bloodthirsty.[2] The King took advantage of the opportunity afforded by the imprudence of the abbot of Croyland to confiscate its treasure.

Vlfric cilt is a tenant in Derbyshire before the Domesday Survey. His name is not found among the under-tenants at the Domesday period. He was, no doubt, a scion of the royal family.

The ill-fated Wallef Comes, also called Walleuus, or Waltef, Waldeuus, Waleuus Consul, Walleter, and Walthews, and by many other somewhat similar names, deserves a word in passing. He was the younger son of Siward, the earl of Northumberland, one of Edward the Confessor's adherents, who died in 1055. His mother was the daughter and heir of

---

[1] Ingulph's "Chronicle," pp. 113, 115, 126–8.

[2] "Cruentissimus." It was abbot Thurstan who, in 1081, poured out, on the altar-steps, the blood of his monks who would not accept his new regulations. "John of Oxenedes," p. 32.

Aldred, the Saxon earl of Northumberland. Fifteen years[1] after his father's death he obtained the earldom of Northumberland, to which he was raised by King William, upon the flight of Cospatrick, the former rebellious earl, into Scotland. Previous to this time, but the exact date has not been ascertained, he had held the earldom of Northampton and Huntingdom, probably[2] between A.D. 1066 and 1068. These earldoms, we are informed, had been at one time attached to that of Northumberland, and were afterwards separated from it, and held distinctly from it by Waltheof. Ingulph, whose unsupported evidence is, according to many writers, rarely to be trusted, states that Waltheof received these dignities on the death of his father, when Tosti received that of Northumberland. Whereas the Chronicle of John of Peterborough distinctly, but incorrectly, records that Waltheof succeeded to Northamptonshire on his father's death in 1055, yet it is known from a charter still extant,[3] that Tosti was then earl of that shire.

It can, therefore, hardly be doubted that the earldoms of Northamptonshire and Huntingdonshire were obtained by Waltheof as a result of the Northumbrian revolt in 1065.

In the year after the conquest, King William took Waltheof, with Edgar Atheling, Eadwine, and Morcar to Normandy on his return to that country.

[1] "The Life and Times of Earl Waltheof," by E. Levien, in "Journ. Brit. Arch. Assoc.," vol. xxx. p. 387.
[2] Freeman, "History of the Norman Conquest," vol. ii. pp. 555–569.   [3] Kemble, "Cod. Dipl." No. Dcccciv.

Waltheof appears in the list of pre-Domesday
tenants as holding lands of considerable extent in
many counties, chiefly Surrey, Cambridge, Huntingdon, Bedford, Northampton, Leicester, Derby,
Rutland, Lincoln, and Essex. The revolt in 1069,
when York Castle was attacked by the combined
forces of the Northumbrians and Danes, joined by
Edgar Atheling, and the earls Cospatric and
Waltheof, naturally made King William an implacable
enemy of Waltheof, but the king appears to have at
any rate abstained at the time from taking retaliation.
He gave the earl his niece Judith—an ominous
name!—to wife; and, according to William of
Ramsey, made a free grant of all his lands to him,
and, further, conferred on him the liberties belonging
to the honours of Huntingdon. At this time it
would appear that Waltheof enjoyed some share of
royal favour. He was appointed by the king,
together with Gosfrid, bishop of Constance, Remigius de Fécamp, bishop of Lincoln, and others, a
commissioner to inquire into the alleged usurpation
of lands belonging to the Abbey of Ely. The text
of the *placitum* has been printed,[1] and forms, with
the text of records relating to the trial at Penenden
Heath, and to the Worcester *Indiculum*,[2] a valuable
insight into the judicial processes respecting the
settlement of land in the Domesday period. Waltheof

---

[1] "Inquisitio Comitatus Cantabr.," ed. Hamilton, p. 192,
from MS. Trin. Coll. Cantab. O . 2 . 1. f. 210 *b.*

[2] Hearne's "Heming," vol. i., p. 287, from MS. Cotton.
Tiberius, A. xiii. f. 132. See further on, chap. xiv.

is also known[1] to have sat with the unfortunate
Walcher, the warlike bishop of Durham, as a judge
in temporal matters, and to have been consulted by
that prelate on matters relating to the Church.
Eventually, however, the earl became involved in the
plot for which he forfeited his life. The exasperation
of the nobility at the king's arbitrary and oppressive,
conduct in A.D. 1074, on the occasion of the marriage of Emma, sister of Roger Fitz-Osborn, earl of
Hereford, son and heir of William Fitz-Osborn, a
favourite of the king, with Ralph de Guader or de
Waet, earl of Norfolk—which was celebrated in
defiance of the king's refusal to sanction their union,
a compact was entered into by the powerful nobles,
then present, who swore to take steps to rid the
country of the Normans. Among the conspirators
was Waltheof; and his wife Judith, on hearing of the
plot, revealed it to the king. Waltheof does not
appear to have entered upon this perilous path of
prodition with any intention of acting upon it. On
the advice of Lanfranc, archbishop of Canterbury,
he proceeded to Normandy to divulge it himself to
the king, and to explain how it had come to pass
that he had a mistaken and unwilling share in it.

Meanwhile the rebellious nobles had risen somewhat prematurely for their plans, and were easily
repressed. To each a share of barbarous punishment
was decreed ; to Waltheof fell the sentence of decapi-
tation, which he suffered at Winchester on April 29,
A.D. 1075. His lands were conferred on his widow,

---

[1] Hoveden.

the countess Judith, whose conduct in denouncing her husband to the king has been viewed in various aspects. Ingulph[1] bestows on her the strong term of "*impiissima Jezebel*," while he looks on the death of the earl as the martyrdom of an innocent and harmless man. His body was hastily buried; after a fortnight's lapse the king allowed Wulketul, abbot of Croyland, to translate the remains to the chapter-house at Croyland, and the subsequent miracles which took place at his tomb cost the abbot his freedom, as we have already shown.

Wigot of Wallingford is another great Saxon tenant before the Domesday Survey was prepared. Ellis, quoting a passage in. Kennett's ".Parochial Anti-quities,"[2] states that William the Conqueror, after the battle of Hastings, passed through Kent and by London, then held by the party of Edgar Atheling, to Wallingford, where the lord of that town, Wigod de Wallingford, went out to meet him, delivered the town up to him, and entertained him there, until archbishop Stigand and many of the nobles of Edgar's party came in and tendered their submission. For this service the king, with a view of ingratiating himself with his newly-acquired subjects, and at the same time to reward his Norman companions, bestowed Aldith, the only daughter of Wigod, in marriage to Robert de Oily or Oilli, who afterwards enjoyed the estates of his Saxon father-in-law.

The names of places and persons mentioned in the Record afford a vast field for the consideration

---

[1] Ed. Birch, p. 126.   [2] Page 55.

of the. philologist. The place-names might be
divided into separate classes, showing the pre-
historic or Celtic ; the Roman ; the Anglo-Saxon ;
the Danish ; and the Norman origin of the names.
But a mere list would require far more space than
can here be devoted to it, and almost every example
would involve controversial and philological argu-
ments unsuited for the popular character of this
work. As a rule, the apparent significance of a
place-name is not the real one. Who,·but those who
study these questions, will believe that Shepherd's
well in Kent is a corruption of Sibriht's Weald, or
Sibertswold; or that Cambridge is not the Bridge
of the River Cam, but Grantabrige.

Many of the names of persons and of places, no
doubt, have been written down by the Norman scribes
incorrectly, perhaps following a phonetic and arbitrary,
rather than any etymological rule. But even allowing for this, there are numerous names which cannot
fail to excite our interest. Some of them are individual appellations, others secondary names, for the
most part descriptive of some personal peculiarity
or indicating some fact in the life of the individual
to whom it was applied. These names in many instances passed on in the family, until they became
finally and firmly established as surnames. It would
be impossible to allude to or discuss all these peculiarities of nomenclature within the scope of the
present work, but no account of the Domesday
Book would be complete without some reference to
them. The following are of striking appearance,
and may be studied with advantage by the light of

such a work as Dr. Ernest Förstemann's *Altdeutsches Namenbuch* : [1]—

TENANTS IN CAPITE.

Adobed, Rualdus (*Dev.*)
Alfhilla (*Dev.*)
Aluuard collinc (*Wilts.*)
Aluuard mert (*Dev.*)
Anschitil parcher (*Somers.*)
Ansger Fouuer (*Somers.*)
Asinus, or Lasne, Hugo (*Worc.*)
Aulric Wanz (*Suff.*)
Bolle (*Hants.*)
Bollo (*Dors.*)
Buge (*Notts.*)
Carbonel (*Heref.*)
Chaua, Leuuiuus (*Buck.*)
Croc (*Wilts.*)
Dalfin (*Derb., Yorks.*)
Esnebern (*Yorks.*)
Forne (*Yorks.*)
Game (*Yorks.*)
Gamel (*Yorks., Staff.*)
Gernio (*Oxf.*)
Hghebernus (*Ess.*)
Hunfridus Vis-de-Lew (*Berks.*)
Jeanio (*Oxf.*)
Ilbodo (*Ess.*)
Ilbodus (*Oxf.*)
Landri (*Yorks.*)
Leuuinus Oaura (*Buck.*)

[1] Published at Nordhausen in 1856.

Liseman (*Wilts.*)
Mal; Malf; (*Hants.*).
Odolina (*Wilts.*).
Osmundus Benz (*Derb.*)
Otha (*Staff.*)
Outi (*Linc.*)
Ramechil (*Yorks.*)
Ravelin (*Hants.*)
Raven (*Leic.*)
Ravenchil (*Yorks.*)
Ricardus Pugnant, or Puignant (*Hants.*)
Roger Deus-salvæt-Dominas (*Ess.*)
Restoldus (*Linc.*)
Sbernus (*Wilts.*)
Schelin (*Dors., Somers.*)
Sedret (*Derb.*)
Siuuard barn (*Nott.*)
Soartin (*Hants.*)
Sortebrand; Sortebrant (*Linc.*)
Sperri (*Staff.*)
Tochi (*Nott.*)
Toli (*Derb.*)
Tona (*Yorks.*)
Tor (*Yorks.*)
Tored (*Yorks.*)
Tovi (*Hants., Wilts., Norf.*)
Turstinus Mantel (*Buck.*)
Vda (*Staff.*)
Vlchil (*Yorks.*)
Vlsi (*Hants, Bedf., Nott., Yorks.*)
Vluric Waula (*Wilts.*)
Wislac (*Hants.*)
Wit, Alwinus (*Hants.*)

TENANTS IN THE TIME OF EDWARD THE CONFESSOR, AND PREVIOUS TO THE DOMESDAY SURVEY.

Aben (*Linc.*)
Abet.
Abo (*Yorks.*)
Achi (*Wilts, Ches., Suff., etc.*)
Acum (*Linc.*)
Acun (*Yorks.*)·
Ædricus grim (*Suff.*)
Ælfag (*Nott.*); Elfag (*Derb.*)
Ærgrim (*Salop.*)
Ailm (*Cornw.*)
Ailmarus melc (*Ess.*)
Aki (*.Suff.*)
Albus, Oslac (*Northt.*)
Aldene tope (*Linc.*)
Algrim (*Yorks.*)
Alli (*Buck., Bedf.*)
Alnod Grutt or Grud (*Hertf.*)
Alric Eduinus in paragio (*Dev.*)
Alric bolest (*Buck.*)
Alric deburch (*Suff.*)
Alric gangemere (*Buck.*)
Alricus Wintremele (*Bedf.*)
Alsius Bolla (*Ess.*)
Aluredus biga (*Kent.*)
Aluric blac (*Herts.*) and other examples of *blac*,
    blacus.
Aluric busch (*Hert.*)
Aluric capus (*Cambr.*)

Aluric pic (*Devon.*)
Aluric uuelp (*Oxf.*)
Aluricus biga (*Ess.*)
Aluricus camp (*Ess.*)
Aluricus campa, and capin (*Suff.*)
Aluricus scoua (*Hertf.*)
Aluricus stari, and stikestare (.*Suff.*)
Aluricus uuand (*Ess.*)
Aluuardus belrap (*Suss., Berk., Dev., Bed.*)
Aluuardus Dore (*Ess.*)
Aluui blac (*Worc.*)
Aluuinus black (*Hunt.*)
Aluuinus Boi (*Surr.*)
Aluuinus coc (*Cambr.*)
Aluuinus cubold (*Northt.*)
Aluuinus deule (*Hants, Bedf.*)
Aluuinus dode (*Hertf.*)
Aluuinus forst (*Hants.*)
Aluuinus sac (*Bedf.*)
Amod (*fem.*) (*Suff.*)
Andrac (*Hants.*)
Anunt dacus (*Essex.*)
Ape (*Somers.*)
Appe (*Wilts.*)
Archilbar (*Linc.*)
Ardegrip (*Linc.*)
Aregrim (*Chesh.*)
Arnegrim (*York.*)
Aschilbar (*Linc.*)
Aseloc (*Nott.*)
Auti (*Suss., Glouc., Norf.,* &c.)
Azor (*passim*); Azor Rot (*Kent.*)

K

Azur (*Oxf.*, *Northt.*, *Warw.*)
Baco (*Linc.*)
Bar (*Yorks*, *Suff.*, *Midd.*, *Norf.*)
Basin (*Yorks.*)
Ber (*Yorks.*)
Biga (*Surr.*)
Bil (*Glouc.*)
Boda (*Hants.*); Bode (*Wilts.*); Boddus (*Ess.*)
Bou (*Norf.*); Bu (*Yorks.*)
Boui (*Northt.*, *Leic.*, *Warw.*, *Nott.*)
Bricstouuard (*Somers.*)
Brictuarus Bubba (*Suff.*)
Brihtuoldus musla (*Suff.*)
Brodo (*Bed.*, *Norf.*); Brodus (*Linc.*)
Bunda, Bonde, Bunde, Bondi, Bundi, Bondo,
    Bundo, and Bondus, Bundus (*in var. counties.*)
Caduualent (*Cornw.*)
Caflo (*Somers.*)
Caua; Caue; Cauo; Cauus (*Suss.*)
Celcott (*Suff.*)
Cheteber (*Yorks*); Chetelbar (*Linc.*); Chetelber
    (*Hunt.*, *Yorks.*, *Linc.*); Chetelbern (*Nott.*,
    Linc., *Norf.*)
Clac (*Linc.*)
Col (*Linc.*); Cola (*Suss.*); Cole (*Suss.*, *Derb.*);
    Colle (*Derb.*); Colo (*Wilts.*, *Somers.*, *Cornw.*,
    &c.)
Coolle (*Wilts.*)
Couta (*Suff.*)
Crin (*Yorks.*)
Dedol; Dedou (*Chesh.*)
Doda; Dode; Dodo (*Var.*)

Don ; Done ; Donne ; Dŏno ; Donnus (*Var.*)
Edlouedief (*Dev.*)
Edmer atre (*Dev.*)
Edmer Attile (*Hertf.*); atula (*Midd.*, *Buck.*)
Edric cecus (*Wilts.*)
Edric grim (*Suff.*)
Edric lang (*Glouc.*)
Edric maners (*Dev.*)
Edric salvage (*Heref.*, *Salop.*)
Edric spur (*Cambr.*)
Edricus pur (*Cambr.*)
Edricus spuda (*Suff.*)
Edricus stirman (*Worc.*)
Eduinus Alferd (*Leic.*)
Eduinus Grut (*Heref.*)
Eduuardus úuit (*Bedf.*)
Eldille (*Dev.*)
Elsi jllinge (*Nott.*)
Epy (*Buck.*)
Ergrim (*Heref.*)
Esber biga (*Kent.*)
Eureuuacre (*Dev.*)
Felaga (*Ess.*)
Fot (*Chesh.*, *Kent.*)
Fuglo (*Bedf.*)
Gam (*Yorks.*)
Game (*Leic.*, *York*); Gameltorf bar, Gamelbar,
  Gamelber, Gamebar (*Yorks.*)
Gamel (*var.*)
Gamelcarle (*Yorks.*)
Gethne (*Salop.*)
Gilepatric (*Yorks.*)

Glunier (*Yorks.*)
Godtovi (*Surr.*)
Golnil (*Buck.*)
Gos (*Hunt.*)
Gribol (*Linc.*)
Giimulf (*Warw.*)
Haltor ; Heltor (*Yorks.*)
Huna, Hunus (*Suff.*) ; Hune (*Yorks.*); Huni,
 Hunni, Huninc, Hunnic, Hunnit, &c.
 (*Salop.*)
Jalf (*Linc.*)
Jaul (*Cornw.*)
Juin (*Dev.*) ; Juing (*Somers.*)
Kee (*Norf.*)
Ketelbern, Ketelbert (*Worc.*)
Lambecarl, Lanbecarle (*Linc.*)
Leswinus croc(*Suff.*)
Leuenot sterre (*Derb.*)
Leuricus coccus (*Suff.*)
Leuuinus calvus (*Suff.*)
Lurc (*Suff.*)
Maban (*Yorks.*)
Mannius swert (*Suff.*) ; Magno Suert (*Surr.*)
Moithar (*Norf.*)
Offa (*Suss.*, *Suff.*)
Osbertus masculus (*Suff.*)
Oslac albus (*Northt.*)
Phin (*Suff. Ess.*); Phin dacus (*Ess.*); Pin (*Glouc.*).
Ram (*Yorks.*)
Ramechil (*Yorks.*)
Roc (*Suff.*)
Rozo (*Wilts.*) ·
Salomon (*Yorks.*)

Salpus (*Suff.*)

Saul, Saulf, Saulfus (*Var.*) ; Seulf (*Somers.*).

Sbern (*Kent, Suss., Cornw., Leic., Linc.*) ; Sberne (*Hants, Warw.,* &c.)

Sbern biga (*Kent.*)

Sbern croc (*Nott.*)

Sbern, Vlmer (*Nott.*)

Scheit, Schett (*Norf.*)

Scotcol, Scotecol (*Yorks.*)

Seiar, Seiardus, or Siuuard bar (*Norf.; Glouc.*) ; Siuuardbar (*Yorks., Linc.*) ; Siuuard barn (*Warw., Nott., Linc.*)

Sessi (*Salop.*)

Sindi (*Yorks.*)

Snellinc (*Cambr.*)

Snode, Snot (*Dev.*)

Sol (*Heref.*)

Spirites (*Kent, Hants, Heref.*) ; Spirtes (*Wilts., Heref., Salop, Somers.*) ; Sport (*Yorks.*)

Stam (*Yorks.*)

Stanker (*Suff.*)

Ster (*Linc.*) ; Sterr (*Yorks.*) ; Sterre (*Hants, Yorks.*) ; Stur (*Linc.*) ; Strui (*Linc.*)

Suartcol (*Yorks.*)

Suenus Suart (*Ess.*)

Thol, Thole, Tholi, Tol, Toli (*Var.*)

Thor (*Northt.*) ; Tor, (*Yorks., Linc., Norf.*)

Tou, Toul, Toui, Touui, Touius (*Var.*)

Turloga (*Yorks.*)

Vluuard Wit (*Dors.*)

Vnfac (*Nott.*)

Wadel (*Kent, Der., Cornw.*) ; Wadels (*Der.*) ; Wadhel (*Cornw.*) ; Wadelo (*Der.*)

Welp (*Yorks.*); Uuelp, Aluric (*Oxf.*)
Wilegrip (*Staff.*, *Salop.*)
Uuit (*i.e.*, "White") as a second name (*Hants,*
Bedf., *Heref.*, *Kent*, *Dors.*, *Oxf.*, *Midd.*)
Wluuardus Leuet (*Bedf.*)
Wordrou (*Der.*)

There is not a single example in the above list
which does not present peculiarities of great interest.
We may trace in these names, and in many others,
which have been omitted in order to keep the list
within reasonable limits, the germs of many of our
modern surnames. We are also able to see how
heterogeneous was the race of landowners in England
before the coming of the Normans. Celts, Danes,
Normans, Anglo-Saxons, Jews, and natives of almost
every European nation are plainly indicated; and
even from among the undertenants at the time of the
formation of the Domesday Book, as the following
list shows, a similar roll of names may be gathered.

UNDERTENANTS IN THE DOMESDAY BOOK.

Abel (*Kent.*)
Adam (*Kent.*, *Hertf.*, *Oxf.*)
Aelous (*Suff.*)
Alde (*Warw.*)
Aluredus Hispan (*Glouc.*)
Aluricus chacepol (*Midd.*)
Aluricus parvus (*Hants.*)
Aluuin ret (*Hants.*)
Amun (*Dors.*)
Ansegis (*Warw.*)

Asso (*Ess.*); Azo (*Var.*); Azor (*Hants.*, *Midd.*,
    Linc.)
Auigi (*Bedf.*)
Baderon (Will.), *Glouc.*, *Heref.*)
Bainard (surname or single name, *Norf.*, *Suff.*)
Balt (surname, *Ess.*)
Basset (surname, *Hertf.*, *Bedf.*, *Buck.*)
Blize (*Kent.*)
Blondus, Blundus (surnames, *Norf.*, *Suff.*, *Ess.*)
Bono (*Somers.*)
Brant (Will.), (*Norf.*)
Buterus (*Leic.*)
Caflo (*Somers.*)
Cheping (*Wilts.*)
Cola (*Derb.*, *Berks.*)
Croc (single name, *Wilts.*; surname, *Hants.*)
Dauid (*Dors.*, *Ches.*, *Ess.*)
Donecan (*Somers.*)
Dynechaie (*Suff.*)
Ehelo (*Linc.*)
Enisan (*Yorks.*); Enisant (*Cambr.*, *Ess.*)
Ernuzon (*Berks.*)
Feggo (*Leic.*)
Flint (surname, *Suff.*)
Fragrin (*Staff.*)
Gadio (*Oxf.*)
Gamas (*Suff.*)
Gerneber (*Yorks.*)
Gleu (*Bedf.*)
Gollam, Gollan (*Cambr.*)
Gulaffra, Gulafra (surname, *Suff.*)
Gunequata (*Suff.*)

Gunter (*Wilts.*)
Hubb' (*Suff.*)
Idhel (*Glouc.*)
Isac (*Norf., Suff.*)
Jacob (*Oxf.*)
Jagelin (*Der.*)
James (*Suff.*)
Jarnacotus (*Suff.*)
Johais (*Warw.*)
Judhellus (*Der.*); Judichel (*Wilts., Bedf.*);
  ·Juhellus (*Warw.*)
Juran (*Hants.*)
Lofus (*Surr.*)
Lunen (*Hunts.*)
Maci (surname, *Hants.*)
Malus Vicinus (*Suff.*)
Marcud (*Ches.*)
Mecheuta (*Leic.*)
Moyses (*Somers.*)
Nauuen (*Staff.*)
Noui (*Heref.*) -
Oddo (*Suff.*); Odo (*var.*); Otho (*Cambr.*); Otto
  (*Ess.*)
Offels (*Cornw.*)
Papaldus (*Hants.*)
Parler (surname, *Worc.*)
Passaq̃ (surname, *Bedf.*)
Phanexon (*Norf.*)
Pugnant, Pungiant (surnames, *Hants., Berks.*)
Rademar (*Dev.*); Rademer (*Somers.*)
Ratho (*Norf.*) ⁚
Rauenesort (*Nott.*)

Robert niger (*Kent*).
Rold (*Linc.*)
Rolland (*Northt.*)
Roricus (*Suff.*)
Salo (*Warw.*)
Sasuualo (*Sus.*, *Berks.*, *Oxf.*, *Northt.*, *Linc.*, *Warw.*, *Derb.*)
Sasuuardes (*Suss.*)
Scudet, Scutet (surnames, *Wilts.*, *Suff.*)
Sinod (*Dors.*)
Stable (*Somers.*)
Tirus (*Norf.*)
Tor (*Linc.*)
Tuder, a Welshman (*Salop.*)
Turmit (surname, *Norf.*)
Uctebrand (*Derb.*)
Venables, Gislebertus de (*Chesh.*)
Vltbertus (*Northt.*)
Vrfer (*Warw.*, *Staff.*)
Uttalis (*Kent.*)
Wala (*Norf.*)
Wast (surname, *Buck.*, *Bedf.*)
Wazo (*Surr.*, *Berks.*)
Werllc (*Suss.*); Werenc (*Suss.*)
Wihuenec, Wihucnech (*Dev.*)
Wihumar, Wihumare (*Cornw.*)

Besides the consideration of these peculiar names, the titular designations and titles of persons, officers, and other distinguishing appellations are of considerable interest. Many of the terms employed are difficult of interpretation, and even the learned Ducange, who has devoted more attention to the subject than any one since his day, is unable to throw light on some of the obscurer names of officers and offices. The following collection of the principal of these terms has been arranged, for convenience of reference, in alphabetical order, with a short account of each as far as may be gathered from the explanations which have been recorded by writers on this branch of Domesday ethics.

The ABBOTS were the heads of the abbeys, and ranked next to Bishops in the importance of their position. There was not a great number of them who find place in the Domesday.

Accipitrarii, or *Ancipitrarii*, officers appointed to attend to the Lords' falcons. Ducange calls this person "accipitrum curator et domitor," "the caretaker and tamer of the hawks."

Aloarii, Alodarii, or *Alodiarii,* were the tenants in *Allodium,* or *Fee Simple,* that is of an hereditary and perpetual estate, free to be disposed of by gift or sale, and subject to the common and constant land-tax of hidage. In Kent, under certain cases, all the allodial tenants, and their men, were liable to a fine or tax, and on the death of the *Aloarius,* the king was entitled to a relief. Although, as a rule, the *Aloarii* were freemen, there are some instances of a qualified kind of allodium, and of undertenants in *allodium.* In Berkshire the *Alodiarus* still exists, at the time of the formation of the survey.

The king was entitled to a *relief* when an *Alodiarius* died, in Kent, with certain exceptions specified by Ellis from the opening account of the survey in the Domesday Book.

.. *Ancilla* was a female slave, much of the same class as the *servus*. They were at the lord's disposal, but protective laws were in force in their favour. The term is derived from a classical source.

There were no less than a hundred and one *ancillæ* in Worcestershire, out of the total number of four hundred and seven specified throughout the survey. Sometimes, however, as in Herefordshire, for example, these persons are mentioned without a definite number being expressed.

The payment to which an *Ancilla* was entitled is quoted by Ellis from the British Museum Cotton MS., Titus A. xxvii., f. 453.

Angli, or *Anglici*, amount in all to twenty-six. They were probably Saxon undertenants. The *Angligenæ* were similar to them. The English, or *Angligenæ* of Shrewsbury stated[1] that at the time of the taking of the survey, they paid the whole local geld for the support of the state, as it was paid in the time of Edward the Confessor, notwithstanding that the castle of earl Roger de Montgomery—who held the city—had occupied the site of fifty-one houses, and fifty others were lying waste. The word was of course also employed in a general and comprehensive sense, as, for example, in the passage in the Chronicle of John of Oxenedes, where he says that the word was used as a term of reproach.

The *Apium Custos*, or Bee-master, was one of the assistants in husbandry. Only two are mentioned, but no doubt the number of persons employed in agriculture was great, honey being a staple article of food among our Saxon and Norman forefathers.

[1] Ellis, i, 201..

Arbalistarii, or *Balistarii,* were cross-bow men. This important section of the military strength has been discussed in detail by J. Hewitt, in his valuable work on "Ancient Armour and Weapons in Europe."

Arcarii, officers whose duties have not been very clearly defined. They were probably archers, sagittarii, bowmen. The same term is used anciently to signify those to whom was entrusted the charge of the public chest or *arca* of the treasury.

Aurifabri, or workers in gold, goldsmiths, occur among the various tradesmen and artificers. The goldsmith appears to have been a privileged person in some cases, not only in Domesday, but throughout the ancient and mediæval world. There were three tenants in capite, and three under tenants at the time of the survey, and one held in the time of King Edward, besides others.

Barons are rarely noticed. They represent in Domesday the king's justiciaries, and the term was also applied to the tenants-in-chief generally.

Batsueins occurs in the survey of Warwick. The burgesses of the town provided four Batsueins, *i.e.,* *Boatswains,*[1] or paid four pounds in money when the king made war at sea against his enemies.

The *Bedel,* or *Bedellus,* was an under-bailiff of a manor. Twenty-two only are mentioned in all. In Leominster, in Herefordshire, the Manor of which had sixteen members, there were eight *prepositi* or provosts, and as many *bedels.* In Bedfordshire the bedels are classed with the king's prefects, and the almoners among the tenants in chief. The bedel had

---

[1] *Batus,* a boat, *scapha cymba.* Ducange.

greater freedom from work than others, because of his frequent interruptions, and was favoured with a small patch of land for his own cultivation.

Bercarii, or shepherds, are considered by Ellis to be equivalent to *Berbicarii*, a word derived from *vervex*, a weather. Only ten in all are specified.

Biga. Ellis considers this word a title of the officer appointed to provide carriages for the .use of the .king. It looks, however, more like a name, derived from the classical *biga*, a vehicle on two wheels. Ducange instances other significations of the word, a beam, a table, &c.

Bordarii. The total number of these amounts to 82,119, according to Ellis's tabulation. This is between a third and a fourth of the total recorded population of all conditions. There are also 490 *bordarii pauperes*, and 15 *dimidii*. The exact status of the Bordarius has formed the subject of much speculation, and Mr. Seebohm has added maps to his work, showing the comparative aggregation of these persons in certain localities by colour deeper or paler in accordance with their more or less frequent occurrence.

From the account given by Mr. H. E. Malden that in some hundreds the *bordarii* predominate, to the exclusion of the *cotarii*, while in others the reverse takes place, it is not improbable that the exact distinction between these two classes of peasants was but slight. It may be that different customs obtained in different hundreds, and that really the terms are synonymous. This is borne out by the Sussex Domesday, which enumerates *bordarii* from the commencement to folio 24, col. 2, line 4 from bottom; these then give place to *cotarii*, who end with folio 25 *b ;* and *bordarii* are again·denoted 'down to the end of the county survey. It is clear, from a charter of King Eadgar[1], that the word *Bord* signified a cottage, perhaps a boarded· or wooden hut. The *bordarii* are considered by Domesday antiquaries to have been drudges, performing inferior services of a miscellaneous character, such as grinding, thrashing, drawing water, cutting wood, and the like. Many derivations have, however, been hazarded for their appellation. Lord Coke calls them *boors,* holding a small house, larger than a cottage, to which some small portion of land was attached. Others consider that they lived as cottagers on the *borders* of a village or Manor, but in some cases, at least, this cannot be correct, for they are found as dwelling near the *aula* or Manor.House, and even as residents in the towns of Huntingdon, Norwich, and Thetford. The city of Norwich, indeed, sheltered no less than four hundred and eighty *bordarii,* who, on account of their poverty, were unable to pay taxes. Kennett considers these peasants to be distinct from the *servi* and *villani,* and to belong to a less servile class, being supplied with a *bord,* or cottage, and some adjacent land, on condition of supplying their lord with poultry, eggs, and other small provisions, for his *board* and entertainment. This, however, is extremely conjectural. Ellis is practically correct in his estimate of the position of the bordar, who were merely cottagers, and the "Inquisitio Eliensis" uses the expression *bordarii* where the Breviate MS. of the same

[1] Dugdale, "Mon. Angl." (new edition), i. 209.

entry in the Domesday uses the term *cotarii*. That they rendered occasional service in return for their maintenance is clear, from the statement in the Domesday, that on the demesne appertaining to the Castle of Ewias, there were twelve *bordarii*, who worked for one day every week. This term of *bord-men*, or *bordarii*, was used down to the end of the thirteenth century.

The *Bovarii*, or Oxherds.

The *Burgenses* or *burgesses* were, as their name implies, the inhabitants of the borough or *Burgh*, and the city. These inhabitants enjoyed a variety of privileges, which probably in very few cases were exactly alike. Domesday Book contains incidental notices of the services, charges, and customs of these Burghs:—

Dover.	Worcester.	York.
Canterbury.	Pershore.	Lincoln.
Romney.	Hereford.	Stamford.
Pevensey.	Cambridge.	Torksey.
Lewes.	Huntingdon.	Grantham.
Wallingford.	Northampton.	Louth.
Dorchester.	Leicester.	Maldon.
Bridport.	Warwick.	Colchester.
Wareham.	Stafford.	Norwich.
Shaftesbury.	Shrewsbury.	Yarmouth.
Taunton.	Chester.	Thetford.
Hertford.	The Wiches.	Ipswich.
Buckingham.	Nottingham.	Dunwich.
Oxford.	Derby.	

For example at Dover, the burgesses supplied the king with twenty ships for a fortnight every year. Each of these vessels contained a crew of twenty-one mariners. For this the burgesses enjoyed the privileges of Sac and Soc : two very important rights, the one of determining causes and disputes, executing laws and administering justice within a certain local area; the other being the term for the area in which the Sac was exercised. Dover being then, as indeed it is now, a port of passage, it is not strange that there were customs connected with the royal messengers. Thus, the burgesses paid threepence in winter and two in summer, when the king's messenger arrived, for transporting his horse. Among other privileges was this, that whoever, constantly residing in the town, paid his customary rent to the king, went free of toll throughout England. These customs were not introduced under the Norman rule, for it is expressly stated that they were found here at the king's coming. This is only one example of many, that the change of government interfered in a very small degree with the ancient and established institutions of the Saxons.

Lewes is another town of which the peculiar customs are set forth with some degree of minuteness. Twenty shillings, a large sum, was collected from every burgess to be paid to the naval forces, when the king sent out a fleet to guard the seas. Specific payments, or toll for selling saleable properties, and specific fines for certain offences obtained here.

Oxford had many peculiar customs, among which was this, that when the king set out on an expedition, twenty of the burgesses went with him for the rest, or the burgh paid a fine of twenty pounds that all might be excused. The tenants of the twenty "mural mansions" held their habitations under the liability to repair the city walls when need required, and the king should call upon them to do so.

The Hereford burgesses exercised customs and privileges which are minutely enumerated. Among them may be mentioned the right of sale by any burgess leaving the city, to any one who undertook to perform the proper services due from the holding, provided the parties obtained leave of the bailiff, who charged the third penny, *i.e.*, $33\frac{1}{3}$ *per cent.* on the transfer.

The moneyers in this city consisted of seven persons, who were bound to coin the king's silver, when he visited the city, into pennies, and for this they had the privilege of Sac and Soc.

The Cambridge burgesses lent their ploughs to the sheriff three times every year in the time of King Edward. But at the time of the survey this demand had been augmented to nine times.

Leicester supplied a contingent of twelve burgesses to the royal army when the king marched through the land, and a relay of four horses as far as London when a foreign expedition was equipped. A curious example of the comparative value of a certain kind of property is seen in the fact that for a hawk the king had the alternative of ten pounds by sale; for a baggage or sumpter horse twenty shillings.[1] A hawk was therefore valued at the worth of ten pack-horses.

[1] Taking the average modern value of a horse at £40, we see, incidentally, that money was worth forty times more then than it is now-a-days.

L

This proportion of valuation is also borne out by the enumeration of the Warwick customs.

Warwick seems to have been a centre of the honey district; in the time of the Confessor, part of the tax due from the town to the king consisted of thirty-six *sextaria*, an irregular, and not uniform measure, of honey. In the time of the Domesday the number of these measures, and the capacity, had apparently altered; but the return was still made in kind. In the city ten burgesses had to accompany the king whenever he went in person in any land expedition. Of the *batsueins* of Warwick, notice has been taken in another part of this work.

The Shrewsbury customs are enumerated with considerable detail. Among them the most interesting are that when the king lodged in the city he had a body-guard consisting of twelve of the principal inhabitants. When the king hunted, the burgesses who possessed horses attended him with their arms, and the sheriff sent thirty-six men on foot to the deer-stand while the king was there. An equal body of men were supplied for a week at the park of Marsetelie. A widow, on her remarriage paid a tax of twenty shillings to the king, while a maiden was only charged half this sum at her wedding.

Chester City possessed a large code of local laws and customs, which Ellis has discussed at length. If any burgess committed the crime of housebreaking and murder, he forfeited to the king the whole of his property and was declared an outlaw. The tax or fine on a widow under certain circumstances here may be compared with the Shrewsbury fine, above-mentioned, of twenty shillings, if she took a second husband. On the arrival of a cargo of martene skins, the king's bailiff was required to give order, under penalty of forty shillings, that no one should purchase them until he had himself examined them, presumably to secure the best specimens for the use of the royal court. False measures and, adulteration of beer involved the offender in a fine of four shillings, and the indignity of the cucking-stool. Provision was made for repairing the city walls, and the bridge by the bailiff, who required the freeholder of every hide of land within the county to supply one labourer, neglect on this behalf rendering the tenant liable to a fine of forty shillings. In this custom we see the survival of the *trinoda necessitas*, of the whole of Christendom, or triple[1] charge, from which no single landowner, of whatever degree he might be, was exempt throughout the Anglo-Saxon era. This duty, which was paramount in the uncertain times of the pre-Norman period, is differently expressed in the text of ancient charters, as for example :— "Liberam . . . exceptis istis tribus expeditione (military operations), pontis arcisue constructione (repair of bridge or fortress)," "Cartul. Saxon." No. 12, A.D. 616.—" Absque triinoda necessitate totius Christiani populi, id est, arcis munitione, pontis emendatione, exercitus congestione liberum," free except the triple need of the whole of Christendom, that is, the munition of the fort, the repair of

---

[1] Cf. also the "quatuor causis;" which included the usual three, and also "singulare prætium solvere adversus alium." "Cartul. Saxon." No. 51, A.D. 680.

the bridge, the reinforcement of the ranks. *Ibid.*
No. 50, A.D. 680.

But under whatever phraseology it might be stated,
the duty which was specified was the same. The
pons, the *arx* or *castellum*, and the *expeditio* can
relate to nothing else than the repair of bridges, a
term probably taken of wide signification, and including the approaches in the vicinity; the maintenance
of the city walls, which were regarded in many cases
as the outer wall of a castle co-extensive with the area
included by the city wall: the castle itself, if there
were one, being, so to speak, a second or inner line of
.defence; and the contribution of men, money, or
horses, as the case might be, towards the reinforcement of the king's army when it was once set in
movement against the common enemy.

Nottingham appears to have been, as it were, an
advance-guard to York, for the conservation of the
River Trent and the way to the City of York were
in the custody of the burgesses, and if any one
hindered the water-way, or ploughed, or dug ditches
within the distance of two perches of the king's
highway, he forfeited the large sum of eight pounds.
We may gather from this the relative breadth of the
marching front of army along the herepad, or war
path, which is synonymous in pre-Norman documents
with our terms of highroad or king's highway.

Derby had two kinds of burgesses; the full burgesses, of whom there were a hundred at the time
of the Domesday Book, and forty distinguished, as
minores, or of less importance. They may be
compared with the burgesses minuti of Tateshale,

the mein burgesses of Norwich, and the poor burgesses of Ipswich.

In three instances, at Cambridge, Lincoln, and Stamford, apart from the ordinary burgesses, we meet with the *lagemen, lagemanni,* or *lesser thegns.* These were, in the two latter of the three cases, only twelve in number. Ellis compares them with the twelve city judges of Chester, and the same number of *Lahmen,* specified in the " Senatus Consultum de Monticolis Walliæ." The twelve lagemen of Stamford, who are, like those of Lincoln, recognised in the laws of King Æthelred and King Edward the Confessor,[1] were reduced to the number of nine in that town when the Domesday Survey was compiled.

Torksey, like Nottingham, was charged with the duty of assisting in keeping up communication with the city of York. When the king's messengers arrived at this town, the watermen conducted them to the city, and the sheriff was bound to supply provisions, both for the messengers and their guides.

At Colchester, among other duties required of the burgesses in return for their privileges, the tax for expeditions, by sea or land, is specially mentioned in the Domesday Book.

Norwich, like Warwick, paid in honey, as well as in cash, for its local privileges. Apart from the specified money payments, there were due to the king twenty-one shillings and fourpence for proven-

---

[1] Thorpe, "Ancient Laws," ÆTHELRED, sec. III. ; EDW. CONF., sec. xxxviii., p. 199 ; compare also p. 151, where twelve *lahmen* were to "explain the law" to the "Wealas" and English.

der, six *sextaria* of honey, a bear, and six bear-hounds—presumably for the royal and popular amusement! of bear-baiting, which did not become extinct until the year 1835, when it was finally prohibited by Act of Parliament. To the queen this city gave a palfrey, in addition to the money payments due to her.

It must be remembered that in some towns, besides the burgesses, who were answerable to the Crown for their respective shares in the duties already mentioned, there were other burgesses under other lords; for example, in the City of Winchester, the Abbey of Romsey had fourteen burgesses, and in the town of Gloucester thirty burgesses owed their allegiance to a foreign body, the famous and wealthy Abbey of St. Denys at Paris. The total number of burgesses is estimated at 7,968.

The *Burs* or *Buri*, of whom sixty-two are enumerated in different parts of the Domesday Book—Berkshire, Buckinghamshire, Devonshire, Herefordshire, Oxfordshire, and Worcestershire. We are fortunately enabled, by means of an ancient manuscript in the British Museum,[1] to estimate the position and duties of the Burs or Geburs. Their services varied in different localities, and consisted of a certain number of days' work in the fields, and money payments at Michaelmas and Martinmas, as well as other charges.[2] In return, the *gebur* received two oxen and one cow and seven oxen and seven acres sown, and *tela* for his use, and furniture (*supellex*) for

[1] Cotton. MS. Titus A. viii., printed in Ellis's "Introd." ii. 425.

[2] *Hunigablum, metegablum,* or *ealagablum,* according to the prevalent custom of the manor.

his house. But on the death of the *gebur*, the lord took all. They were synonymous with the *Coliberti.*

The *Buzecarls*, mentioned in Domesday under Malmesbury, county of Wiltshire, were mariners. In the Anglo-Saxon Chronicle,[1] they are called Butse-carlas.

The Canons, Chaplains, or domestic priests of the king, the bishop or the earl, Clerks,[2] in some cases the same as *capellani*, Deacons,[3] Prebendaries,[4] Presbyters, the half-Presbyter, scarcely need an explanation of their condition.

Camerarii were chamberlains, but it is difficult to say whether they were royal or borough officers, or merely domestic servants of the lord's household.

Campo, or Champion, that is, a soldier, also occurs among the many terms used in the Domesday Book, representing condition of men. The quasi-surname Cemp or Camp, which occurs in the Cambridgeshire Survey, is the same.

The *Capicerius* of the church of Winchester was an officer thought to correspond with the sacrist of later times.

The *Caprarum mediator*,[5] one who attended the she-goats—presumably in a veterinary capacity—occurs in the Hampshire Domesday.

---

[1] Page 172.

[2] It is curious that as *Ecclesia* has a diminutive form, *Ecclesiola*, so *clericus* has in one instance a diminutive *clericolus*, who held a church worth one shilling at Westberie in Wiltshire.

[3] Walter the Deacon, an Essex tenant in capite, was married, and left two sons and a daughter.

[4] One only is recorded in the Domesday Book.

[5] Ellis, strangely enough, reads *venator* in his index, ii. 519.

The *Carpentarius* was an important artisan. His range of work was probably far wider than would now be included in the term of carpenter. Like the goldsmith and the huntsman, the necessities and the customs of the Domesday period rendered the skilled carpenter a man of repute and consideration. In accordance with this view, we find two of the king's carpenters among the tenants-in-chief in Cambridgeshire.

The *Cementarius*, bricklayer or stone-mason, also occurs. According to Ducange the word signifies "qui victum manibus quæritat," he who earns his food by handiwork.

There were 159 *Censarii*, *Censores*, or *Censorii*. They were those villains who paid *censum*, or a kind of relief by which they redeemed their estate, and so obtained possession of it.

The *Centenarius*, or Hundredor, appears in the Survey as *Custos*, *Prefectus*, or *Provost of the Hundred*. Ellis states that the Centenary was an officer retained among the Franks, Lombards, and other continental peoples, as well as among the Anglo-Saxons. Ducange mentions a variety of duties attached to this office, which was certainly of some local dignity and responsibility.

The *Cerevisiarii* were employed in the manufacture of *cerevisia* or beer, as their name implies. There are forty of these inferior officers in all mentioned in the Domesday Book.

The *Coci*, *Coqui*, or *Koci*, were cooks, and it has been suggested[1] that Tezelinus, the cook at Addington in Surrey, may have originated the tenure of "Malpy-

[1] Lysons, "Environs."

gurnon," produced by the owner of that manor at the royal coronation banquets.

The *Coliberti* amount in all to eight hundred and fifty-eight. They are derived [1] from the Roman civil law. One writer describes them as " Tenants in free socage by free rent." Another considers the *colibertus* as "a middle sort of tenants, between servile and free, or such as held their freedom of tenure under condition of such works and services," that they were a class of landholders who appear in later times as *conditionales*. Ducange [2] discusses the condition of the *Coliberti*.

The *Bures* or *Gebures* were equivalent to the *Coloni* and *Coliberti*, and over the latter word in one passage in the Domesday Book there is written in a contemporary hand the gloss " *vel Bures*," which sufficiently establishes the equality of the two appellations.

The *Commendati* and *dimidii commendati* were a class of freemen, a broad term with many local qualifications and restrictions, but either from choice or necessity placed (commended, *i.e.*, joined) under the protection of great lords. They were free, or partially free as the case might be, in person and blood, their property being guaranteed by the lord or patron to whom they were attached; and for this protection they paid an annual stipend, or performed some duty or services required of them by the lord. In this respect they resemble the coliberti, and, like them, are a survival from the social classes created by the provisions of the Roman civil law. They repre-

[1] Ellis, "Introd.," vol. i., p. 85.   [2] "Gloss," *sub voc.*

sented, in fact, the client, while the lord represented their patron. The *dimidii*, of course, had two masters, who shared the responsibility and enjoyed the benefits which their patronage acquired. Ellis thinks that it is not unlikely that some of the manorial rights at present existing may be traced for their origin to the commendation customs found in the Domesday.

The *Constable* was an officer of superior degree, but his duties and position are not very clearly laid down. Perhaps he was equal to the *stallere*, of whom some account is given further on.

The *Consul* or *Comes*, for there is little doubt that the first of these terms was only occasionally used as a synonym for the latter, will be referred to under the term *Earl*.

Coscets, *Cotsedæ*, *Coscez*, *Cozets*, or *Cozez*, amount in all to 1,749 for the whole area covered by the Domesday Book. They were apparently the same as the *Cottarii* and *Cotmanni*, being simply small cottagers paying rent for very small pieces of land. Their duties and privileges are described at length in the Cottonian MS., to which notice has been drawn under a previous title. Their position differed according to local customs; in some places they were required to work for their lord on every Monday throughout the year, and for three days every week in the month of August; in other places they worked every day in this month for the lord, mowing an acre of oats for a day's work, for which he had a sheaf and other rewards. The *coscet* was free of land gable, and entitled to five acres of land or more. He paid "heord penig," or hearth-penny, on Holy Thurs-

day, or Ascension Day, as every freeman should, and
"scyrisceat" at Martinmas; and was answerable to
the lord for "inland" and other charges.

The Cottars, *Cotarii, Coteri*, or *Cotmanni*, with
their diminutive Coterellus[1] (a term analogous to the
clericolus, æcclesiola, and other Domesday diminutives), amount in total to 5,070 and upwards. Some
mention of these inferior tenants has been already
made,[2] under the account of the *bordarii* and *coscets*.
Ellis records his opinion against the conclusions of
Kennett, Spelman, and Dufresne, who declare the
cotarius to have been of servile condition; and
considers this tenant to have enjoyed a free socage
tenure, and paid a rent in money or produce as well
as rendering some customary services. On the other
hand, the *coterellus* was held in absolute villenage, and
was entirely at the will and pleasure of his lord. The
cottar's position and services depended on the pleasure
of the lord under certain bounds. His duties were
of an uncertain kind, but he could "nihil proprium
habere nec acquirere nisi ad promotionem domini
sui," hold nothing of his own, nor acquire anything,
except with the assent of the lord.

The *Cubicularius* was an officer of superior condition, but his position and duties are not clearly
defined. The word is, however, derived from the
Byzantine Court. Perhaps, in the Domesday, the
cubicularius was a kind of chamberlain or guardian
of the royal treasure.

---

[1] Not used in Domesday, but discussed by the authors mentioned below.   [2] Pp. 141, 154.

The word *Custos*, warden, guardian, or keeper, occurs with several qualifying words. There were, for example, the bee-keepers, *custodes apium*, two in number. The term *bocher* was applied to this person in later days. He delivered six sextaria of honey or more, and was liable to be called upon by the lord to perform a variety of agricultural duties.

The *Custos Cuneorum*, or keeper of the dies, superintended the work performed by the *monetarii*, or moneyers, of whom more will be said in another place.

The *Custos Domus Regis*, in the New Forest, occurs in one passage; the *custos hundret* in another; the *custos molini*, the *custos silva* require but little explanation.

Dapifer, or steward, was an officer of superior domestic position. As his name implied, he carried the meals in to the banquet; but the title soon became purely honorific.

The *Drenchs*, or *Drengs*, were a kind of allodial tenants, who occur in the survey of the land between the Ribble and the Mersey Rivers in Lancashire. They were military vassals, and the allotments of land which they owned were held as manors. The peculiar services rendered by these tenants was known as *Drengage*, and it is found in existence, in one locality at least, as late as the close of the thirteenth century. The *Dinges* are believed to have been persons of a similar class.

Dispensator was an officer of condition in the lord's domestic establishment. He may be conjectured, as his name signified, to have exercised some rule over the maintenance of the provisions in the house, and to have superintended the expenses.

The Norman equivalent was the *major-domus* or *maître d' hôtel.*

The *Earl* is of frequent mention throughout the Domesday Book. At his creation by Royal Charter, he was invested with the "third penny of the county," and girded with the sword of the county, or earldom. The earl's "relief" consisted of eight horses harnessed and bitted, two breast-plates, four helmets, and as many shields, spears, and swords, *veredi*, and palfreys. This may be compared with the bequests made by Saxons of noble degree to their kings, as recorded in some of the few wills which are still extant.[1] Among the earls and countesses mentioned by name are :—

Alberic, Earl of Northumberland, a tenant in capite.
Alveva, Countess   "   "
Boulogne, Countess of (Ida)   "   "
Eustachius, Earl of Boulogne   "   "
Goda, Countess   "   "
Godeva, Countess   "   "
Hugo, Earl of Chester   "   "
Judita, Countess of Huntingdon, &c. "   "

[1] Leof Æthelwold the aldorman, for example, in his will, preserved in the "Codex Wintoniensis," Brit. Mus., Add. MS. 15,350, f. 87, printed in Birch's "Cartularium Saxonicum," No. 819, vol. ii. p. 583, A.D. 946–955, bequeaths "to the king my heriots, four swords and four spears, four shields and four rings, two worth a hundred and twenty mancuses, and two worth eighty mancuses, and four horses, and two silvern vessels," "þam cinge minne hære geatwa . feower sweord. and feower spæra. and feower scyldas. and feower beagas. twegen on hund twelftigum mancosun. and twegen on hund eahtatigum 7 feorwer hors. and two sylfrene fata." See also Thorpe, "Diplomatarium," p. 499.

Moritoniensis, Robert, Earl of Moretaine, a tenant
   in capite.

Radulfus Waher, Earl of Norfolk and Suffolk, a
   tenant in capite.

Rogerius de Montgomery, Earl of Arundel, &c., a
   tenant in capite.

W——, Earl, holding land in Oxfordshire, a tenant
   in capite.

William Fitz-Osbern, Earl of Hereford, a tenant
   in capite.

Among the earls holding lands in the time of
King Edward the Confessor, and previous to the
Domesday Survey, are:—

Ædgeua, Countess.

Ælueua, or Alveva, Countess.

Albericus, Earl.

Algar, Earl of Mercia.

Balduinus, Earl.

Edduinus, Earl.

Edgarus, Earl.

Ghida, or Gida, Countess, mother of Harold.

Goda, Countess, sister of King Edward the
   Confessor.

Godeva, Countess.

Goduinus, Earl.

Guerd, or Guert, Earl, brother of Harold.

Gudeta, Countess.

Harold, Heraldus, or Heroldus, Earl.

Leuric, or Leuricus, Earl.

Leuuinus, Earl.

Morcár, Earl.

R——, Earl.

R——, the old Earl Ralph, father of Radulfus
    Waher, or de Guader, mentioned above.

Radulfus, Earl.

Siuuard, or Siuuardus, Earl.

Tosti, Earl.

W——, Earl.

Wallef, Wallenus, &c., of whom some account has
    already been given.

Out of these the earls who occur as under-tenants
at the time of the survey are :—

Alanus, Earl.

The Earl of Eyereux.

Eustachius, Consul and Earl of Boulogne.

Hugh, Earl.

The Earl of Mellend or Meulant.

Ralph, Earl.

Robert, Earl.

Rogerius, Earl (of Montgomery).

Rogerus, Earl.

William, Earl.

The *Equarius Regis*, or king's equerry, is an officer
of rank and importance, whose duties seem clearly
explained by the term itself to have been connected
with the stud and stable.

Esne is the Saxon name for *servus*, and these will
be mentioned further on in their proper place in this
category.... See also under the account of the
Villains.

The *Examinatores*, or Assayers of the *moneta* or

mint, like the Custodes, or *cuneorum*, with whom they
were connected, had it in charge to take care that
their coins answered to the standard of weight and
quality.

The *Faber*, or smith, who could make ironwork and
shoe horses, was an important personage in the Domesday social and manorial life, although Ellis ranks him
with the trader and inferior officer. The term was
applied not only to the blacksmith or ironworker, but
also to those employed in working iron ore and
smelting. Among the persons who held lands in the
time of King Edward, and previous to the Domesday
Survey in Essex, " one smith," " unus faber," occurs,
who had been put to death for larceny. The names
of two Saxon smiths also occur in this list; they are
Bunda faber in Suffolk, and Eduuinus faber in the
same county. Among the under-tenants of the Domesday period are the " Fabri " of Berkshire.

The king's *Famuli*, or servants, occur in the second
volume of the Domesday Book, but their position
and duties have not been ascertained.

The *Figuli*, or potters, are mentioned among the
inferior trades.

· The *Forestarii*, or foresters, were officers of superior
grade; occasionally they occur as tenants-in-chief;
as for example, " the Forestarii Regis," or king's
foresters in Gravelinges Forest, *Wiltshire ;* Peret, the
Forester, *Hants ;* Richard, the Forester, *Warwickshire.* The knowledge of forestry, the laws of the
forest and the chace, would make them of value to
the king or the lord whom they served. Three, without
names given, held lands in the time of Edward the

Confessor in *Somersetshire*, Bundi, the Forester, *Oxfordshire;* and Leuuinus in *Hants,* also occur in this category. Herbert, the Forester of *Hants*, was an undertenant at the time the survey was made. Kelham states that the king appointed a forester to take care of his forests in every county, who answered for such a part of the Crown revenue as was under his care. But if so, they were not entered in the Domesday unless they held lands.

One *fossarius* occurs, also a *fossator*, Hereberd, in Norfolk ; he was, perhaps, an artisan employed about the ditches. The *fossarius* was also a grave-digger, the word *fossa* being anciently employed in that sense, as in the celebrated epitaph of the Venerable Bede, sculptured on his tombstone in the Galilee of the Cathedral at Durham.

Fifty Franci, or Franks, are the total of these, but the *Francigenæ* and *Francones* are difficult to be distinguished ; there were two hundred and ninety-six of the former, and but three of the latter in the Survey. The Francigena has been considered to be a general term for any one who could not prove himself to be English. The Francones held freely, " libere," in the time of Edward the Confessor, but their condition appears to have altered for the worse under the new government, for they re-appear on the same manor as if attached to the manor along with the villani and bordarii.

The *Homo*, or " Man," was a term which appears to have had a specific signification in England at this time. The word occurs in almost every page of the Survey, and included, in a very comprehensive

M

manner, all kinds of feudatory tenants. One of their most important privileges was, that their causes and persons could be tried only in the court of their own lord, to whom they were bound by submission and dependance. Hence the term *homage*, which, apart from its sentimental meaning of spiritual submission, indicated in the middle ages the duty, right, and claim of appearing at the court with the lord's *homines*, or "men," the word sometimes being used to denote the body of persons thus assembled.

. It was possible, but probably it did not often happen, that a *homo* might hold a manor in his own possession. The half *homo*, or *dimidius*, was the man who held part of his land under one lord and part under another. There are 1,287 homines, and 11 dimidii homines in the Domesday Book.

: Seventeen *hospites* occur. Ducange considers the *hospes* an inhabitant of a vill or village, and equivalent to the *mansionarius*, paying a yearly rent, like other inferior tenants, but not a *servus*.

: *Hostiarius*, an inferior officer, probably the same as *usher, husher, huissier, apparitor*, or *somner*. The *hostiarius* in some cases would answer to our *porter* or *gatekeeper*.

The *Huscarli* were domestic servants, and also military retainers, sometimes of the king, or an earl. Among them Thanes and higher tenants occur. The Huscarle who was a tenant in capite in Somersetshire may have had the name only, but not any office. Several occur by name, as Ingulfus, Leuric, or without name in Somerset, Surrey, and Gloucestershire, in the time of Edward the Confessor,

Ingeniator, an officer of unknown duty, perhaps charged with the care and construction of military machines, such as battering rams and catapults; or of farm implements.

Joculator, and the feminine form *Joculatrix,* a minstrel, jongleur, or an improviser of songs, one of the indispensable adjuncts of the Court. Hence the modern "juggler," which has acquired a somewhat different meaning.

Inguardi was charged with the duty of the Inward, that is guarding the person of the king when he lodged in the city; or attendance upon a sheriff. This also implied certain works about the king's demesnes or lord's inlands, *i.e.,* lands taken into culture with the old demesne, yet not absolutely apart of it.

Interpres, an interpreter, would be naturally a person of considerable use in Domesday times. " David interpres " occurs in *Dorsetshire,* and "Hugolinus interpres" in Somersetshire, among the tenants *in capite.* The former also of these re-appears as an undertenant. The term *Latimer* was of similar signification, and occurs as *Latinarius,* "The Latinist." Radulfus Latimarus of *Essex,* Lewinus Latinarius of *Hereford,* are among the tenants in capite ; and Robert *Latin'* or *Latinus* of *Kent,* along with the above-mentioned Leuuinus, are undertenants.

Lagemanni or *Lagemen,* Lawmen, " explainers of the laws," or Lesser Thegns, appear in Lincoln, Stamford, and other towns. According to Whitaker, the historian of Whalley, the *Lageman* who had *soc* and *sac* over his men, was the same who afterwards was termed " Lord of a Manor."

Lavatores—Laundrymen (?), or fullers.

Legati, a term applied to some officers of unknown capacity; was also used with the word *Regis* to denote Royal Commissioners, to whom the formation of the Domesday Book was intrusted.

. Of the *Liberatores* not much is known.

: Of the *Liberi*, or " free men," a great number are recorded. .Ellis gives the following table :—

Libera feminæ subcommendata ...		1
Liberæ feminæ		31
Libera femina commendata ...		1
Liberi homines	...10,097	
„ „ commendati ...	2,041	
„ „ faldæ	21	
Dimidii liberi homines	224	
Dim. lib. homo commendatione tantum	1	

The "freeman" was a term of considerable latitude—freemen or freeholders of a manor, holders of land for military service, tenants in capite. The half-freeman with *commendatio* only probably held half his land as free tenant, and the other half under protection of a lord.

. *Loricati;* two are mentioned in Windsor ward. Probably breast-plate makers ; if so, the word would be equivalent to Loricarii. But certain monks were called *loricati*, who put on an iron lorica or breast-plate next the skin, for mortification sake, and removed it on no account. Ducange mentions several remarkable instances, and a parallel case is described by William of Malmesbury.

Lorimarii, or *Lorimers*, makers of small iron and brass fittings.

Loripes, a term for one who had a twisted foot, perhaps used as a name in Domesday.

Two hundred and seven *manents* at St. Edmundsbury are entered among the Domesday class list of population. They are resident burgesses.

Matricularii, officers of ecclesiastical duty at St. John's Church, Chester.

Mellitarius, perhaps the same as *mellitor*, whom Ducange notices as occurring elsewhere. A honey and wax manufacturer.

Mercatores, merchants. Twenty-four occur. There were forty-eight merchants' houses in the town of Nottingham, held by William Peverell.

Mercennarius, a hired servant perhaps. But Ducange attributes to *mercenarius* the signification of merchant of small wares, a mercer; another mercenarius was a priest who received a stipend for his duties connected with a church.

Miles, a soldier; only 137 in the total, with two Anglici, and as many Francigenæ, are mentioned. There does not seem to have been any very precise meaning attached to the word. The *miles* may have been a high commander in some cases, and an inferior in another case. Some of them held large areas of land. The soldiers of Westminster Abbey held 30 houses. A salary appears to have been paid to the milites, at least in some cases. Hence the term *soldarii*, of similar import, used in the account of Colchester. The word is a synonym of *minister*, or thegn, in late Anglo-Saxon charters.

Molinarii, millers.

Monachi, monk.

Monetarii, moneyers, have been noticed in the chapter relating to money.

Moniales, nuns.

Nativi, or *niefes,* children of villains, in the same state of serfdom as their parents.

Piscatores, fishermen.

Pistores, bakers.

Porcarii, generally swineherds, but ranking as free occupiers who paid rent in money or kind for feeding their pigs in the woodlands.

Portarius, an inferior officer who kept the gate.

Prebendarii, purveyors.

Prefecti, or *Prepositi;* provosts, reeves, bailiffs, or stewards of manors. This was an important officer; he collected rents, carried on the affairs of the manor over which he was set, kept the peace, and performed all the offices of equity and right between lord and tenant. To some were attached the bedelli, bedels, beadles, or under-bailiffs. The provost of the town, or *burh-gerefa, præpositus villæ,* had a great power for good or ill over all the persons under his control in the manor.

Presbyter, or Priest, occurs frequently in the Survey; there were nine hundred and ninety-four, and a dimidius presbyter. From the occurrence of the presbyter in places where no church is mentioned, some writers have conjectured that the entry of the presbyter includes the existence of the church in the same place. But this is open to considerable doubt. The object of the Domesday was by no means to

ascertain the condition of the Church or her ministers; hence, as Ellis correctly remarks, "Domesday
cannot be decisively appealed to for the existence
or non-existence of parish churches, in the age in
which it was compiled."

In another place the same writer finds that those
priests are occasionally classed with the inferior
tenantry, such as the villani, bordarii, and buri. The
parish priest probably did not occupy any very exalted
position in the parish, except in cases where patronage
or individual excellence brought him in contact with
the lord, who forwarded his promotion in the
church.

Radchenistres, or *Rachenistres*, perhaps the same as
the *Radmanni* or *Radmans*, belong to the class of
socmen, some being possessed of a greater degree
of freedom than others. Some derive the name from
Rad, a riding, a road; and they were a class of
freemen who served on horseback only.

Rustici, a general term for hinds or *coloni
glebæ adscriptitii*, an agricultural workman, who
passed with the land from one owner to the other.

"Rusticus a rure quoniam rus est sibi curæ."

The term is used in opposition to the *noble*,
nobilis.

Salinarii, employed in the salines or salt works;
or those who engaged in the sale of salt.

Servi, although distinguished in the Domesday
Book from the villani, were of a still less free class.
They represent the Saxon *Esne*. Though protected
by law from injury by the lord, their lives were spent

in his service, for which they received wages or maintenance, at his discretion. Occasionally they were able to obtain their manumission, and then became *liberi*, freemen.

Servientes, serjeants. Ducange gives a long account of the various kinds of *servientes*. Among them the *Servientes feodati* were liable to certain definite services, in return for the possession of fees and farms; others again appear to be serjeants of manors, or bailiffs.

The *Sochemanni*, or socmen, were inferior landowners, who had land in the *soc*, or franchise of a great lord. Their freedom consisted in various privileges; they rendered fixed service, they could not be put out of their tenements unwillingly; they held the pleas of the manor courts. There were various degrees of *sochemanni*, some could not dispose of their estate, nor remove without permission of their lords. Some were required to perform certain services of husbandry, and in this respect they resembled the lower grades of the agricultural population.

Stalre, master of the horse, constable, or standard bearer. Some account of this noble officer has been given in a former chapter.

Teini, Taini, Tegni, Thanes, or *thegns* — the *ministri* of the Anglo-Saxon charters, were the highest class of tenants; in fact, the nobility or barons of pre-Norman times. There appear to have been king's thanes, such as archbishops, bishops, abbots, and the great lords; *Thani mediocres*, secondary thanes, lords of manors, or vavassors; and lesser thanes, the lowest class of freeholders. But there were also many intermediate grades, and some of the great thanes had dependants, also called by the same title. The title of Thane afterwards became that of Baron.

Vaccarii, probably persons employed in the management of cows, and Ducange calls these persons "qui vaccarum curam habet in prædiis rusticis."

Vavassores were next in dignity to the higher thanes and barons. They were also called *valvassors*. The title seems to have sunk in the general name of Liberi homines, or free men. They were not tenants-in-chief, but held of the superior lord or of the king as lord of a manor or honour. The vavassor was superior in degree to a knight.

Venator, the huntsman, appears in some cases to have been a favoured person. His knowledge must have been extremely valuable to his lord, who would in return take care to admit him to corresponding advantages. It is not unlikely that among officers of the king's household the huntsman occupied a place of some considerable importance. Waleran and Croch, the huntsmen, held lands in capite in Hampshire, and there are other corresponding examples showing the importance and dignity of the office.

Of *Villani* or *Villains*, much has been written. Blackstone considers that their new tenure was not strictly feodal, Norman, or Saxon, but compounded of them all, and, from the heriots which they were liable to, somewhat Danish in composition. These men, with their families, were in servitude to the lord of the soil, like the rest of the cattle and stock on it,

and held the folk-land, by which they supported
themselves and their families, and from which they
would be removed at their lord's will, but not their
own. At the coming of the Normans, the condition
of these peasants may have been slightly improved.
Two classes have been observed; the villains reguar-
dant, annexed to the manor, or the land; and the
villains in gross, annexed to the person of the lord,
and transferable by deed, of which several examples
are still extant in the vast collection of charters in
the British Museum. The villain performed practically the same services in his day, for kind, as the
agricultural labourer now-a-days performs on a farm
for a weekly wage. But he could acquire no private
property, land nor goods; his female children could
not be married without the lord's consent to what was
considered a damage to the property; his sons
naturally grew up in the same state of bondage. The
law, however, protected the villain from atrocious
cruelties of the lord. He could acquire freedom in
several ways; most usually by a formal deed or act
of manumission (of which several specimens are still
extant), or by any act on the part of the lord such as
granting him an annuity or an estate, or bringing an
action at law against him, by which the manumission
is implied. In course of time, the condition of many
villains became considerably ameliorated in those
instances where under a benevolent lord they and
their families enjoyed their holdings in a regular
course of descent, uninterrupted by enforced removal
or other interruption which tended to retard their
improvement, and eventually the will of lord as to

their tenure merged into a will agreeable to the usual custom observed in the manor, "which[1] customs are preserved and evidenced by the rolls of the several courts-baron in which they are entered, or kept on foot by the constant immemorial usage of the several manors in which the lands lie. And as such tenants had nothing to show for their estates but these customs, and admissions in pursuance of them, entered on those rolls, or the *copies* of such entries witnessed by the steward, they now began to be called tenants by *copy of court roll*, and their tenure itself a *copyhold*."

The villain must not, however, be confused with the still more abject *servi* or bondsman. The former being the equivalent of the Saxon *Ceorl*, the latter of the *Theow* or *Esne*. Ellis finds that the degradation of the *Ceorls* and the improvement of the *Theowas* and *Esnen*, the two classes, at first distinct, were gradually brought nearer together in the social scale, until finally, under the oppressive military system of the Normans, all degrees of tenants and servants were amalgamated into one common slavery in this respect, or at least into strict dependence, and fell into a class generally denominated as villains re-guardant.

---

[1] Ellis, i. 78.

CHAPTER X.

THE LAND—CLASSIFICATION AND CONDITIONS OF THE
COUNTY POPULATION—CITIES AND TOWNS.

A FEW remarks on each county, the general aspect
of the survey, the population, and the principal
features of note, will be useful to the reader. Ellis
has carefully summed up the various totals of population from which the following facts are derived, and
to them have been added some accounts of the
various works and bibliographical treaties[1] connected
with each county. The population mentioned in
Domesday only imperfectly represents the true population of the county, no notice being taken of the
women and children, the inferior servants not concerned with the land tax, the clergy, the manufac-
turing and trading classes, the religious and other
inhabitants of monastic institutions, the mercenaries
and rank and file of the soldiery, and a floating
residuum who probably then, as now, managed with
little trouble to avoid being entered into the census of
any particular locality. There are also certain places,
known, from the antiquity of their names, to have
been in existence prior to the taking of the survey,
of which nothing is recorded to show that they

[1] See p. 315.

were visited by the Commissioners. These different omissions would probably swell the grand total to at least five times that arrived at by Ellis, viz., 283,242, that would give the true population of England, as far as the Domesday Survey extended, at about 1,400,000 souls.

KENT.[1] This large and important county is called CHENTH in the Domesday Book, which can only be accounted for on the principle that the scribes were either foreigners writing from dictation, and attempting to re-produce the sound which they heard, according to the phonetics of their own language, or that they were singularly ignorant of the names of the English counties. The survey of the county begins with the account of Dover, and has no numbered list of chief tenants. It then proceeds with the *terra regis,* or king's lands, the archbishop of Canterbury's lands, the lands of his milites or knights, and the rest of the chief tenants. The recorded population consisted, among other persons, of 13 chief tenants (of whom some account follows below), 212 under-tenants, 1 *mulier paupercula,* 3,118 bordarii, and 6,597 villani; in all 12,205 inhabitants. The principal towns, if we may judge from the number of burgesses, are Canterbury, Romney, Sandwich, and Dover. In Sandwich were nearly four hundred *masuræ,* or houses. The burgesses of *Burgus Hedæ,* Hythe Borough, numbered 231, of whom six belonged to the Manor of Leminges or Lyminge, and 125 to the archbishop of Canterbury's

---

[1] From the Celtic word *Kant, Cant* (Portuguese *Canto*), a corner; *Cantium* is the classic name.

Manor of Salteode, or Saltwood. In Romenel or Romney, were 156 burgesses, some belonging to outside manors. In Fordwic or Fordwich, near Canterbury, a *"parvus burgus,"* belonging to St. Augustine's Abbey, were six burgesses, "a hundred masures of land wanting four," in pre-Domesday times, but at the survey only seventy-three. The castles of Canterbury and Rochester are mentioned.

The chief tenants of this first county surveyed in the Domesday are as follows :—

1. The king himself, holding his lands in ancient demesne of the Crown.

2. The archbishop of Canterbury, most of whose lands stood as they were in the time of King Edward the Confessor.

3. The monks and men of the archbishop, that is, the lands of the Priory of Christ Church or Holy Trinity, and St. Martin in Canterbury.

4. The bishop of Rochester, whose lands remained mostly as in the time of the Confessor.

5. The bishop of Bayeux, all his lands being grants from the Conqueror, increased by his own spoliations.

6. The Abbey of Battel, or Battle, holding the Royal Manor of Wye, part of the ancient demesne of the Crown, granted to the Abbey by William the Conqueror. The charter granting this manor is preserved among the Harleian charters in the British Museum, 83 A. 12. There are some curious

stipulations respecting the division of the "piscis qui *adspeis*[1] vocatur" if one be caught.

7. St. Augustine's Abbey, Canterbury.

8. The Abbey of St. Peter's, Gand, or Ghent, in Flanders, whose land consisted of the Manor of Lewisham, Greenwich and *Woolwich* [Lievesham, Gronewic et Uuluuich], (not *Combe*, as Tanner, and Dugdale, and Larking following them, state), granted to the Abbey by King Alfred's niece, Elthruda, or Elstrudis (the original charter I have printed in the "Cartularium Saxonicum," No. 611, 11th September A.D. 918).

9. Hugh de Montford, who accompanied the king to Hastings, and was trusted by the king in important offices. He was one of the barons assembled at the Penenden controversy[2] to adjudicate between Lanfranc and Odo. He had received, as the reward for his fidelity, more than a hundred different lordships in England.

10. Eustace, earl of Boulogne, also present with the Conqueror at the battle of Hastings, wherein he was severely wounded.. His subsequent rebellious assault on Dover Castle, which ended in his discomfiture and hasty retreat, has been graphically described by Ordericus Vitalis, and is referred to at length by Larking.

11. Richard de Tonebrige, called also Richard de Benefacta, or Richard filius Gisliberti, or Richard de Clare; eldest son of Gilbert, earl of Brion, in

---

[1] Sometimes called *Craspeys, i.e., crassus piscis*, "a huge fish."   [2] See Chapter xiv.

Normandy, also at the battle of Hastings, and a large landowner.

12. Haimo the Sheriff, an extensive holder of land in the county.

13. Albert the Chaplain, the king's Secretary and Chancellor; these offices were, in early days, one and the same, being always held by an ecclesiastic who had also the care of the king's Chapel.

2. SUSSEX, called Sudsex, *i.e.*, the South Saxon (territory), has a list of fifteen tenants-in-chief prefixed to the survey of the county; there were 534 under-tenants, 2,497 bordarii, 5,898 villani, and other inhabitants, making a total of 10,410 in all. The towns with burgesses are, Pevenesel, 110; Novo-Burgo, 64; Lewes, 53; Bolintun, 20; Cicestre, 9; and Hastinges, 4. Chichester in King Edward's time had 98 *hagæ* or ground plots, on each of which one or more houses stood; sixty more had been added by the time the survey was made. In the burgh of Steyninges there were 124 *masuræ*. Mr. F. E. Sawyer, F.S.A., read before the Domesday Commemoration a valuable notice of the county as it appears in Domesday Book, in which he considers that the true population was ten times that recorded, or 104,100—ten inmates of one holding not being an exaggerated number. He attributes the increase of buildings in Chichester to the removal of the cathedral to that city from Selsea in A.D. 1075, or between that year and the formation of the survey.

The castles of Hastings, Borne, Ferle, Brembre

for Bramber, and Lauues, Lawes, and La quis for Lewes, are incidentally mentioned.

3. SURREY is called by the writers of the Survey SUDREtE. Of the total of recorded inhabitants, 4,383, there were 44 tenants in chief, including the king, 108 under tenants, 2,363 villani, 968 bordarii, 1 Anglicus, and 1 forestarius. Southwark was an important place, bishop Odo of Bayeux had there a monastery and a watercourse. Guildford was the only other place that had any pretension to the name of a town. There were a hundred and seventy-five burgesses in it; but it is remarkable that no mention is made of any corporate privileges therein. The notices of Bermondsey and Lambeth are interesting. A paper on the county was recently read by Mr. H. E. Malden before the Commemoration, in which he showed that there was no southern boundary of the county except the undefined tract of the primeval forest of the Andreds-weald. In the same way Sussex could have had but a doubtful northern boundary. This has led to some remarkable results in the Survey, where land in Compton, co. Sussex, is rated in Surrey, while Worth—the "Orde" of the Domesday Book,—now in Sussex, is taken as in Surrey. Lodsworth, then in Surrey now in Sussex, is another example.

Geological conditions here, as doubtless elsewhere, considerably affected the cultivation, the unfertile Wealden clay being, as a rule, uninhabited, but the fertile greensand is almost coterminous with the Domesday life of the county. A portion of the

N

north-west of ' Surrey ' was also uninhabited, on
account of the unmanageable and unfruitful characteristics of the soil. Mr. Malden computes fifty-nine
places where churches are mentioned, and that on
the average there was a church for every seventy
men, or, say, for every three hundred and fifty of
population, for he only allows five to a household,
which is just half the total conjectured by Mr. Sawyer
for Sussex. This may be taken as an independent
indication of the probable area of Anglo-Saxon
churches, the extant examples of which would have
much difficulty to find room for half that number. Mr.
Malden puts down the true total of population at
about twenty thousand. Some of the old Saxon
holders still held land here in the Domesday times,
and some were despoiled by bishop Odo, the king's
kinsman. Among these ancient tenants occur a goldsmith, an interpreter, and two huntsmen—men whose
occupations were probably too useful to allow of
their being dispossessed. He also pointed out the
unexplained fact that the bordarii predominate in
some hundreds in which the cotarii are but few;
while in others, not contiguous, the reverse is the
case. This has been shown more clearly in Mr.
Seebohm's well-known work. It may be that there
were different customs in-force in different hundreds,
or perhaps the two terms were, for most purposes,
practically synonymous.[1] Some isolated homesteads
in the great forest had been overlooked, or unsur-
veyed, by the Commissioners. On the Church lands,
the proportion of *servi* was about $5\frac{1}{2}$ per cent. of the

[1] See also p. 141.

population, while on the lands of the bishops, lay lords, and other tenants in chief, it was 16 per cent., or nearly three times as much. From this it may be inferred that the monasteries had already commenced to ameliorate the condition of the lower classes of the people.

4. HAMPSHIRE is styled Hantesscire by the Commissioners. Excluding the New Forest and the Isle of Wight, there were 128 tenants in chief, 174 under-tenants, 3,466 bordarii, 3,416 villani, 1,458 servi, 3 presbyters only, and others, which enable Ellis to state the total recorded population as 9,032. Burgesses occur in the following towns:—Thuinam (Twinham), 31; Wincestre, 14, belonging to the abbey of Romsey; Sanburne (King's Somborne), 9; Houston and Bromelai, 3 each,

In the *Burgus* of Hantune or Hantone (Southampton), the king held 76 *homines;* there were 96 Francigenæ and Angligenæ *hospitati*, or indwellers; and 49 houses, of which the great persons of the Court received custom. Winchester is not separately treated in Domesday Book. It contained, by computation of the scattered notices throughout the County Survey, seven houses, thirty-nine hagæ, thirty-two masuræ. The comparative condition of this city in the time of Edward the Confessor and in that of Henry I. (as recorded in the "Liber Wintoniensis," published by the Record Commissioners, among the additions to Domesday Book, vol. iii. 1816, edited by Sir Henry Ellis) enable the historian of Winchester, by the light of Domesday, to see the pro-

·gress and decay of the town for three separate
, periods.

..: .The Survey of this county contains a separate
heading of "Item in eadem Hantescire circa Nouam
Forestam et intra ipsam." In this forest the total of
recorded population is only 217, composed of 17
tenants in chief, the same number of subtenants,
·87 bordarii, 66 villani, 22 servi, 7 homines, and one
custos of the king's house.

The Isle of Wight, which is also separately sur-
·veyed as "Insula de With," contained but 1,124
inhabitants mentioned specifically. This total is
made up of 37 chief tenants, 45 under tenants, 441
· bordarii, 360 villani, 232 servi, 8 homines, and one
: vavassor, who is described as "possessed of two
cows." A castle at Alwinestune in this island is identified with Carisbrook by Ellis.

5. BERKSHIRE, called Berrochescire, contained a
total population of 6,324: among them 80 tenants in
capite, 185 undertenants, 10 merchants stationed in
front of the gate of St. Helen's Church at Bertone, in
Abingdon, 1 radchenistre with his plough. Wal-
·lingford was an important town. It had a merchant-
guild in the time of King Edward the Confessor, and
276 hagæ, or plots containing houses belonging to the
king; the total houses, including 24 belonging to
manors in Oxfordshire and elsewhere, amounted to
·491. Old Windsor had 100 hagæ; in Reading the
king had 28 hagæ. The smallness may be accounted
for by the burning of the town by the Danes sixty
years before the survey was made. The castles of

Wallingford and Windsor are incidentally mentioned.

The Domesday of Berkshire is being prepared for
publication, with descriptive notices, by Mr. H. J.
Reid, F.S.A., of Donnington.

6. WILTSHIRE, or Wiltescire as it is called in the
Record, was a well-populated county, the total enumerated inhabitants amounting to 10,150, which may
be multiplied by five or six to show the probable actual
census at the time under consideration. Of these
there were 156 chief tenants and 286 undertenants,
3,049 villani, 2,754 bordarii, 1,539 servi, 1,418
coscez, but only 1 presbyter, a plain indication that
the Church dignitaries are only incidentally introduced into the Domesday, it being no part of the
duty of the Commissioners to ascertain the number
of the clergy. The number of burgesses in thirteen
towns is entered as follows:—Cauna or Caune, 73;
Theodulveside, 66; Crichelade, 33; Bradeford, 33;
Guerminstre (Warminster), 30; Bedvinde (Bedwyn),
25; Wiltune, 17; Malmesberie, 8; Sudtone, 5;
Domnitone, 2; Draicote, Smitecote, and Gordone,
1 each.

Domesday Book does not afford very much information as to the condition of Wiltshire cities and
boroughs.[1]   Two, Wilton and Malmesbury, are
expressly called *burgi*, but others must be included,
as Sarum, Marlborough, Cricklade, and " Bade,"
perhaps Bedwin, unless Bath, in the contiguous

---

[1] Rev. W. H. Jones, "Domesday for Wiltshire." Bath,
1865, 4to.

county of Somerset, had been thus placed[1] in the farm or collectorship of Wiltshire. In each of these, the third penny or third part of the proceeds of taxation belonged to the king, so that he stood in the position of comes or earl so far as the county was concerned separately. In Calne, Ambresbury, Warminster, Chippenham, and perhaps Tilshead, the king claimed the "firma unius noctis," a night's farm or hospitality for himself and his concomitant court. Add to these, Bradford-on-Avon, Westbury, Melksham, Mere, Ramsbury, and Aldbourn, which would also fall into this category of boroughs. On the other hand the recorded presence of burgesses in Domnitone (Dinton), Draicote, Gardone, Smitecote, and Sudtone (Sutton Mandeville), does not necessarily imply that these places, never more than small market towns at best, were boroughs. Malmesbury borough, one of these, is distinguished in the Domesday Book by having its survey placed before the numbered list of 68 tenants, or groups of tenants, which precedes the general text. Even this, however, is short and meagre. Like Wallingford, in Berkshire, Malmesbury furnished soldiers for the king's army. The town's military service amounted to twenty shillings for the support of the king's sailors (buzecarls), or in furnishing him with one man for each honour of five hides, a statement which tends to prove that the service of one man was rated at or commuted for by twenty shillings.

Jones considers that Wiltshire is an exception to

---

[1] Morgan, "England under the Normans," p. 191.

the general rule that the king's lands were more highly valued than before the Conquest, and his rent from the cities and boroughs increased; that a few of the larger tenants had improved their property, but that on the whole the rental of the kingdom represented little more than three-fourths of the Confessor's estimate. In this county he finds the value of the greater holdings greater than, if not the same, as is reported in the days of King Edward the Confessor. This he makes evident by a selection of examples taken from different portions of Domesday Book, in which is given the estimated value of a large number of manors held by various persons at either period:—

		ANNUAL VALUE.					
		T.R.E.			T.R.W.		
	HIDES.	£	s.	d.	£	s.	d.
Bishop of Winchester	260	196	0	0	268	10	0
Bishop of Sarum	267	231	10	0	233	10	0
Abbot of Glastonbury	258	167	10	0	223	0	0
Abbot of Malmesbury	194	154	19	0	170	19	0
Edward of Salisbury	157	158	7	0	220	17	0
Humphrey de L'Isle	157	108	9	3	115	19	0
Waleran the Huntsman	43	42	6	0	45	16	0
Osbern Gifard	69	43	10	0	52	0	0
	1,405	£1,102	11	3	£1,330	11	0

From this we see that the annual value of land in Wiltshire had risen by twenty per cent. since the days of Edward the Confessor, and that at the Domesday era the average annual value of a hide of land under cultivation was about nineteen shillings.

7. DORSETSHIRE, or Dorsete, has no preliminary

schedule or list of tenants. Ellis tabulates the
recorded population at 7,807, including among
others 146 chief tenants, 195 under tenants, 2,941
bordarii, 2,613 villani, 1,231 servi, 151 burgesses in
Sceftesberie (Shaftesbury), 8 in Winburne, 3 in
Warham, and only 1 in Dorecestre, belonging to the
bishop of Salisbury's Manor of Cerminstre. The
principal towns were Dorchester, Bridport, Wareham,
and Shaftesbury. The 172 houses in Dorchester in
the time of Edward the Confessor had decreased to 88
at the Domesday Survey. There were two moneyers
in this town. But its prosperous condition may
perhaps be estimated from the fact that it paid geld
for ten hides, thrice the rating of the city of Exeter.
In Bridport the houses had similarly diminished
from 120 to 100, the other twenty so far "wasted"
that their inhabitants were unable to pay the geld.
Here there was one moneyer. Wareham, which
possessed 143 houses on the king's demesne in the
time of the Confessor, retained only 70 at the survey.
The total of houses in the town, 285, had fallen to
135 when the Commissioners took the census. Two
moneyers were in this town. Shaftesbury also shows
a similar decrease of houses, from 257 in the time of
King Edward to 177 in the year 1086. The 151
burgesses, dwelling in 91 manses, shows that the
number of burgesses in a town might exceed the
number of houses. Wareham Castle is stated to have
been built by King William in the survey of this
county.

Eyton, who has carefully analysed the Domesday Book for this county, finds that constant refer-

ence is made to two distinct systems of measuration :—1, the old system of hidation, based on the Saxon *hide;* and 2, the contemporary and more exact system. He finds the Domesday hide of Dorsetshire represented on an average by nearly 240 statute acres,[1] the hidage, or valuation by hides, indicating liability, capacity or intrinsic value, and. adventitious or extrinsic value. The hide liable to geld in Dorsetshire is by this writer technically divided into these parts :—

1 Hide = 4 Virgates = 16 Ferndels = 48 Acres.
1 Virgate = 4 Ferndels = 12 Acres.
1 Ferndel = 3 Acres.

These have reference to the original assessment for the Danegeld by Ethelred the Unready, A.D. 979—1016. Thus an estate geldable as one or two virgates, simply means that it was assessed to Danegeld as a quarter or half of one hide—the ordinary acre of Norman and actual measurement applied in the Domesday to meadows, pastures, and woods, being quite different to the *acra ad gheldum,* which represented about 5 modern acres. The carucate in Dorsetshire, as a precise areal measure, is probably represented, as it is in Lincolnshire, by the same number, 240, of modern acres as is the average hide. The *terra ad unam carucam,* or plough-gang, was a still more constant quantity, not exceeding, and probably equivalent to, 120 measured acres.

Eyton's calculation of the lineal measures of the

---

[1] But varying from 4,000 to as little as 84 acres.

Dorsetshire Survey are of great interest. Assuming the length of the *pertica* or *virga* (nowhere defined in Domesday) to be 16½ ft., or 5½ yds., he constructs the following table :—

16½ ft. = ½ yds. = 1 *Virga* or *Pertica*.
66 ft. = 22 yds. = 4 Virgæ or Perticæ = 1 Acra (lineal, not [extant).
660 ft. = 22 yds. = 40 Perticæ = 10 Acres = 1 Quarentina.
7,920 ft. = 2,640 yds. = 480 Perticæ = 120 Acres = 12 Quarentinæ.
[= 1 Leuua, Leuga, or Leuca.

The lineal acre occurs in the description of the wood at Wichemetune, or Wichampton, which is set down as 1 quarentine long, 8 acres broad. (*D.B.*, f. 79*b*.) The areal or superficial measures are exactly deduced from these, as has been shown in a forthcoming part of the work :—

30¼ sq. yds. = 1 Pertica square.
4,840 sq. yds. = 160 Perticæ = 1 Areal Acre.
48,400 sq. yds. = 10 sq. Acres = 1 sq. Quarentine.
580,800 sq. yds. = 120 sq. Acres = 12 sq. Quar. = 1 Areal League.

This corresponds with the modern system of area measure, which, however, employs other denominations.

8. SOMERSETSHIRE, called Sumersete, or Summersette, has 47 entries of 80 tenants in chief, 368 under tenants, 5,298 villains or villans, 4,770 bordarii or boors, 2,110 servi, and other classes, amounting in all to 13,764 recorded population. Of royal boroughs in Somersetshire, Bath had 154 burgesses, of whom 64 belonged to the laity, and 24 to the Church; Alsebruge, or Axbridge 32; Givel-

cestre, or Ilchester, 1o8; Lanporth, or Langport,
39; Brinnetune, or Brumetone, now Brewton, 17;
Milbourne, 67; and Tantone, or Taunton, 64. Among
the farming stock of the county, Eyton, who has
carefully digested the Survey, notices *equæ silvestres*
or *indomitæ*, wild brood-mares; the *animalia*, plough-
or store-cattle; *caballi* or riding horses, kept by Alured
of Spain; the *roncini* or packhorses, and the *berbices* or
wether sheep. Two castles of Somersetshire find
incidental notice in the Domesday Book, "Mon-
tagud" at Biscopestune, and Torre..

9. DEVONSHIRE, styled Devenescire, contained a
total recorded population of 17,434, consisting of 77
tenants *in capite*, 402 under tenants, 8,070 villani,
4,847 bordarii, 3,294 servi, the large number of 294
porcarii, and others. Exeter is signalised by having
its survey prefixed to the numbered schedule, which
goes before the general text. Six towns had burgesses,
viz., Totenais (Totnes), 110: Lideford, 69, this was
apparently a walled town, and forty houses lay waste
in it before the Normans came to England; Barn-
staple, 67: of thirty-eight wasted houses in this
town twenty-three had fallen into this condition
since King William came to England; Exeter, 13,
but the city is computed to have possessed 463
houses in King Edward's time, and 411 at the
time of the survey. This city was rated as for five
hides upon any naval or military expedition taking
place. The little village of Lupridge, called Lupe-
rige, in North Huish, had one burgess, who, with
one villani, held "1 car et una acr. prati." Two-

castles are incidentally spoken of by Domesday,
"Cornuali," and Ochementone or Oakhampton.

10. CORNWALL, called Cornvalgie and Cornvalia,
completed the first or southernmost zone of the
Domesday Commissioners' work. This county had
5,438 recorded inhabitants, among whom are 7
tenants *in capite*, 97 under tenants, 2,355 bordarii,
1,730 villani, 1,160 servi, and as many as 40 cer-
visarii, or brewers. Here were two castles, Dunhevet
or Launceston;[1] "the strongest,[2] but not the biggest,
that ever I saw in any auncient work in England,"
and Tremetone, which latter had a market.

11. MIDDLESEX, or Middelsexe, commences the
second zone or rank in the arrangement of counties.
Here was a population of 2,302, including 30 tenants
in chief, 62 under tenants as mesne lords, 46
burgesses on the abbot of Westminster's manor in
Stanes; 1,141 villani, 464 cotarii, 343 bordarii, and
112 servi. London was probably exempt by
charter from the notice of the Commissioners. The
first charter extant[3] was granted to the city by
William the Conqueror, in the second year of his
reign over England, at the instance of William
the Norman, bishop of London, on the occasion of
the royal entry into the City. This is written in
Anglo-Saxon, and is drawn up in accordance with

---

[1] The "History of Launceston and Dunheved," by R. Peter
and O. B. Peter, 1885.   [2] Leland, "Itin."
[3] The "Historical Charters and Constitutional Documents
of the City of London." Lond., 1884, 4to.

the conventional usages of Anglo-Saxon diplomatics, and these circumstances have been regarded by historians as great concessions to English feelings, seeing that it was issued at a time when the Norman language and Norman forms of legal deeds were supplanting the native language and methods of formulation. The two chief privileges granted in it are, that the burgesses were declared to be law-worthy, *legales homines*, and that their children should be their heirs. Hence it may be conjectured that the burgesses of London had obtained of the Saxon monarchs several liberties and immunities, among others this one, that they were to be so far free as not to be *in dominio*, or under any lord's power, but that they might be law-worthy, that is, have the full benefit of the law. In this respect, the king's charter is but a confirmation of the pre-Norman condition of the London burgesses. Hume, following Dalrymple on Feudal Property, considers this famous charter little better than a charter of protection, a declaration that the citizens should not be treated as slaves. But even this was a considerable immunity at a time when all persons who were not possessed of land were included in that class. What enhanced the value of these charters was, that they were granted at a time when the feudal system obtained a firmer and more extensive establishment by the settlement of the Norman barons in England under the military tenure.

12. HERTFORDSHIRE, is called Herfordscire in the Domesday Book. There is a record of 4,927 popula-

tion, comprising, among others, 55 chief tenants, 184 under tenants as mesne proprietors, 1,830½ villani, 1,107 bordarii, 837 cotarii, 550 servi, 1 fossar, 48 presbyters. The town of Hertforde is stated to hold 18 burgesses; but in the time of Edward the Confessor there were 146 burgesses under the king's protection, the town being rated at ten hides. Other towns held the following census of burgesses :— Berchamstede, 52 ; St. Alban's, 46 ; Escwelle or Ash-well, near Baldock, once a market-town, granted by Edward the Confessor to the abbot of Westminster, 14; and Stanstede or Stanstead Abbot, near Hoddesdon, 7. The proximity of this place to the River Lea (the boundary of division between Alfred's Anglo-Saxon subjects and Guthrum's Danes at the close of the ninth century) may account for the trade which appears to have flourished here.

13. BUCKINGHAMSHIRE, called Bochinghamscire, only contained 5,420 persons, among them 70 tenants-in-chief, 223 under tenants, 26 burgesses in the town of Buckingham who belonged to certain of the barons, 1 salinarius, 2 vavassors. The Survey prefixes the account of the county town of Bochingeham cum Bortone to the preliminary numbered list of 57 tenants and groups of tenants.

14. OXFORDSHIRE, or Oxenefordscire, as the Survey calls this county, renders a recorded census of 6,775 persons. Among them, 84 tenants-in-chief, under 59 groups in the tabulation prefixed to the general text ; 207 under tenants and occupiers, 3,545 villani, 1,889 bordarii, 963 servi, and but 1 presbyter. The

account of the city of Oxford is placed first, but it supplies no enumeration of the inhabitants of the city. The houses amounted in number to 243 paying geld, within and without the walls, for this was a walled city of considerable strategic importance; 478 dilapidated and unable to pay geld; there was one burgess at Wistelle.

15. GLOUCESTERSHIRE, styled Glowecestrescire in the Domesday Book, records a census of 8,366 in all, comprising, among other classes, 102 tenants-in-chief, under a numbered tabulation of 78 heads; 166 under-tenants, 3,627 villani, 30 half villanis 2,044 servi, and 1,792 bordarii. Burgesses occur in Bristou, or Bristol, without stated number; Gloucester, 72; Wincelcumbe, 18; Teodekesberie, or Tewkesbury, 13; and *homines* dwelling in *foro de Berchelai*, Berkley market-place, 17. Ellis thinks that the entries relating to Gloucester and Evesham, in the Register of Evesham, in the Cottonian Manuscript, Vespasian B xxiv., may be possibly those originally laid before the Commissioners, who prepared from them the abridged Domesday Survey. Under this county are mentioned the Castle of Estrighoiel, with lands between the Wye and the Usk, and lands in Wales. The notice of four vills wasted by King Caraduech, or Trhearn ap Caradoc,[1] in A.D. 1074, is also of interest to Welsh history in the eleventh century. The Castles of Nesse and Gloucester are incidentally mentioned; and in the county the Survey places Estrighoiel Castle which is really in Monmouthshire.

[1] Ellis, i. 321.

16. WORCESTERSHIRE, called Wirecestrescire, held a total recorded population of 4,625 persons; among them, 28 tenants-in-chief, 129 undertenants, 1,728 bordarii, 1,520 villani, 677 servi, the large number of 101 ancillæ, 59 presbyters, 1 huntsman, 1 widow, and 3 salt manufacturers owning as many salines or salt pans in Wich, *i.e.*, Droitwich. These pans or salt boileries paid three hundred *mittas* of salt, for which they received, in the time of King Edward, as many cart loads, *caretedes*, of fire wood from the wood-wardens. The City of Worcester, Wirecestre, commences the survey, before the numbered list of chief tenants, and its rents, customs, and services are set forth, but not the census of its burgesses; eight, however, are known from other places. The houses in the city, which was rated at fifteen hides, consisted of ninety appendant to the bishop of Worcester's Manor of Norwiche or Northwich. Urso, who held twenty-four of these, held also twenty-five in the market-place of Worcester, which paid a hundred shillings yearly. Five of the twenty-eight masures belonging to the Abbey of Evesham, in Worcester, had been *wasted.* There were, too, three masures in Worcester paying thirty pence yearly, belonging to the Church of Hereford as appendant to its Manor of Cotingtune. The houses and salines in Wich were numerous; there were 113 burgesses in this town; 28 in Pershore, belonging to the Abbey of Westminster, lord of the Manor. One monk alone appears in Domesday to represent the powerful and opulent Benedictine Abbey of Evesham, which, nevertheless, contained

at this period at least a hundred inmates. The chartulary[1] of the Worcester monk, Heming, throws considerable light on the Domesday Book of the county. It has been printed by the assiduous antiquary, Hearne. In like manner the Evesham chartulary[2] contains valuable information respecting the Abbey lands at the time, but it yet awaits an editor. The British Museum also contains many scattered documents which illuminate the early history of Pershore Abbey. Dudelei, or Dudley Castle is mentioned in the Survey.

17. HEREFORDSHIRE, or Herefordscire, has been confused with Hertfordshire by Mr. Ewald.[3] The Domesday name of the latter, Herfordscire, certainly resembles that of the county of Hereford, but does not take the second *e*. Ellis tabulates 5,368 total population, comprising among the number, 37 tenants-in-chief, 282 undertenants, 2,124 villani, 1,407 bordarii and 10 poor boors, 691 servi, 99 ancillæ, 104 bovarii as well as 12 free, a carpenter, a bee-master, a miller, 2 cowmen, 21 bedels, and 42 Welshmen. The state of the city of Hereford is prefixed to the schedule of 36 numbered classes of tenants-in-chief. In this city were six smiths, each provided with a *forgia*, or forge, and bound to work at his trade for the king to a specified extent, for which he received a payment. There were two classes of burgesses here: the English retaining

[1] Brit. Mus., Cotton MS., Tiberius, A. xiii.
[2] Brit. Mus., Cotton MS., Vespasian, B. xxiv.
[3] "Encycl. Brit.," new edition, s. v. Domesday Book.

O.

privileges which they had enjoyed in the time of Edward the Confessor; and the francigenæ or foreigners who had certain exemptions. The Hereford moneyers had the right of *sac* and *soc*; their inmates were therefore under their own keeping. Wigmore was a borough; there were 16 burgesses of Cliford held in demesne by Ralph de Todenei; 10 in Hereford, and 1 in Hanlie. The castles of Wigmore, Monemude, Clifford, Ewias, as well as *domus defensabiles*, are noticed in the County Survey. This county finishes the second row or rank of counties as taken in order by the scribes of the Exchequer Domesday.

18. CAMBRIDGESHIRE, or Grentebriscire, held 5,204 persons. Among these, 45 tenants-in-chief, including two carpenters and 257 undertenants, 29 burgesses in Cambridge, 15 fishermen, 4 priests, 3 foreign-born soldiers. The description of the town precedes the numbered list of 44 sections. It contained 373 *masuræ*, was rated for a whole hundred, and divided into ten wards. In the time of King Edward the Confessor the burgesses gave the sheriff the use of their " carrucæ," or carts, three times a year. Of the " Inquisition of the county of Cambridge," the original return from which the Cambridgeshire Domesday was prepared, an account has been given in a former chapter. The " Inquest of Ely," bound up with this in the same volume, and edited together with the former text by Mr. Hamilton, describes the lands of the Abbey of St. Etheldrida, Ely, in this and other neighbouring counties, and these two records must

be studied in connection with the Domesday account for the county. Cambridge Castle, *castrum*, finds a notice in the Domesday Book, which states that twenty-seven houses were demolished for it.

19. HUNTINGDONSHIRE is termed Huntedunscire in the Domesday Book. There was a population of 2,914, including 35 tenants-in-chief, 85 sub-tenants, including *homines* and *milites*; 1,933 villani; 490 bordarii, and 47 presbyters. The town or burgus of Huntingdon, notice of which stands first in the survey of the county, seems to have been of considerable resort, no less a number than 296 burgesses being recorded in two divisions, each consisting of two *ferlinges*, or fourth parts. In the first, 116 burgesses and 100 bordarii, to assist in paying the geld; in the second, 140. Eustace, the sheriff, held 22, and Gislebert de Gant 18 burgesses. The whole borough paid geld, as if it were a fourth part of the hundred of Hyrstingstan, rated at 50 hides; but this rating was changed by William the Conqueror. Huntingdon Castle, apparently of recent construction, occurs.

20. BEDFORDSHIRE, called Bedefordscire in the manuscript, was not a populous county, numbering 3,875 persons in all. There are 56 titular owners, or county burgesses, and other officers 104; 229 under tenants, the remainder bordarii, servi, socmen, and villains. The town of Bedford paid tax as for half a hundred. The description of it precedes the numbered schedule of tenants in the text, but the burgesses are grouped last but one, followed by the "Prefecti regis

et bedelli et elemosinarii," whose description closes
the county record.

21. NORTHAMPTONSHIRE, Northañtscire, records
a census of 8,441, according to Ellis's computation,
inclusive of 66 chief tenants, 261 undertenants, including 33 milites of St. Peter de Burgo, or Peterborough; 3,952 villani, 2,056 bordarii, 1,062 sochemanni, 59 ancillæ, 66 presbyters.   The description
of Northantone, or Northampton, heads the County
Survey.   Here King Edward the Confessor had sixty
burgesses in demesne, holding as many mansions.
There appears to have been a new suburb of this
town (called "Novus Burgus," in the Domesday
Book), in which King William had forty houses,
besides 47 in demesne in the other quarter of the town.
221 houses were in this new quarter in possession
of various tenants-in-chief, of which 21 were _wasted_,
so that there were at least 287 inhabited houses in
Northampton in A.D. 1086.   The castle of Rochinge-
ham is mentioned as having been built by King
William on wasted land.

22. LEICESTERSHIRE, the Lægreceasterscyre and
Lædecæstrescire of the "Anglo-Saxon Chronicle," is
called Ledecestrescire in the Domesday Book. Ellis
computes the population census at 6,772, which included 63 tenants-in-chief, 196 under tenants, 2,665
villani, 1,914 sochemanni, 1,345 bordarii, 23 ancillæ,
42 presbyters, a clerk, and a deacon.   Notice of the
"Civitas de Ledecestre" precedes the numbered
table of 44 tenants, among whom Comes Hugo

occupies two places, the 13th and the 43rd. The burgesses of Ledecestre numbered 65, but there were 318 houses and 4 wasted; 71 houses were assessed to the king's geld.

23. WARWICKSHIRE, or Warwicscire, contained, according to Ellis's valuable digest, a population of 6,574, among whom were 55 chief-tenants, 176 under tenants, 3,500 villani, 1775 bordarii, 845 servi, 22 burgesses in the burgh of Warwick, and about 225 houses; 10 burgesses in Tamworth, which border town also held Staffordshire burgesses. An account of the burgus de Warwic is prefixed to the numbered schedule of tenants-in-chief. Four masures were wasted in the town of Warwick for the site of the castle.

24. STAFFORDSHIRE, called Statfordscire, but in the "Anglo-Saxon Chronicle" Stæffordscyre, only held a population of 3,178, 32 of these being tenants-in-chief, 138 undertenants, 1,728 villani, 912 bordarii, 212 servi, 1 ancilla, 6 teini, including 1 designated by name, Chenuin; 12 burgesses in Tamworth, others being in the Warwickshire part of this town; 36 burgesses in the burgus de Stadford, a notice of which town commences the survey before the schedule of tenants-in-chief. The Conqueror held in this borough 18 burgesses, besides 8 waste manses, and 22 manses as of the honour of the earldom. The other 18 burgesses were parcel of the manor of Mertone, held by the Monastery of St. Evroul in Normandy. Five canons of Lecefelle or Lichfield,

and 18 in Statford are enumerated; and in the
market of Tutbury there were 42 homines, all probably engaged solely in the pursuit of various trades.
Eyton's "Analysis of the Staffordshire Survey" must
be carefully studied in connexion with the record of
that county.   He finds three remarkable peculiarities
in the method of the Staffordshire Commissioners
which distinguishes their work from that of the
Commissioners which examined the counties adjacent, Worcester, Shropshire, Cheshire, and Derbyshire.   These are :—

1. In dealing with plough lands and teams, special
formula different to those used in the above-
mentioned counties.

2. They do not use the word ecclesia, but signify
the church by mere mention of a resident presbyter.

3. They do not make written mention of the
geldability or non-geldability of an estate; they speak
of a hide, a virgate of land, a carucate of land, but
not of a hida geldabilis, or hida ad geldum.

These peculiarities are found to be also used
in the Surveys of Warwickshire and Oxfordshire.
Thus, these three counties, Oxfordshire, Warwickshire, and Staffordshire were in the same circuit.
The king's land, *Terra regis*, in this county, has
been distinguished by Eyton into three sections.
1. The "*Vetus Dominicum Coronæ*," the estates of King
Edward descended to King William; 2. The lands
escheated to the king by Edwin, last earl of Mercia,
and earl Harold; and 3. Estates, uniformly waste,
which had gone to the Crown by forfeiture or eviction
of Saxon thegns.   The Domesday Book notices the

castles of Toteberie, or Tutbury, and Stadford in the manor of Cebbesio.

25. SHROPSHIRE, or Salop, the Sciropecsire of the Domesday Book, had a total recorded population of 5,080 individuals; among them only 9 chief tenants, 199 under tenants, 1,788 villani, 1,157 bordarii, 871 servi, 384 bovarii, 52 ancillæ, 167 radmans, 1 bee-master, 67 Welshmen. The survey of the "Civitas de Sciropesberie" heads the County Survey. Here were 252 houses, inhabited by as many burgesses paying gable as for 100 hides in the time of Edward the Confessor. In the time of the taking of the Domesday census the castle of earl Roger occupied the site of 51 masures, and 50 more were wasted, 43 foreign burgesses paid no share of the tax, and 39 burgesses who did not pay were transferred by the earl to the abbey. This large proportion of loss entailed upon the remaining burgesses a very heavy individual share in the assessment, at which they naturally complained. In this county Domesday notices the following castles :— Shrewsbury, Lvvre, Stantvne, and Montgomery, the last built by earl Roger of Montgomery.

26. CHESHIRE, Cestrescire, has no numbered list of tenants-in-chief. The text of the general survey is preceded by the account of the City of Cestre, and closed with that of the land "inter Ripam et Mersham," between the rivers Ribble and Mersey (in Lancashire), which had belonged to Rogerus Pictaviensis, Roger of Poictou, but were in the king's hands when the Com-

missioners dealt with them, and the castle of Peneverdant is incidentally mentioned. The rest of Lancashire to the north of this district was but thinly peopled and sparsely cultivated. In this respect we may compare some parts of Surrey. This section of the Survey comprehends parts of Flintshire, including, incidentally, notices of the castle of Roelent or Ruthelan, Denbighshire, and a few townships in Cumberland and Westmoreland, as is shown by Mr. W. Beaumont, in his work on the Domesday for these parts, in 1882. In all, Ellis sums up 2,349 total recorded population of this county, inclusive of 2 tenants-in-chief only, 167 undertenants, 797 villani, 635 bordarii, 193 servi, 172 bovarii, indicative of the grazing qualities of the land; 6 drenghs. Chester city was rated at 50 hides, and sheltered 7 moneyers and a corporation of 12 *Judices*, bound to attend the hundred court under a penalty; perhaps a kind of standing jury. The total of houses was 487 in King Edward's time, but these had dwindled to 282 in A.D. 1086. Two churches, St. John's and St. Werburgh's, had houses in the city.

27. DERBYSHIRE, Derbyscire, does not record a very large population, Ellis's total being but 3,041. The numbered schedule of tenants-in-chief prefixed to the text has seventeen titles, including 25 tenants. There were 75 under tenants, 1,840 villani, 719 bordarii, 128 sochemanni, 49 presbyteri, 20 servi.

This county was evidently connected in some remarkable manner with that of Nottingham, which follows it in the Domesday Book; but we do not know the exact character of the links which united them. Mr. Pendleton, the latest historian of this county, has overlooked this fact, apart from there being but one sheriff for the two counties, which is parallelled in other pairs of counties; the account of the *Burgus Derby* follows that of the *Burgus Snotingeham* in the Nottinghamshire Domesday. The fine for breach of the king's peace in the two counties is thus expressed: "In Snotinghamscire et in Derbiscire pax regis manu vel sigillo data, si fuerit infracta; emendatur per viii hundrez. Vnumquodque hundredum . viii libris. Hujus emendationis habeat rex . ii . partes, comes terciam. Id est . xii . hundreda emendant regi et vi . comiti ." Another connexion between the counties is seen in the paragraph which records the names of those "In Snotingeham scyre et in Derbiscyre" who enjoyed the four great, indeed paramount, privileges of "*socam et sacam et Thol et Thaim*, et consuetudinem regis . ii . denariorum." Ellis thinks this connexion is due to the commercial relations between the two towns of Derby and Nottingham. Mr. Pendleton notices that in A.D. 1204 Derby, which had been a royal borough since the time of King Edward the Confessor, received a grant of additional privileges, *such as Nottingham had*, and these included the monopoly of dyeing cloth,[1] the creation of a merchant's guild, and the freedom of serfs unclaimed by their lords, after one year's

---

[1] "Nec aliquis infra decem leucas in circuitu de Derebi tinctos pannos operari debet nisi in Burgo de Derebi, salva libertate Burgi de Nottingham."

residence. The homines of the two counties were to come to the burgus of Derebi on Thursdays and Fridays "cum quadrigis et summagiis suis." In the time of King Edward the Confessor there were two hundred and forty-three burgesses in the county town; one church with seven, another with six clerks, each church holding lands free; and fourteen mills. But in A.D. 1086 only 100 greater and 40 lesser burgesses, four churches, 10 mills, 103 *wasted* mansions or houses, and 16 masures possessed of *sac* and *soc*, ten of which belonged to the king. Forty-one burgesses held twelve geldable carucates, cultivating their lands with twelve ploughs, "although eight could do the work."

28. NOTTINGHAMSHIRE; Snotingĥscire, of the Survey, which perpetuates the ancient orthography of the Saxons,—Snotingaham, a patronymic or tribal name,—held at the time of the Domesday a recorded population of 5,686, including 50 tenants-in-chief, 138 undertenants, 2,603 villani, 1,516 sochemanni; 1,101 bordarii, and 64 presbyters. In Newerche, or Newark, Remigius, bishop of Lincoln, had upon his demesne 56 burgesses, as well as villani and bordarii. Nottingham Town, in the time of King Edward the Confessor, held 173 burgesses and two moneyers. This number had been reduced by the time of the formation of the survey to 120 *homines manentes*, or burgesses holding six carucates, and tilling the area with fourteen ploughs. The shrinkage is remarkable, because the recovery from the devastation of the county in A.D. 1016 seems to have reached its height

in the Confessor's time, after which time the prosperity again fell away, and was falling at an earlier period in the reign of the Conqueror. Here were 214 houses, 4 merchants, 48 *domus* of the merchants held by William Peverell, 12 *domus* of knights in the same possession, 13 held by Ralph de Burun. The king had certain thegns reckoned among the tenants-in-chief. The Domesday Survey of Nottinghamshire and Rutland is now being edited by Mr. W. H. Stevenson.

29. RUTLANDSHIRE, Roteland, had the small recorded population of 862 persons. This includes the following seven tenants-in-chief. 1. The king, 2. Judita, the countess, 3. Robert Malet, 4. Ogerius, 5. Gislebert de Gand, 6. Hugo the earl, 7. Albert the clerk. There were four undertenants, 730 villani, 109 bordarii, 7 presbyters, 5 sochemanni. This, of course, relates to the shire land entered under its own title in the Domesday. Other parts of the county have been described in the Surveys of Northamptonshire and Lincolnshire. This may, perhaps, be accounted for, as in other Domesday instances, on the grounds of convenience or juxtaposition of properties, as Ellis suggests. It may, perhaps, be that the strict limits of the county had not yet been defined. The tithe of this county, "Decima de Rotelanda," was granted by William the Conqueror to the Abbey of St. Peter, Westminster, in one of the shortest and most laconic charters on record, still extant in the Cottonian collection, No. xvi., 2 in the British Museum.[1]

[1] Birch, "Seals of William the Conqueror," in Transac. Roy. Soc. Lit., vol. x., new series.

30. YORKSHIRE, called Evrvicscire, or Evrvice-
scyre, in the Domesday Book, does not present so
large a return of inhabitants and cultivation as the
great area of the land would appear to demand.
The reason of this, the desolation of the year
1080, has been mentioned in another place in this
work. The *tredings*, or threefold sub-division, existed
at the Domesday period, but the description of
their component manors are not kept separate.
There are twenty-nine entries in the numbered list
which precedes the general text, representing the more
important holders of land, but 105 tenants-in-chief
in all ; only 222 undertenants, 5,079 villani, 1,819
bordarii, 447 sochemanni, 136 presbyters, 1 clericus.
35 villani and 8 bordarii occupied the large number
of 411 manors, a clear indication of the thorough
harrying which the county had undergone. There are
no undertenants on the Terra Regis, and only two
on the whole of the earl of Moretaine's lands.

The city of York has its survey prefixed to the
numbered list of tenants. From it we learn that it
comprehended 6 shires at the date of Edward the
Confessor. One of these was abolished, to make
room for the castles. The others contained 1,418
"mansiones hospitatæ," inhabited tenements. The
archbishop's shire held 189 others ; thus bringing up
the total to 1,597. King William's shire contained
391 rent-paying houses, 540 vacant, 400 occasionally
inhabited, 145 in occupation of the francigenæ,
and other dwellings. It was evidently a large com-
munity, of upwards of 1,000 inhabited tenements.
The city held 4 *Judices*, of whose probable official

capacity some notice has been given in the account
of Chester.   The geld was levied on 84 carucates
within the city bounds.   Burgesses are also entered
by number as follow :—Bretlinton, or Bridlington,
4; Dadesleia, Stantone and Helgebi, 31; Pocling-
ton, 15; lesser burgesses in Tateshale, 60.   Incidental Domesday notices of, or allusions to, castles
occur in the survey of the county.   Among them are
two at York, one at Pontefract, and one at Richmond.
A paragraph in the Domesday records the names of
the great tenants of the county who possessed the
privileges of "soc and sac, and tol, and thaim, and
all customs."

31. LINCOLNSHIRE or Lincolescire, and Lindesig, or
the parts of Lindsey, follows Yorkshire in the Survey.
The numbered schedule comprises seventy titles, and
there are also the separate notices of Civitas Lincolia,
Stanford "Burgū Regis," and Torchesey.   The fine for
breaking the king's peace in Lincoln city resembles
that already described at Derby and Nottingham.
Some of the lands in the Yorkshire Ridings have been
placed in this county.   It was a populous district.
Ellis finds a population of 25,305 recorded ; consisting of 92 chief tenants and *Taini regis*, 414
undertenants, 11,503½ sochemanni, 7,723 villani,
4,024 bordarii, 131 presbyters, among others.   The
burgesses are set down as follows :—City of Lincoln,
about 900 ; Stanford, 136 ; Grantham, 111; Torkesey,
102 ; Ludes (or Louth) 80.   Lincoln city held 1,150
inhabited houses in the time of Edward the Confessor,
and, from the names of some of those who held the

houses, Ellis conjectures that the city had served as
a resort for partisans of Merlesuain, Ulf, Morcar, and
Harold, opposed to the Conqueror at the beginning
of his reign.   About a fifth of these had been
wasted in building the castle, or from misfortune,
poverty, and fire.   The 12 lagemen here may, perhaps, compare with the twelve *judices* of Chester.

Stanford must have been a populous town in the
days of Edward the Confessor.   The castle was
erected[1] by Edward the Elder in A.D. 922, on the
south side of the River Welland.   But it would seem
that another castle had taken the place of this from
which the Danes were expelled by King Edmund[2] in
A.D. 942, for the town wards held 141 inhabited houses
in the time of Edward the Confessor; 5 were
destroyed at the re-erection of the Castle, 136
remained for the survey of A.D. 1086.   The Domesday takes special notice (by a separate paragraph) of
the great lords who held the four important jurisdictions of sac, soc, tol, and thaim.   Here also were
12 lagemen, reduced to 9 when the Domesday was
prepared.   70 mansiones here, which had belonged
to Queen Editha, are said to be in Rutlandshire.

Torkesey had possessed 213 burgesses in the
Confessor's day.   When William the Conqueror's Commissioners assessed the town they found but 102, for
111 lay waste.   There were castles at Lincoln and
Stanford:

The first volume of the Domesday then reverts to
YORKSHIRE, and contains entries which tend to show

---

[1] "Anglo-Saxon Chronicle."   [2] *Ibid.*

that there was considerable confusion with that county and Lincolnshire, or, at any rate, that returns were taken in common. The arrangement of the materials is as follows :—

Clamores de Evrvic scire. Claims in Yorkshire.

Clamores in Nort Treding. Claims in the North Riding.

Clamores quæ sunt, in Sud Treding Lincoliæ. Claims in the South Riding of Lincoln.

Clamores in Nortreding, again.

Clamores in Chetsteuen, Kesteven, co. Lincoln.

Westreding. "In geldo civitatis Eboracensis sunt quaterviginti et quatuor carucatæ terræ quæ tempore regis Edwardi geldabant unaquaque quantum una domus civitatis." The city geld comprised 88 carucates of land, each rated as a house.

Nortreding.

Estreding.

The second volume is occupied with the three great counties of Essex, Norfolk, Suffolk.

32. ESSEX, or Exsessa, commences with the titled schedule of 88 tenants, to which follow the title of *Liberi homines*, or freemen, and the Invasions. Here Ellis finds a recorded population of 16,060 ; including 95 tenants-in-chief, 520 undertenants, 8,002 bordarii, 4,087 villains, 1,768 servi, 33 presbyters, and the following burgesses :—Colchester, 401 ; Melduna, or Maldon, 180 ; Sudberia (or Sudbury, now in Suffolk), 20.

The notice of Colchester is full and interesting.
294 burgesses had, for the most part, 1 house each.
some 2, a few 4, and one, as many as 13 ; with more
or less land attached.   Among those holding houses
are Hamo Dapifer, he is entered in the Survey for a
house, a *curia*, a hide of land, 15 burgesses ; the
bishop of London, 14 houses, free except for *scot*.
The king is credited with 102 acres in demesne, with
10 boors.   Sixpence yearly was assessed to every
house when the king mobilised his army.   There
was a corporation of the burgesses here which held
land, the proceeds of which (60 shillings), if not
wanted for the service of the Crown, was divided in
common. The church of St. Peter here, is mentioned
in the Domesday.

Maldon was the only other place in Essex containing burgesses, some of which held land, others only
their houses within the borough.   There were 1 king's
house, 180 burgesses' houses, held of the king, 18
waste houses.   The Domesday notices the castle of
Rageneia, or Rayleigh, in Rochford hundred.

33. NORFOLK, is called Norfulc, and Nordf.   Here
was established the large recorded population of
27,087 persons, which may be multiplied by 5 or 6
to represent actual total, including women and
children.   We do not know at what age the youth
put off his legal infancy, and was reckoned as an
adult.   Perhaps not very far from the age adopted
by modern English law for the attainment of majority.
In the enumeration of the Israelites by Moses,[1]

---

[1] Numb. i. 1–3 ; Exod. xxx. 14. .

those under 20 years of age were not counted. When David numbered the people, the same limit of age was observed.[1] This is noteworthy, as being the custom of a race who, like other inhabitants of low latitudes, arrive at an earlier maturity than is the case in England. This large Norfolk population is composed of, among others, 63 chief tenants, mentioned by name in another part of the work; 435 under-tenants, 9,537 bordarii and 480 in Norwich too poor to pay custom, 4,656 villani, 4,571 sochemanni, 17 half-sochemanni, 4,277 liberi homines, and only one Anglicus. The burgesses follow the proportion of inhabitants, and are fairly numerous, viz., in Tetford (Thetford), whither bishop Herfast, of Elmham, had transferred his see eleven years previously, 725; English burgesses in Norwic, 665; and in the Novus Burgus, or newly included suburbs, 124; in Gernemuta, or Yarmouth, 70.

Thetford was the most flourishing town, if we may judge by the number of burgesses within it. There had been even more, 943 in the time of King Edward the Confessor, but the difference in the time of the survey is accounted for by the return of 224 vacant houses. Of these burgesses, 21 held six carucates and sixty acres. The king here held two-thirds of the royal revenue, as of the Crown, the other third went to him as of the forfeited earldom of Ralph Guader. But if the tale of inhabitants and tenements had diminished, the tax had increased, for while in the time of the Confessor it amounted in all to £30, in the report of King William's commissioners

[1] 1 Chron. xxvii. 23.

P

it stood at £50 to the Crown by weight, £20 blanched
money, £6 by count, £40 in coin de moneta, from
the mint, and 16 sh. for provender; making in all
£116 16s., or nearly four times as much as under
Saxon government.

Norwich city, or rather town, for the cathedral did
not rise until the transfer by bishop Herbert Losinga
from Thetford here in A.D. 1094, had recently suffered
much. The forfeiture of earl Roger, conflagrations,
the king's geld, and other retarding agencies had,
however, left 1,320 burgesses, the greater part to the
king, 50 to Stigand, who had been ejected from his
See of Elmham, 32 to Harold. The town was rated
by itself as for a whole hundred. The payments in
the time of Edward the Confessor were the same
as those of Thetford, but they were increased at
the time of the survey to upwards of three times
the amount. The empty houses were very numerous,
for some of the burgesses had transferred themselves
to Beccles, which belonged to the Abbey of Bury St.
Edmund's, others to the Hundred of Humbleyard,
where they held eighty acres of land, and a few elsewhere. Norwich Castle is mentioned incidentally.

Yarmouth had remained stationary, in point of
numbers, for both in the reign of King Edward the
Confessor and at the time of the survey it sheltered
seventy burgesses, whose financial condition was so
far bettered by the change of government that the
rents could be slightly increased, and they paid four
pounds to the sheriff as a free gratuity or stipend.

34. The survey of SUFFOLK, called Svdfolc, or

Svdfulc, completes the second volume of the Domesday Book.

· This, like Norfolk, is a populous county. Ellis
finds a recorded population of 20,491 at least, which
would yield over a hundred thousand souls. The
numbered list of chief tenants contains seventy-six
entries, the last three being :—74, the Vavassors, also
termed *free men* ; 75, the King's free men ; 76, the
encroachments or *invasiones* upon the King. The
total is made up of 73 tenants in capite, 625 under-
tenants, 6,205 bordarii and 11 half-bordarii, 5,344
free men, 1,895 free men under choice protection,
commendati, and other sub-divisions of this class ;
2,812 villani, 998 sochemanni, 909 servi, 103 homines,
9 presbyters, and others.

The Abbey of St. Edmund de Burgo, or Bury St.
Edmund, was a large and important factor in the
life of the Suffolk people at this time, and made its
influence felt in many ways. In it were 30 presbyters, deacons, and clerks; 28 nuns, *nonnæ*, and
poor persons; 75 serjeants, or perhaps lay servants;
13 in-dwellers, probably engaged in trade or business;
27 bordarii, and 34 milites; in all, 207 persons,
besides monks. In King Edward's time there had
been 310. The whole number of houses belonging
to the abbey property was 342. They were probably
occupied by lay tenants, who, however, do not figure
as burgesses.

Six towns in this county possessed burgesses.
Dunewic or Dunwich, the primal seat of the Christian
Church in these parts of England, wherein Felix of
Burgundy had sown the Gospel seed, and endeavoured

to soften the barbarian habits of the nations by
establishing schools, in which he could teach Latin to
his missionary band, in the first half of the seventh
century, under the protection of Sigbert, King of the
East Angles, subsequently. parted with a moiety of
its episcopal area with Elmham, A.D. 673, which in a
later age, after the hostile incursions of the Mercians,
led by Ludekan, then King, was re-joined to it, and its
own name suppressed. Here the Domesday Book
places 316 burgesses; and the town appears to have
been improving, for in the time of Edward the Confessor there were but 120. Eighty of the Domesday
burgesses belonged to the Abbey of Ely; the others
were held by Robert Malet. They paid £50, and sixty
thousand herrings, which throws a light on the condition of the fisheries of England and the nature of
the food of the inhabitants.

Gipewiz, or Ipswich, records 210 burgesses, but in
King Edward's day there had been nearly five times
that number; between the two periods of rule 328
geldable tenements were wasted. The third penny
had gone to earl Guert in the days preceding the
Conquest. It was rated probably as a half hundred.
Sudberie, or Sudbury, part of the survey of which
town is entered under the county of Essex, contained
118 Suffolk burgesses, with a market and moneyers.
Its chief rent had been nearly doubled under the new
government.

Beccles, in the holding of the Abbey of Bury St.
Edmunds, contained 26 burgesses and a market; one
fourth part of its proceeds went to the Crown. There
were 30 sochemanni, with 20 bordarii in their soc.

Clare sheltered 43 burgesses ; Eye, 25 ; and at Cara-
halla mention is made of a free market granted by
the king. Incidental mention is made of a castle at
Eia or Eye. Here, or at any rate within the Manor
of Hoxne, the See of Dunwich, which had been over-
whelmed by the sea at some time between the reign
of Edward the Confessor and the formation of the
survey, had been removed.

CHAPTER XI.

MEASURES OF LAND — DENOMINATIONS — JURISDIC-
TIONS — FRANCHISES — TENURES — SERVICES.

Measures of Land.

THE land measures of the Domesday Book have always been the subject of considerable discussion among students. Even so lately as the Domesday Commemoration of this year, the principal readers of papers and members were found to take up positions irreconcilable with one another's opinions, and it would, therefore, perhaps be unwise in this place to lay down any very hard and fast theories upon the details and comparative values of superficial and linear measures.

The following principal terms are employed in the text of the surveys for land measures.

(1) Acra.

(2) Bovata.

(3) Carucata.

(4) Ferding.

(5) Furlong.

(6) Hida.

(7) Jugum.

(8) Leuca.

(9) Perca.

(10) Pes.

(11) Quarentena.

(12) Solin, or suling.

(13) Virgata.

(1.) The *acra*, or acre, appears to be the equivalent of the Saxon *Æcer* and Roman *ager*,[1] and, like other areas mentioned in Domesday, to have originally signified no specific quantity of surface. There appears also to have been a Norman as well as an English acre, a natural consequence of the difference of computation employed by the two nations. In the time of King Edward the First,[2] the acre consisted of a hundred and sixty perches, and the proportions of the sides of the rectangle, which measured, as a rule, forty perches one way by four the other, were tabulated in MSS. in detail, so that, for example, when the length was ten perches the breadth was sixteen perches; when the length was eighty perches, the breadth was two, and so on. This rectangularity could not, however, have always been practicable, on account of the varying conditions of each locality, but probably it obtained in places where open land and pastures were first marked out for tillage. The *furlong*, or "furrow's length,"[3] was the length of the long side of the normal acre of forty perches by four. This, which was one course for the plough, was found to be the most convenient in practice, and the most humane for the beasts employed in ploughing, which required breathing time at the end of each furrow. The late Mr. J. B. Davidson,[4] who had

---

[1] "*Dimidium agrum* quod nostra lingua dicimus *healve aker*." Birch, "Cart. Sax.," No. 460, A.D. 850.

[2] 33 Edward I., s. 6, A.D. 1305.

[3] But Ellis considers the furlong to have another value, which will be mentioned further on.

[4] "Note on the Measures of Domesday, especially as applicable to Devonshire."

made considerable researches into the composition of Domesday measures, finds that the *quarentena* and *leuca* depend on the acre, as will be shown in treating of these terms.

Even as late as the seventeenth century the acre was an imaginary quantity,[1] as is testified by the line of the pretty little Shakesperean song :—

"Between the *acres* of the rye."[2]

2. The *bovata*, or "Oxgang," as Ellis translates it, must have originally consisted of as much land as an *ox* could till, an *ox's worth* of land, for the word is formed with a termination *ata*, analogous to the terms librata, solidata, denariata, carucata, virgata, signifying a pounds' worth of land, &c., that is, so much land as should pay one pound, and so on. Ellis considers it to have been originally as much as an "ox team" could plough in a year, but the explanation is obscure, as he does not inform us how many oxen went, in his understanding, to such a team. He admits, moreover, that the number of acres which composed a *bovate* are variously stated in different parts of the Domesday Book; no doubt in proportion to the manageability of the soil. Records of the time of Edward I. mention eight acres to the bovate at Doncaster in Yorkshire, and other bovates of sixteen and seventeen acres respectively. There can be no question that the proportion of a *bovate* (one ox's worth) to a *jugum* (a pair's worth), is as

[1] See Halliwell's "Archaic Dict.," *s.v.*
[2] *As You Like It*, act v., sc. 3.

one to two, and of the *bovate* to the *carucate* as one to four, the number assigned to the plough, but of this more hereafter.

3. The *carucate*, or plough's worth, that is, the area that one plough could till annually, is a word introduced by the Normans, and is probably one of the most interesting subjects in the whole of the Domesday Book. Beamont tersely puts it that the hide was the ploughable land; the carucate, that which was actually ploughed. We must first consider the *caruca* before we can justly arrive at an appreciation of the *carucata*.

It is remarkable that the common Latin word *aratrum*, a plough, is not used in the Domesday, although the verb *aro*, to plough, is of frequent occurrence. We must, therefore, admit that the synonym *caruca* suggested itself more readily to the scribes because of its similarity to the vernacular word in use among the common people at the period, for it can hardly be suggested that they had no acquaintance with *aratrum*. The Greek κάρρον, and Latin *carrus*, do not appear to have any part in the derivation of *caruca*. But from the Low-Latin form, or, at any rate, post-classical form, *carruca*,[1] used by Pliny and others to signify a sort of four-wheeled travelling carriage,[2] several Romance languages

---

[1] Genus vehiculi tum in urbem, tum extra in itineribus adhibiti, et non solum a viris, præsertim honoratioribus, sed etiam a feminis.

[2] The carrucæ, or carts of the Cambridge burgesses, which were customarily lent to the sheriff three times yearly, belong to this category.

formed cognate words, such as the Italian *carrozza*, the French *carrosse*, and, by the ordinary processes of derivation, the English *carriage*.

The cardinal fact in all these words is that they represent a four-wheeled vehicle. The words used in the Romance languages for plough, are :—carruca, Ital.; carruga, Provenç.; charrua, Portug.; kérue, Picardy; quiérue, Normandy (Valogne); chèrowe, Walloon; chèreuwe, Namur; kèrue, Rouchi. Setting aside for the present the termination, which is a very common one in the languages of Western France, our task is directed to elucidating, if possible, the meaning of the root *car*. Comparing other words in Romance languages, the following immediately strike our attention :—

Portuguese, *catle* or *catre*, a bed, a "four-poster" (*quatuor*).

French—*Car*, why = Latin *quare*.

    „   *Carême*, Lent = Latin *quadragesima*.

    „   *Carrefour*, a cross road = Latin *quatuor* fori; English, *Carfax*.

    „   *Carré*, squared = Latin, *quadratus*.

    „   *Carriere*, *career*, *quarry*.

    „   *Carillon* = Latin, quadrilio.

Latin — *Carta* = quarta; a quart.

        Carteria = quarteria.

From this list, which might be easily extended, the root *car* in *caruca*, may fairly be taken to represent the Latin *quatuor*. But a plough would not from its nature be provided with four wheels. In some of the earliest representations of a plough, for

example, those in the Utrecht Psalter (a manuscript
which has been attributed to periods ranging from
the sixth to the ninth century), the ploughman holds,
the tanged or turned-over end of the ploughshare,
which has no woodwork or wheels. The idea of *four*,
therefore, cannot refer to wheels, nor can it refer to
the men employed with it. It remains, therefore, to
represent the beasts yoked to it, and this is exactly
what is found in two manuscripts contemporary with
the Domesday Book, in the Cottonian Library of the
British Museum. In the first of these, Julius A. vi.
f. 3, the plough is of an elaborate and elegant form;
the body consists of a solid beam to which a wheel
(indicating two, of course, the second being supposed
to be behind the first) is attached at the front part.
Behind this a curved ploughshare or knife, something
like the blade of a Turkish scimitar, is represented,
the haft going through the beam and standing a little
above it right through the thickness of the wood.
There is a thong or tie hanked round the beam
in front of this metal portion, which seems to be
attached to the blade at about one-third from its
point. The use of this was apparently to cut into,
but not to turn over the earth, as the plough passed
up the furrow. Behind this knife-like portion, and
at the rear end of the beam, comes the true ploughshare, of angular form, with sharp cutting point
shaved off at an angle from the blade, and having a
square hole into which the end of the beam is fitted.
The metal work is then carried up, and forks into
two horn-like handles, one of which is grasped in
each hand by the ploughman, who is thereby enabled

to steer the plough along its proper course. Between
these two blades, the latter of which is evidently
adapted to turn over the earth, is a small peg or nail
with an uncertain object like a blade attached to it,
partially hidden behind the large blade. Two pairs
of bullocks attached in some obscure manner to the
beam draw it along over the rough and hummocky
ground. These pairs are not united together, nor is
any harness or gear introduced into the illustration.
Over the necks of the two in front, as also over the
necks of the two behind, a yoke or rail is laid, apparently with the object of keeping the rank of two
abreast in their work. In front of the beasts walks
the man, backwards or nearly so, provided with a
long, straight goad or stick with which he is pricking
the right-hand animal of the second row, or "off-side
wheeler."

The second illustration, that in Cottonian MS.
Tiberius B.V. part 1, f. 3, looks almost like an enlarged copy of the first. But it has the advantage of
being coloured. The wheel has eight spokes,
alternately plain and turned, its circumference is
coloured of a pale blue, perhaps to represent iron or
steel; the beam also is of the same colour. The front
blade or knife is plain and uncoloured; the tie
silvered; the hinder blade red, with white streaks;
the blade carried by the middle peg, blue. Between
the two oxen of the front pair is a straight line, indicating apparently a pole or bar between the oxen, but it
is merely a line, and has not any thickness or substance. It is not seen in the other drawing.

In the Utrecht Psalter, of which an excellent

photographic copy has recently been prepared, under the direction of the trustees of the British Museum, the illustration to Psalm ciii. (civ. of the authorised version), "Man goeth forth unto his work and to his labour until the evening," v. 23, "Exibit homo ad opus suum et ad operationem suam usque ad vesperum," is represented by a picture (fol. 120 of the facsimile), of a man ploughing with two oxen, which he directs by means of a long goad held in the right hand. His left hand holds the handle of the primitive plough, which is turned over into hook-like form, while the part that enters the ground performs, by means of its pointed end, the part of blade, or culter, and share. Through this blade passes the beam or a rope; it is difficult to determine which of these two is signified by the thin straight line which issues from behind the oxen and runs into the iron plough.

A similar representation of the early plough is contained in the same manuscript (folio 126 of the facsimile), where it is introduced to illustrate (in that remarkably realistic manner in which the whole of the pictures have been designed throughout the volume), Psalm cvi. (cvii. of the authorised version). "And there he maketh the hungry to dwell, that they may .... sow the fields," &c., v. 36, 37. "Et seminaverunt agros," &c. The picture in this place is very similar to that which has been already mentioned, but the ploughman has no goad. The bar or beam is represented of more substance, and has two lines to it. The draughtsman of the Harley MS. 603, which is a copy of this manuscript, executed about the time of the Norman conquest, and therefore strictly contem-

porary with the formation of the Domesday Book,
has introduced the same subjects, at the corresponding places of his work, folios 516-5, 216.

The celebrated Bayeux tapestry, a faithful representation of the manners and customs of the Saxons
and Normans at the time of the Conquest, contains
on its lower border a panoramic view of four chief
agricultural pursuits arranged in reverse order of
event, viz., slinging at birds from the young crops,
horse-harrowing with a square frame with four rows
of teeth, sowing in a furrowed field of which the
boundary is composed of single stones set at regular
distances, and ploughing. The picture, as given in
Mr. Fowke's valuable work on the tapestry, is somewhat indistinct, but shows a long beam drawn by a
single animal with long ears (whether intended for
ox, cow, horse—vastly different, however, from the
finely drawn horses throughout the tapestry, and
from that in the same scene drawing the harrow—
or ass, who shall say?) One shaft and some harness is
depicted. The beam is furnished with two front
wheels; between them sits the driver, holding a long
goad in the right hand, his left hand extended as if
pointing to a distant object, his head turned back in
converse with the ploughman. The beam goes on
behind the wheels, and carries a knife blade set
through it, as in the other examples described; and
at the back strides the plodding ploughman, with
both hands occupied in guiding the long curved turn-
over or plough-share, the point of which reaches
nearly to the tip of the knife in front. This representation appears to be quite conclusive as to the

number of animals employed to draw the plough. The ladies, who worked with intelligent assiduity at the smallest and most unimportant details all through this illustrative needlework history of their own times, would not have hesitated to render the picture of the ploughing strictly correct as to the complement of animals usually seen under these conditions.

The Royal Manuscript in the British Museum, 12 F. xiii., a work of the thirteenth century written in England, containing excellent illuminations for a "Bestiary," or "Natural History," gives at folio 37 a fine picture of ploughing with two oxen. Here the beasts are drawing, by means of a rope between them (but with no other visible appliances) attached to the beam, into which is inserted the share or knife, the tang or haft of which passes right through the substance of the beam; behind them is the share, which is of triangular form (coloured a pale slatey blue, like the knife, to represent steel), let into a wooden handle, which is held by the ploughman with the left hand, who is apparently guiding the oxen by his voice, and with a long staff or goad in the right hand. The peg in front of this latter part of the machine is of light red colour, and set into the beam at an angle. In this picture the accessories that have been introduced, viz., the conventional tree and the hummocky ground, clearly show that the artist has derived his inspiration from an older prototype.

An illuminated manuscript in the Additional Collection of the British Museum, 28,162, written in France at the beginning of the fourteenth century, has at folio 86 a very remarkable picture of the process of ploughing. There are two oxen, turning round the plough at the end of the furrow. They are attached to the pole or beam of the plough by three ropes or traces, which carry a bar across the plough beam, each ox being harnessed solely with a collar round the neck to hold the traces. The blade of the plough is formed like a knife, the tang or hilt of which passes through the body of the beam. It is illuminated with silver, and evidently represents steel. The wheel, which has eight spokes, as in the former cases here, is placed behind the blade; the handles, of which there are two, pass upwards out of the beam, which increases in bulk as it approaches this end, and below the handles is a box-like object, with two square sockets or holes of uncertain use. There is no ploughman or ox-herd in the picture, which is a very fine work of art of the period, and evidently faithful in detail, as far as can be expected in the pictorial work of the period.

The "Chronicon Roffense," or Chronicle of Rochester, an important manuscript written in the fourteenth century in England, preserved among the Cottonian MSS. Nero D. ii., has at page 11 *b.* an outline drawing, somewhat roughly and irregularly drawn, of a plough, worked by two oxen in a collar and rope-trace. The ploughman appears to be guiding the work by two reins, one held in each hand. There are no wheels, and the blade has the knife-like form seen in most of the other illustrations. The furrows at the base are drawn quite straight, but the details of the beam and the manner in which the knife is inserted into it are not very clearly defined.

The combined evidence, therefore, of these manuscripts, ranging in point of date from the ninth to the
fourteenth century, reacts strongly against a remarkable theory which was expressed—not, of course, as a
novel idea—by the Rev. Canon Isaac Taylor, at the
recent Domesday commemoration. It amounts to no
less than this. That cultivation was performed by
eight oxen—whether four abreast or in four pairs the
Canon did not state—led by their respective owners on
a co-operative system, drawing an immense plough,
and having their heads so pulled round by the head
gear when they reached the end of their furrow
that it caused the furrow itself in course to take the
form of a reversed S. Another writer on the metrology
and agricultural aspects of Domesday speaks of acres
broken up into strips, which were distributed into
two-fields, indicating a two-field or two-course shift,
where half the estate lay fallow every year in alterna-
tion with the other half, or (as in after times) into
three fields, indicating a three-course shift, where
similarly one-third of the property lay idle every year
in rotation ; and continues to state that the strips
were not, as a rule, straight or at right angles to the
common base from which they sprang, nor was the
base itself straight,—on the contrary, they were
generally wavy in character, and of the shape shown
by the inverted letter S., as any one can very well see
in passing through the grass country of the midland
counties. Canon Taylor believes that half ploughs
drawn by four oxen were occasionally used, but the
fact that a Domesday carucate is invariably equivalent
to eight bovates, shows that a team of eight oxen was

Q

the regular complement. The fallacy here is evident on reflection. Why should not the plough of eight oxen be one of double strength? Professor Nasse, whose testimony is invoked by Canon Taylor, says, "The team of a plough consisted, *as a rule*, of not less than eight draught oxen." He cannot therefore have attached much value to the contemporary, the older, or the newer evidence of illuminated manuscripts, not one of which, as far as I know, attaches eight oxen to the plough. Mr. Seebohm's declaration is similarly qualified, although Canon Taylor relies firmly on it. "The team of eight oxen *seems to have been* the normal manorial plough throughout England, though in some districts still larger teams were needful." No doubt Mr. Seebohm is right as to the concluding proposition, for large ploughs and stiff claylands might well require more than eight beasts to work them, but it would be needless waste of strength to employ eight oxen on the average quality of English-land, where two horses or four oxen could do all that was required.

Many writers, besides Beamont, see in the *carucate* a mere synonym for the *hide*, which they accept as a hundred acres, that is, six score acres, English measure. This may be so if the hide were, as we cannot deny it to have been, the amount of land required for one family, and that family, at any rate in the older days of occupation, possessed but one *caruca*, then the *hida* and the caruca's worth, or *carucata*, must have been co-extensive in every sense.

Canon Taylor, relying upon the twofold system of agriculture in use, as he believes, at the Domesday period, viz., the two-field shift and three-field shift, lays down that the open arable field is the key to the interpretation of the record. He states that the Domesday geldable carucate—unit of assessèd arable —does not really signify what it is usually held .to signify in contemporary literature, the total quantity ploughed yearly by one plough, but the quantity tilled yearly in one arable field. He places the size of the carucates thus :—

180 acr = 1 carucate in a three-field manor.
160 acr = 1 carucate in a two-field manor.
60 acr = 1 geldable Domesday carucate.

4. The *Ferding* occurs as a measure of land in a few Domesday entries. Ellis considers the term equivalent to *Ferling*, a word used in the Somersetshire and Devonshire Domesday as a feordling or farthing. It was a small area only. Agard, quoted by Ellis, allows to this measure about fifteen acres, or the same as the bovate or ox gang. The Cottonian MS. Faustina E.V. deduces from the Liber Rubeus that a ferling is equal to ten acres. This word must not be confused with the *Ferlings*, or four town wards, into which the town of Huntingdon was divided ; nor with the *ferlingel de frumento*, or " quarter " of corn. Throughout the Devonshire Domesday, the hide is reckoned as consisting of four virgates, and the virgate of four ferlings.[1]

5. *Furlong*, the measure of length equivalent to

---

[1] Davidson ; but he attributes very large areas to the ferling, in some instances.

a measure of forty perches, would represent the
length of the *furrow*, in a field containing ten acres
square, the acre being a rectangle 40 perches, or a
furlong in length, and 1-10th, *i.e.*, 4 perches in width.
This proportion of 1-10th is significant.

6. *Hida.* The hide[1] is, perhaps, the oldest, his-
torically speaking, of all terms connected with the
geodesic aspect of the Domesday Book. It occurs
in the laws of Ina, in the seventh century. It has
formed a favourite theme with many writers, and its
origin and meaning are evidently wrapped in some
uncertainty and doubt, because almost all have varied
more or less in their estimate of its value as a measure.
Some fanciful writers, such as Polydore Virgil, look
at the English hide in the light of the Virgilian mytho-
logical origin of the city of Carthage, which sprang in
the first instance from an artifice by which the grant
of land to the new comers was to extend :

" Quantum taurino possint circumdare tergo."

This must, however, be rejected as an etymology,
for we have no reason to admit that the seventh
century inhabitants of Britain were aware of the
existence of Carthage centuries before the time, much
less of the fabled origin of the city. That etymology
is far more worthy of acceptance which refers the
hida to the Anglo-Saxon word *hyd*, a house or habitation, from *hydan*, to hide or cover (analogous to *tectum*,
a roof, from *tego*, to hide). The word still exists in
two modern English words, *hut*, a cottage, *hat*, a

---

[1] Or *higid*: "novem higidæ." Birch, "Cart. Sax.," No.
452.

head covering. Beda uses the term *familia* for a homestead, and its circumjacent land, sufficient for the maintenance of a family of some importance that is, for the lower-class tiller of the soil would not and could not form a family to himself, he and his suit, his wife, children, and property, being an accidental item in the familia of the lord, who defended him from extermination by his enemies. King Alfred translates the Latin word *familia*, by *hydeland*. The quantity of it was sufficient for the work that could be done by one plough, for in the remoter periods, before the congregation of adherents under the ægis of a kinglet, or even a semi-heroic head of a clan, one plough would till sufficient land for the moderate number of persons forming the group of the familia. The quantity of the hide was never expressly determined, nor is it so fixed in Domesday. The calculations which work out one value of it in acres in one place, or in one county, will not give satisfactory deductions elsewhere, and all attempts to fix the exact acreage of the hide have necessarily failed, because the expression represents a quantity which varies in direct proportion to the fertility, arability, and convenience of the land to which the term was applied. For example, the *Dialogus de Scaccario* makes the hide equal to a hundred acres; the Malmesbury manuscript cited by Spelman, ninety-six acres; the Liber Rubeus, a hundred and seventy acres; Agard, calculating by the *Anglicus numerus*, or "great hundred," gives six score acres to the hide. Mr. Davidson finds that it is clear that the Normans used the word hide in Domesday to express some fixed area of land, and he instances the case of Otri, in Devonshire, where it is said there were 24 acres of meadow, and 1 acre of wood, and 1 hide of pasture. His computation of the hide in Devonshire varies between 480, 960, 1,920 acres, with a preponderance in favour of the first number. Some writers compare the hide, the measure of land in the reign of Edward the Confessor, with the carucate, that to which it was reduced by the Conqueror's new standard. Other entries seem to work out the hide to be equivalent to 13$\frac{1}{2}$ carucates, 18 carucates, 6 carucates. Kemble, in his masterly work on the Saxons in England, has attributed an excessive value of area to the hide, which has been criticised somewhat severely by Eyton and later writers. Beamont finds that for South Lancashire the hide stood to the bovate in the relation of one to six, but in the rest of England generally, of one to eight, and in Cheshire, of one to four, and this because the number of carucates to the hide in these two specified counties was smaller than elsewhere, not because the hide was less, for if anything it was greater, but the greater size of the acre occasioned the difference, thus :—

4,840 square yards = 1 statute acre.
7,840 „ = 1 Lancashire acre.
10,240 „ = 1 Cheshire acre.

With such acres fewer carucates were required to raise the hide to the standard which prevailed in other parts of England.

The hide, as one of the oldest terms of areal value, occurs in the Anglo-Saxon charters of a very remote

period. This term by no means disappeared with
the Saxon rule on the invasion of the Normans, but
lingered on in some parts of the country at least as
late as the close of the twelfth century. The word
occurs frequently in the charters entered into the Chartulary of Lewes Priory, co. Sussex (British Museum,
Cotton MS. Vespasian F. xv.), about the time of.
King Henry II. In a collection of original charters
of great intrinsic interest, which have been inlaid as
a volume in the same Library (Nero C. iii.), the word
hida frequently occurs[1] in early charters connected
with the great and rich Abbey of St. Martin at
Battle, co. Sussex. At folio 189 is the counterpart,
which exactly corresponds with the original charter
in the collection of Lord Frederick Campbell, vii. 4,
now also in the British Museum, whereby Odo,
abbot of Battle (A.D. 1175–1199), grants to Nicholas,
son of Ældwine the Palmer, four solidatæ, or shillings'
worth of land, and other three solidatæ of land at
Bromham in Wiltshire, charged with certain services
of three days' work "*in autumn*" to assist in carrying
the lord's crops, and of ploughing one acre, in exchange for half a *hide* of land in Bromham, which the
said Nicholas and Ældwine, his father, used to hold.
We cannot assume from this that half a hide was
equivalent to seven shillings' worth of land, but the
interest of the passage lies in the late use of the
hide, which was still, as we are thus enabled to prove,
of occasional use in some parts of England.

The Chartulary of the Benedictine Abbey of
Abingdon (Cotton MS. Claudius c. ix.), compiled in

[1] Cf., also folios 186, *a b*; 187, *a b c*.

the twelfth century, mentions (in the titles of folios
113, 114) the amount of certain lands by hides,
which in the text of the same are called *cassati* or
mansæ, the three terms being used as equivalent.

. Another example of the late use of the term *hida*
is that afforded by the Ad. Ch. 24,613 in the
British Museum collection. In this deed John,
abbot of St. Peter's monastery at Hyde, or New-
minster, outside the city of Winchester, confirms a
grant to William de Pirelea, son of Osbert de Pirelea,
of "dimidiam hidam terre in Sandestuda," or San-
derstead, co. Surrey. The date is about A.D. 1200.
Another charter by the same abbot grants to Hugo
de Wiengeham also "dimidiam hidam," which is
confirmed in the above charter. This latter charter
is facsimiled in the "Surrey Archæological Collection," vol. vii., 1880, p. 2.

In a charter among the collection of Lord Frederick
Campbell in the British Museum of the time of
Henry III. (L. F. C. I. 9), a passage occurs which
equates the half-hide at two virgates :—"Sciant tam
presentes quam futuri quod ego Radulfus Brito dedi
Jordano fratri meo .... *dimidiam hidam* terræ in
Stretone (? Sturton-in-Aberford, co. York) scilicet
virgatam quam Dolewinus tenuit, et *virgatam* quam
Willelmus filius Sirun et Alexander tenuerunt . . .
pro una libra piperis annuatim reddenda," etc.

7. The *Jugum* was a land measure confined to
Kent in the Domesday Book. Its value has not been
ascertained. Some mediæval chroniclers write as if
the jugum were a mere synonym of the *hida*. I am
inclined to think that the word represents a *pair* of

oxen's worth, *i.e.*, two bovates. In corroboration of this view, there is a passage in Agard's work, quoted by Ellis, to the effect that a *jugum* was equivalent to half a carucate, which latter, as I have shown before, irrespective of the area, would be a plough's worth, *i.e.*, four oxen's worth of land; in other words, the *jugum* would be the land that a pair of oxen could till. On the other hand, Ellis refers to a passage when a certain manor (Eastwell, in Kent) is rated at 1 solin, of which three *juga* are placed under one lord, and one under another. The *jugum* (pl. *juga*), must not be confused with *jugera*, which are mentioned in the statement of claim of archbishop Lanfranc against bishop Odo of Bayeux, of which some account will be found in another place.[1]

In the notice of the pictorial illustrations of the plough, the reader will find the yoke, *jugum*, or bar, which harnessed the two oxen together abreast, described.

8. The *Leuca, leuga, leuua,* for all three forms of this word occur, was a term generally employed to denote an areal superficies of woodland. According to the Register of Battle Abbey, the *leuca* consisted of four hundred and eighty perches, or twelve quarentines. It therefore contained a hundred and twenty acres. Mr. Davidson considers that the lineal leuga is a length of four hundred and eighty perches, and, therefore, as a mile consists of three hundred and twenty perches, the lineal leuca is a mile and a half in length. Others, however, have reckoned the leuga from a mile, as Ingulph, to two miles, as Blomefield.

[1] P. 291.

9. *Perca*, or *Pertica*, has been variously estimated at 10, 16, 20, 25, and 27 feet. In later times five and a half yards went to the perch, according to the king's standard measure. Ellis shows that a larger perch than that fixed by the statute of Edward III., as above, is still in use for woodlands.

10. *Pes.* There is no difficulty in the use of this word, which consisted then, as now, of twelve inches. That the foot originally was set out greater than the human foot, is a question which cannot be discussed in this work.

11. *Quarentena*, or as it is called in the Exon Domesday *quadragenaria*, was a length of *forty* perches, *i.e.*, a furlong. There was also an areal *quarentena*, or square *quarentena*, consisting of forty[1] acres, which, if in one rectangular field, would measure forty perches, or two hundred and twenty yards on each of its four sides.

12. The *Sulin*, or *Solin*, is a measure of land area found only in Kent, and from a passage in the Register of Battle Abbey among the Cottonian manuscripts in the British Museum (Domitian A. ii.) the *swulinga* is shown to be equivalent to the *hida*. Another passage in the Domesday Book itself equates 450 acres with two solins and a half. This would give two hundred and sixteen acres (about) to the solin in English measure, or 80 acres Norman measure. A Domesday passage, quoted by Ellis,

---

[1] Davidson states that the square or areal quarentena was ten acres, but this would give only 160 acres to the square mile, instead of 640.

seems also to show that seven solins were equivalent to seventeen carucates.[1] But the number of carucates to the solin evidently varied; and in manors which paid for one solin the *terra* is variously stated at 6, 3, 5, 4, or 2 car̃. This measure occasionally occurs in Anglo-Saxon charters of Kent, but not very often. It is derived from *sulh*, a plough, that is, the land that could be tilled yearly by one plough: hence it was a plough land, but not, as Mr. Davidson infers, a carucate.

13. The *Virgate*, a measure of considerable antiquity, occurs constantly in the Domesday Book, and was used long subsequently to the date of the survey. Like all, or almost all, the measures which have been already discovered, its actual area was uncertain, irregular, and varied at different places, in accordance with the sliding scale of the hide and the acre. The following areas have been respectively attributed to the virgate: 4 *virgæ* or virgates to 1 hide in the Ely and Exeter MSS. and in the Campbell charter i. 9, referred to under the notice of the hide in an earlier part of this chapter; 8 virgates to the hide in the Battle Abbey Register; 15, 16, 18, 20, 24, 30, 32, or 60 acres to the virgate, according to Agard. With these conflicting valuations, it would be useless to attempt any solution of the difficulty.[2]

How far these Domesday measures of land correspond with pre-Norman measures, it would be

[1] Vol. i., p. 154.
[2] The *wista* appears occasionally in the *Chron. de Bello*, and Sussex charters (see B. M. 20,161). Some consider it equal to 1 virgate; others to 4 virgates or ½ hide.

difficult to determine. Among such early terms the following occur :—

Agri[1] jugera,[2] cassati,[3] mansæ,[4] manentes,[5] mansiones,[6] aratra,[7] segetes,[8] virgæ,[9] fundus,[10] perticæ,[11] familiæ,[12] mansiunculæ,[13] sulunga,[14] tributarii.[15]

The *agri* are found in a passage which equates them with *jugera*.

The *cassati*, or *cassatæ*, were equal to hidæ.[16] A hundred cassates composed the *fundus* of land. at Myceldefer, or Micheldefer, co Hants.

The *Mansa* was the same as the *cassata* ;[17] sometimes it called the *Mansa* agelluli,[18] or aseluli.[19] It was also equivalent to the *hida*,[20] to the *sulung*, and

---

[1] Birch, "Cartularium Saxonicum," Nos. 577, 578, A.D. 898.
[2] *Ibid.*   [3] *Ibid.*, Nos. 508, 509, 525, and many others.
[4] *Ibid.*, No. 533.
[5] Exiguam portiunculam v. manentes. No. 511 cf. exig. port. x. man. No. 482.
[6] *Ibid.*, No. 481, A.D. 854.
[7] Aliquam partem terræ . . . hoc est viii. *aratra* in illa loco. *Ibid.*, No. 507, A.D. 863; cf. also No. 13, A.D. 618.
[8] cc. segites cum gramite toto. *Ibid.*, No. 513, A.D. 866.
[9] *Ibid.*, No. 515.   [10] *Ibid.*, No. 596.
[11] *Ibid.*, No. 723, "dabo . . . sex perticas, ubi," &c.
[12] *Ibid.*, No. 696, A.D. 933.   [13] *Ibid.*, No. 667.
[14] vi. *mansas* quod Cantigene dicunt *syx sulunga*" at Wichham, Kent. Stowe Charter, A.D. 948, in British Museum.
[15] "terram . . . id est, xii. tributarios terræ." No. 198. A.D. 762-5.
[16] Cf. *Ibid.*, Nos. 466, 525, 526, 587, 590, 591, 648, 705, 706.
[17] *Ibid.*, Nos. 596, 597 ; 721, 722.   [18] *Ibid.*, No. 743.
[19] *Ibid.*, Nos. 776, 728.   [20] *Ibid.*, No. 729 ; 705, 706.

the *manens*.[1]   The *familia* (or hida) occurs as late
as the tenth century.

The *aratrum* was equivalent to the *sulung*[2] of
Kent, and therefore to the *Mansa;* and to the
viculus[3] of the same county.

The *pertica*, in one passage, at least, is a square
measure.

Denominations, jurisdictions, franchises, tenures,
and services in connexion with land are all of
interest, but they may only be touched on lightly
within the limits of this work. *Terra*, or arable land,
consisted of slips or pieces, *Particulæ, frusta, culturæ ;*
it was called *planum*, to distinguish it from *silva*, or
woodland.   On the rare mention of *terra arabilis
duplex*, or *ad duplum*, much of the novel theory that
farms were cultivated on a two-field or three-field shift
is founded, that is, that one-half or one-third of the
ploughed land was suffered to lie fallow every year.
Can this have been so, when we know the difficulties
our forefathers must have had to reclaim the land ?
With no recorded knowledge of rotation of crops,
of manuring the land, or of improving its quality by
admixture, the cultivators probably went on year
after year, cropping their fields, with little systematic
attention to fallow.   We will not say that they did not
let the land lie fallow, perhaps for rest, perhaps to
allow of clearing away tenacious weeds, but to put the
fallow at one-half or one-third, as Canon Taylor does,

---

[1] Stowe Charter, No. 627.

[2] *Ibid.*, No. 214, A.D. 774 : "aliquam partem terræ *trium
aratrorum* quod cantianice dicitur *threora sulunga*."

[3] *Ibid.*, No 439, A.D. 842.

is far too expensive an estimate. *Silva* and *nemus*, sometimes *silvula*, and *nemusculum*—for diminutives were favourite images of diction with the Survey Commissioners—represent woodland, always carefully estimated, because of the important item of beech-mast and acorns, a food so indispensable among the Anglo-Saxons that Kentish lands not provided with it within the precincts of the estate conveyed by charter, usually had *dens*, *dænu*, *denbæro*, pig-feeding tracts of woodland, far away from the land itself, specially set apart and named as belonging to it.[1] The right of feeding hogs was called pasnage, pannage, or *pasnagium ;* and, as usual with terms formed after this model in-*agium* signified also the price, charge or cost of the feeding. *Pastio* is sometimes used synonymously with pasnagium. *Herbagium* represents the right or cost of grass-feed in the woods.

Then there were the unfruitful woods; woods for fire-wood ; wood without pannage ; wood for enclosures or palings ; wood for repairing fences, woods supplying timber suitable for house-building, underwood, or brushwood, and other kinds. Among the trees known in English woods before the Norman advent, are the oak, the sour apple, the apple, the thorn, the elder, the maple, the willow, the bramble, and the furze bush; and plantations of osiers, the tracts of furze (compare Spinæ, the Roman name of Speen in Berkshire), and *roncaria*, *roncetum*, or patches of brambles and briers must be noticed. *Essarz*, land grubbed up or "projectæ de silva," indicate the progress of breaking up the forest and reclaiming the soil.

[1] See Birch, "Cartul. Saxon."

Pastura ad pecuniam occurs over and over again as pasture for the cattle of the village, and common pasture not so frequently. Sometimes the pasture was converted into sown land, at other times the *duna*, or down, appears to have been utilised for cattle feeding. The term *Pratum bobus*, or *carrucis*, signified pasture enough to keep the plough oxen. The marsh, or fen-land, occurs in the same parts as now, the flat lands of Huntingdon, Cambridge, and Lincolnshire, left as alluvial soil by the shrinkage of the great primæval river, whose embouchure we call the Wash. Woods, parks, and forests were naturally more frequent throughout the Domesday world than they are with us, who stand removed by eight centuries further away from the days when by far the greater portion of the land was covered by the untrodden or rarely trodden wood.

The forest, not being an object of enquiry by the Commissioners for assessment, is, like the Church, only found incidentally mentioned. Thus it is, that of the great number which the map of England discloses, some of vast proportion, as Braden, Sherwood, Hainault, Epping, Needwood, Arden, Dartmoor, Exmoor, Andred's Weald, and Savernake, five only are directly mentioned, viz., Windsor, Berkshire; Gravelinges, Wiltshire; Winburne, Dorsetshire; Hucheuuode or Whichwood, Oxfordshire, and the New Forest, Hampshire, the latter of especial care and enjoyment to the Conqueror (who has been, perhaps, too much blamed for the reputed manner of its formation), and separately surveyed for the record. Several topographers have estimated the damage to

agriculture and loss of property which the formation
of this forest is believed to have occasioned. The
total area of land thus affected, appears, according to
some, to be little short of seventeen thousand acres,
added to an ancient nucleus of forest, known by the
name of Ytene, involving with it the destruction of
many habitable places. Ellis computes a reduction
from upwards of two hundred and fifteen hides, producing about £364 in the time of Edward the
Confessor, to little more that seventy-six hides producing £129 in the time of the Conqueror. Other
calculations, perhaps more strictly accurate, reduce
the quantity of land to half the amount. *Stabilitio*,
or stalling the deer, was practised. *Haiæ* were parts
of a wood or forest, staked and paled off, into which
capreolæ, goats, beasts, and wild animals could be
driven for slaughter. These are found noticed in four
western counties, Worcester, Hereford, Salop, and
Cheshire. A hare-warren we find mentioned in
one passage. Parks also possessed very spacious
dimensions. Several are mentioned, and they were
favourite kinds of property in the tenure of the more
important tenants-in-chief. The term was *parcus*, a
very old word with a Latin termination added to it ;
pearroc and *pearruc* (*clausura, septum ferarium*), of
perhaps Celtic origin, and of occasional use in Anglo-
Saxon charters. Within them were the *feræ silvaticæ*,
the wild beasts of the wood. The forest laws of
Cnut and other monarchs have formed the subject
of special and minute research. The fact of their
existence as an independent code, shows the political
importance that was attached to the conservation of

these woodland features of the country; and the rigorous penalties which were laid down, in some cases, to follow infraction of the various regulations, point to the frequency of unlawful doings on the one hand, and to the determination to exclude trespassing and poaching on the other. Notwithstanding the spirit of preservation and love of the chace, which the forests afforded, and which had called into existence a large class of huntsmen, verderers, and other wood-cunning officers, the felling of timber for boards, and beams, and fuel proceeded apace; and it was only by availing themselves of the vast quantity of firewood supplied by the forests of Sussex, Kent, and some other counties, that the manufacturers of iron and salt were enabled to keep the supply of their productions equal to the demand.

The vineyard, *vinea*, often disputed, but doubtless maintained in England in the Domesday period—for the book notices at least thirty-eight examples, chiefly in southern half of the realm, and William of Malmes-bury[1] described the method of cultivation and the flavour of the wine made very minutely—must not be forgotten. Here the standard of measure was sometimes the acre, but generally the *arpenna* or *arpent*, of two virgates, each of forty perches, as some calculate it, or an acre or furlong according to others, but probably variable, like almost all other Domesday measures, a term seldom used in connexion with other land. The vineyard,[2] the orchard, *hortus*, *ortus ;* the garden, the common pasture for the store

---

[1] " Gesta Pontif.," pp. 292, 326.
[2] *Builder*, vol. li., No. 2,283.

and draught cattle and the sheep; the fish-pond or *vivarium*, the sheep-fold, the growing crops, the ripening grain, the blossoming fruit-trees, and many another rural detail, were features quite as familiar to the eyes of those who lived in the times of the Domesday as they are with us; and the mention of them, "casually[1] introduced into the formal entries in which the estate of the principal owners in the parish was described for assessment, plainly indicates that, after all, in a very great measure, the aspect of the country has undergone but little modification during the last eight hundred years, notwithstanding the development of special agricultural principles, such as drainage, levelling, hedge clipping, wire fencing, and the more universal adoption of rectilinear limits of enclosures."

The mill belonged to the lord. It was called *moliñ, molinum, molendinum,* a water mill, and the site of the Domesday mill is generally still furnished with one now—an example of the long duration of rural employments. The produce, for the lord's advantage, is calculated sometimes in money, at other times in grain, and in eels taken from the mill ponds. It was a valuable property, particularly when the dependants were compelled to grind their own corn at their lord's mill. Even the site on which a mill had stood had an appreciable value, perhaps it carried with it the right of re-erection and re-assertion of its exclusive privileges of thus grinding the corn grown in the neighbourhood. The windmill does not appear to be noticed in Domesday.

Of Jurisdictions, Domesday notices the *Thrithing, Treding,* or Riding, *the third part* of a county, found

---

[1] *Builder, l.c.*

in Yorkshire and Lincolnshire, with a *Tridingmot*, or special court, answering to its degree, inferior to the county, superior to the wapentake.

The *Last*, *Lest*, or *Lathe*, a word derived from *Geladian*, " to assemble," occurs only in Kent, where the following seven are found, but they do not embrace the whole county between them :—

1. Ailesford.
2. Borvart, Borowart, Borwar, or Borwart.
3. Estrea, Estrede, Estrei, or Estre-lest.
4. Limowart, Limwarlet, Linwarlet, Linwart-lest.
5. Middeltone, Middeltune, or Mildetone, dim̃ lest.
6. Sudtone lest, and dim̃ lest.
7. Wiwarlet, or Wiwart-lest.

The *Rape* of Sussex seems to resemble the Last of Kent. There were several in the county, of which four names occur in Domesday, viz. :—

1. Arundel Rap̃.
2. Hastinges, Rap̃ de.
3. Lewes, Rap̃ de.
4. Pevenesel, Rap̃ de (sometimes called a hundred).

Besides these territorial Rapes, several are mentioned as of important chief tenants. Ellis considers the word cognate with the Icelandic *hrepp*, a territorial division, and adds, that it is not improbable that the Rapes of Sussex were military districts for the supply of their respective castles.

The *Wapentake*, one of the earliest terms used by
the Saxons in this county for a definite district, has
been conjectured by Lye,[1] and other Anglo-Saxon
scholars, to be the district where a certain number of
persons in each county were accustomed to meet for
training and military exercises, a " weapon-teaching."
This kind of division is recorded for Yorkshire, Lincolnshire, Nottinghamshire, Leicestershire, Northamptonshire. It was the synonym of the hundred of
other counties. As related in the laws of Edward the
Confessor, the prefect of the wapentake met the members at an appointed day, and, with lance uplifted,
suffered each to touch it with his own, as it were a
" weapon-touching," a confederation, or "confirming
of weapons." Other explanations and derivations of this
ancient territorial division have been suggested, and
the laws of the Anglo-Saxon monarchs contain much
material for the elucidation of the term. One of the
latest theories is that of Canon Taylor, who claims an
entirely new discovery as to the nature of the old
hundreds and wapentakes. The Canon seeks to
show that at the date of the Domesday Survey the old
Anglo-Saxon *hundred* was in process of transformation
into the Danish *wapentake*, that the process had
been completed in some districts (it is to be presumed
those in which they are found), was in progress in
others, and elsewhere had not commenced at all. The
organisation of the hundred, he thought, had indeed
survived a Saxon designation, but the Danish wapentake was the area that was superseding it. Three of
the old hundreds, if the Canon be right, went to make

[1] Lye rejects the idea of *tactus*, touching.

a wapentake, the former being identified by him as the basis of military assessment, the wapentake being the unit of naval assessment. This may be so, but at any rate the conversion cannot have made much progress, from the comparatively small area in which the wapentake occurs as compared with the hundred. It is, too, directly at variance with a passage in the laws of Edward the Confessor—"Quod Angli vocant *Hundredum* supradicti comitatus vocant *Wapentachium*"—"That which the English call *a hundred*, the counties of York, Lincoln, Notts, Leicester, Northampton, call a *wapentake*." The wapentake had its proper court or wapentacmot, presided over by twelve elder thanes and their prefects; it paid the third penny, like the hundred.

The *Hundred* (the origin of which is wrongly ascribed to King Alfred, but far older traces of the institution are extant) is thought to have derived its name from being composed of a hundred hides, but some attribute more, others less, than this number. The "Black Book" of Peterborough, now preserved in the Library of the Society of Antiquaries at Burlington House, contains an Anglo-Saxon enumeration of the hundreds of Northamptonshire in the time of Edward the Confessor, entitled "Certificatio hundredorum in comitatu Northampton," in which many of the hundreds [1] are represented, as containing 100 hides, those which paid gold being separately entered. Ellis prints this document at length, but is wrong in writing that every hundred is composed of the full contents of a hundred hides.

---

[1] Ellis states " every hundred."

In the account of the lands belonging to Evesham
Abbey a passage occurs, also instanced by Ellis [1]
which indicated, or appears to indicate, that in the
hundred of Fissesberge

The Church of Evesham has ...... 65 hides
   (12 being held free)
There are of Dodentreu .... 20 ,,
There are of Worcester .... 15 ,,
                      —————
                     100 hides.
                     —————

These make up the hundred—"*perficiunt hundret.*"
But, on the other hand, the Worcester Chartulary of
Heming, Cotton MS., Tiberius A. xiii., describes a
hundred of 300 hides, "In vice comitatu Uuireceastre
habet Sancta Maria de Uuireceastre *unum* hundred
quod vocatur Oswaldes lau in quo jacent ccc hidæ." [2]

Another class of writers has considered that the
hundred of district was made up of 100 men; others,
of 100 villages. Such a proportion, if it were true at
first, could but last for a very short time.

The Castles of England find frequent mention in
the Domesday. Some notices of the principal
among them will be found in the descriptions of the
separate counties. Ellis finds that they amount to
forty-nine: one at Arundel, earlier than the Norman;
eight built by William; ten by the greater barons;
one by an under-tenant; eleven probably new.
Several of these were built on the sites of prehistoric
fortified mounds, which had been successively occu-

[1] Preface, vol. i. p. xviii.
[2] Fo. 132. Printed in Hearne's Edition, vol. i. p. 287.

pied by the rulers of the district in which they lay. In A.D. 1153, there were 458 castles in England destroyed according to the treaty between Stephen and Henry I.[1] At the time of King Henry II. the number of castles had increased to the enormous number of 1,115. A Survey of England in the thirteenth century, in the British Museum (Cotton MS., Cleopatra, A. xii. f. 46; Vespasian, A. xviii. f. 157, entitled "De partitione Angliæ per Comitatus," etc. (but evidently incomplete), only enumerates 124.[2] The prototype of this Survey is the late twelfth or early thirteenth century "Mappa Mundi" of Gervase of Canterbury.[3] In this only a hundred castles are named as standing in England. Ditched and walled towns are not numerous. Three only, Canterbury, Nottingham, and York, were surrounded with a foss; and seven were protected with walls—Oxford, Hereford, Leicester, Stafford, Chester, Lincoln, and Colchester; remains of these may still be inspected by the archæological pilgrim.

Of private lands and estates, the *Manerium*, or manor, demands the first place in our consideration. The word has been derived from *manoir*, Fr.; or from *manere*, Lat., as the usual residence of the owner on his land. I am, however, inclined to suggest a connexion of the term with *manus*, Lat. "hand," which gives the clue to *manœuvre*, *i.e.*,

[1] See table by G. T. Clark, F.S.A., in *Antiquary*, 1887 (Apr.), p. 112.

[2] Birch, in "Journ. Brit. Arch. Assoc.," vol. xxviii. (1872), p. 49.

[3] *See* his works, edited by Dr. Stubbs, Rolls Series, 1880, vol. ii. pp. 418 *et seq.*

"manus opera," and, by a change of idea, to *manure*, which originally signified any improvement effected in the condition of land by handiwork, and afterwards acquired the more circumscribed and current signi-fication of a fertilising substance applied to the soil. If this be the derivation of manor, the word will represent that portion of an estate which was worked by the hand labour of those dwelling upon it. The word is not found in connexion with English estates before the reign of Edward the Confessor. The king, we are told, held in ancient demesne 1,422 manors, at least ; and Ellis mentions several instances of large proprietors whose holdings I have tabulated below for more easy observation.

1. The King ....1,422 manors.
2. The Earl of Moretaine .... 793 „
3. Alan, Earl of Bretagne .... 442 „
4. Odo, Bishop of Bayeux .... 439 · „
5. Gosfrid, Bishop of Coutances... 280 „
6. Roger de Busli .... 174 „
7. Ilbert de Laci .... 164 „
8. William Peverel .... 162 „
9. Robert de Stadford.............. 150 „
10. Roger de Laci .... 116 „
11. Hugh de Montfort, upwards of 100 „

Eleven proprietors, therefore, held 4,242 manors, or an average of 385 manors to each of the above-mentioned principal tenants. How far the distribu-tion of these and the rest of the possessions of the Saxon thanes was systematically carried out, on what rules the division was based, whether by considera-tion of native rank or in accordance with individual

prowess and liberality of co-operation with the object
of William's expedition, we know not. Caprice probably actuated and dictated many of the royal grants
of land, which at first must have been so over-
whelmingly extensive that they would almost seem
inexhaustible. The manor could be amalgamated
with another, divided, or reduced, and instances of
all occur. Its parts, either animate or inanimate,
could be transferred to other manors, or they could
be removed to other hundreds. There were also subordinate manors.

In the *Dominium*, or demesne, that part of an estate
held to the lord's proper use, Ellis, with good
reason, sees the Saxon *Inland*, which occurs also in
the Domesday Book; in the tenemental land of the
Normans, the Saxon *Outland* or *Neatland*. Other
titles of land are Bocheland, Book-land — that is,
charter-land—land held according to a royal *boc*, or
charter. The term Book-land, or Buckland, has now
become a place-name.

Reveland, perhaps land improperly taken from the
tax-paying land system, and placed by the sheriffs to
their own advantage.

Tainland, or Thegn land, hereditary land.

On the estate, the principal edifice was the *aula*,
halla, or *haula*,[1] a stone-built house, where the lord
lived, and the skilled servants plied their industry.

---

[1] The use of the aspirate by Domesday scribes is of little
importance, when they depended so largely on the ear. The
h, in the Roman languages, has now become little better than
an etymological symbol. Its uncertain use among the lower
classes in England has often been ridiculed, but in this respect
they have Domesday on their side.

The term now frequently forms the second member of a place-name, and points to the existence of one of these houses on the spot. The *Curia*, or Court, may have been a mansion cr a courtyard.

The *Villa* was another term for manor or lordship; a *villata*, a large vill, or more than one united together. A Berewic or *Berewite*, was a member of a manor separated from the main body. Some manors had a large number of these isolated members. *Mansio* is another term for manor, or member of a manor, but its Anglo-Saxon meaning has been described in another place.

Markets do not occur frequently, very probably only those yielding toll to the king are returned in Domesday; the free markets would not enter into the scope of the Commissioners' work. We may best glance at the most important of these by a table.

County.	Name of Place.	Yield.		
		£.	s.	d.
Kent	... Favreshaunt	4	0	0
„ ... , ...	... Newedene	0	39	7
Hampshire	... Neteham	8	0	0
„	... Basingestoche	0	30	0
„	... Ticefelle	0	40	0
Berkshire ...	... Wallingford			
„ ...	... Cocheham (Cookham)	0	20	0
„ ...	... Bertune	0	0	40
Wiltshire ...	... Bradeford	0	45	0
Somersetshire	... Frome	0	46	0
„	... Mileburne			
„	... Givelcestre (Ilchester).	11	0	0

County.	Name of Place.	Yield.		
		£.	s.	d.
,,	... Cruche (Creech) ...	4	0	0
,,	... Milvertone	0	10	0
,,	... Tautone	0	50	0
,,	... Ileminstre	0	20	0
Devon ...	... Ochementone			
Cornwall ...	... Matele			
,,	... St. German's (held on Sundays, against the laws)			
,,	... Launceston			
,,	... Bodmine			
,,	... Liscarret	0	4	0
,,	... Tremetone	0	3	0
Oxfordshire	... Bentone	0	50	0
Gloucestershire ...	... Berchelai (Berkeley)...			
,,	... Teodekesberie(Tewkesbury)	0	11	0
,,	... Turneberie (Thornbury)			
Herefordshire	... Etune			
Bedfordshire	... Lestone	7	0	0
,,	... Loitone (Luton) ...		100	0
,,	... Alriceseie (Arlsey) ...	0	10	0
Northamptonshire	Vndele (Oundle) ...	0	20	0
,,	... Hecham (Heigham) ...	0	20	0
Leicestershire	... Medeltone			
Staffordshire	... Tutbury			
Lincolnshire	... Chirchetone			
,,	... Ludes (Louth)	0	29	0
,,	... Bolingbroc			
,,	... Spallinge	0	40	0

County.	Name of Place.	Yield. £. s. d.
Lincolnshire	... Bertone	4 0 0
,,	... Partene (Bardney) ...	0 10 0
Norfolk	... Dumham (Downham) (a half market)	
,,	... Coleneia	
,,	... Turchetel (a quarter market)	
Suffolk	... Tornai	
,,	... Beccles	
,,	... Entberie	
,,	... Eia	
,,	... Carahalla	
,,	... Hoxana	
,,	... Clara	
,,	... Haverhella	0 13 4
,,	... Aspella (a fair or *feria*)	

Tol, or *Thol,* or *theloneum,* signified the liberty of buying and selling, of keeping a market, the money paid to the lord for his market profits, a tribute or custom for passage. The word is still used in the latter sense.

Among tenures and services the following are the most important: Tenure in frankalmoigne or in free alms; under this the tenant was free of all but the triple need, from which no one was exempt, as has already been described. Prayers for the safety of the soul of the donor, ("pro salute animæ" in the charters), his ancestors, and his heirs, were only stipulated for. The *Firma unius noctis*, or entertainment for one night (and occasionally for three nights) to be rendered to the lord and his followers, was an old form of tenure. The uniform Domesday commutation for this was £13. 8s. 4d. in white money. This firma noctis was rendered by Sir James Thynne, lord of the Royal Manor of Warminster, in Wiltshire, to King Charles II. in A.D. 1663; and by viscount Weymouth (at Longleat), to King George III. on 13th September, 1786. Rent severally of cheeses, dog-bread, or biscuits " ter mille panes canibus," and a cup of beer occur.

The *Auera* was a day's work with the plough; the *inward*, service in the local royal body-guard. Smaller services include the following varieties :— the price of ironwork for two ploughs; four ploughshares; mending the ironwork of the king's ploughs; tending hounds; teaching the sheriff's daughter how to make gold lace, or orphrey;[1] presenting the lady of the manor with 18 ores of pennies, that she might be in a good humour;[2] and giving the king, if he came to the manor, two hundred *hesthas* or loaves, a tub of ale, and a rush basket of butter.

Of civil and criminal jurisdiction, the principal terms are *sac* or *saca*, power and privilege of adjudicating causes, levying fines, executing laws within the definite extent of the same, called *Soc* or *soca*. This latter word also signifies a rent paid for using land.

Team or *theam*, right to have, and judge, bondmen

---

[1] " *Aurifrisium.*"

[2] " Ut esset ipsa læto animo."

and villains, with their children, goods, and chattels, in the lord's court.

Some of the terms for delinquencies, fines, and other expressions illustrative of the manners and customs of the inhabitants of England in the Domesday Book, will be noticed in a future chapter of this work.[1]

[1] p. 287.

CHAPTER XII.

THE CHURCH—ANGLO-SAXON CHURCHES STILL EXTANT—BISHOP AND CLERGY.

THE English Church, *ecclesia*, finds frequent notice in the pages of the Domesday Book ; but, as the Book was not a survey of the condition or statistics of Church property and edifices, but only of those places which the Crown had to look to for a payment of some kind, either in services, rents, or produce, those churches only find a place which incidentally fall into this category, notwithstanding the vast quantity of land held by the Church at the period. We know, also, that there are many still extant churches and parts of churches which indicate by their archæological evidence, for every building has its history written on its walls although we may not all be able to read it, and by their antiquarian characteristics, an erection and establishment before the Domesday period. Some writers, like Ellis and Eyton, have put forward the suggestion that in some counties, at least, the mention of a presbyter or priest in any locality implies the existence of a church in that locality, and they would thus endeavour to account for the apparent fewness of churches in some counties, forgetful of the fact that notices of churches and presbyters are alike accidental and not intended to

be taken as comprehending all the edifices nor all the
clergy of the realm. For example,[1] in the county of
Cambridge only one church is mentioned, two in
Staffordshire, three each in Buckinghamshire and
Hertfordshire. On the other hand, by consulting
the copious indices of the Record Commission
edition of Domesday Book we shall find that Norfolk,
Lincolnshire, Yorkshire, and Hampshire have a proportionately large number of churches, and the
Suffolk churches amount in number to 364. Strange
to say, a diminutive form, *ecclesiola*, "a small or
little church," occasionally finds mention in the
Domesday Surveys of Kent, Dorsetshire, Hampshire,
and Sussex. It would be difficult to estimate the
dimensions of these small churches when few or
none of the Saxon churches of which we have any
knowledge put forward any claims as to spaciousness
of size.

Three highly interesting and undoubted Saxon
churches have been discovered in comparatively
recent years, which may serve as examples of average
size. We may consider them in point of their
antiquity. The first is that of Escombe, near
Bishop Auckland, in the county of Durham; here
the nave measures 43 feet 6 inches long, and 14 feet
wide, inside measures; and the square chancel 10
feet. The flat-headed windows, battering-sides, and
other remarkable details of this edifice indicate a remote antiquity, not far from touch with Roman times.
Next comes Bradford-on-Avon, where stands the
ecclesiola, or little church of St. Laurence, referred

[1] *Builder*, 1886, p. 653.

to by William of Malmesbury, writing in A.D. 1125, reaching back to the days of St. Aldhelm, the earliest years of the eighth century. Here the nave measures 25 feet 6 inches long, and 13 feet 4 inches wide. Ecclesiology may well be proud of the rescue of this relic of early Saxon days from the degrading condition of being cut up into cottages and squalid tenements. The third church of the triad referred to, is that of Deerhurst, near Tewkesbury, in Gloucestershire, only just recently recovered from the disguise of a farmstead, which has masked its true ecclesiastical character for several centuries, until the casual glance of an archæologist revealed its true nature. The measures of this are, for nave, 25 feet 6 inches by 15 feet 10 inches; for chancel, 14 feet by 11 feet 2 inches. In one southern county a recent writer estimates seventy male adults, perhaps representing 350 total souls, as the proportionate number to one church. From this may be deduced an idea of church dimensions in the Saxon period.

No doubt, many of the so-called early Norman churches are but enlargements of pre-existing Saxon buildings. In some cases we may even trace out the respective outlines, as at Walmer, near Deal, in Kent. Perhaps, too, the primitive structure was but an oratory or chapel, and the existing parish church has absorbed, utilised, and modified the original plan, as at Patrixbourne, near Canterbury, which is said to have a most diminutive nucleus; and at Barfreston, a gemlike church, almost unique in its appearance, and certainly, if Norman, then of the very earliest

S

Norman type. Mr. M. H. Bloxam[1] states that the triangular-headed or straight-lined arch is generally considered a characteristic of the Anglo-Saxon style, where it is often to be met with of plain and rude construction. The semicircular arch, in like manner, prevailing from the time of the Romans to the close of the twelfth century, is in some degree considered to be another characteristic of the Anglo-Saxon and Norman styles. As the Anglo-Saxon church architecture derives its origin from later Roman edifices, we should naturally find a greater or less approximation to Roman modes of building. Hence the brickwork arches of the Romans in England, as at Leicester, Castor, and Vinovia near Bishop Auckland, Durham, are the prototypes of the arches at Brixworth Church, Northamptonshire, perhaps the most perfect existing specimen of an early Anglo-Saxon church after that of Escombe. From existing vestiges of churches of presumed Anglo-Saxon construction, it is found that the walls were chiefly formed of rubble and ragstone, covered on the exterior with stucco or plaster, with long and short blocks of ashlar or hewn stone, disposed at the angles in alternate courses. Narrow vertical ribs or square-edged strips of stone, bearing from their position a rude resemblance to pilasters, and corresponding horizontal strips or string-courses, are also found in the churches of this age. Specimens of this style may be examined in the churches of Barnack, Stowe, Wittering,

---

[1] "Principles of Gothic Ecclesiastical Architecture," fifth edition, 1843, p. 20. The illustrations are particularly valuable.
[2] "Journ. Brit. Arch. Assoc.," 1887.

and Earl's-Barton, Northamptonshire; Barton-upon-Humber, Lincolnshire; St. Benedict's, Cambridge; Worth and Sompting, Sussex; Repton, Derbyshire; Stanton-Lacey,·Salop; North Burcombe and Brytford, Wiltshire; St. Michael's, Oxford, and elsewhere. The peculiar details witnessed in many parts of Anglo-Saxon churches seem to point to traditional types of wooden construction and ornamentation, as in the architectural remains of ·Egypt, Greece, India, · and Persia, where the influence of a wooden prototype is plainly discernible. Some ecclesiologists see in the arches of the naves and aisles a resemblance, perhaps fanciful, to the branches of trees in an avenue, meeting overhead. The first recorded church in England, that of Glastonbury,[1] in Somersetshire, was of wattle and wood.[2] Perhaps the wood-haunting worship

---

[1] "Ecclesia de qua loquimur, quæ pro antiquitate sua celebriter ab Anglis Ealdechirche, id est, Vetusta Ecclesia,. nuncupatur primo *virgea*."—William of Malmesbury, "Gest. Reg." i. 32 (Ed. Hardy).

[2] The wooden boarded structure seems to have been placed over the wattle, by Paulinus, Bishop of Rochester, A.D. 633–644. "Paulinum . . . episcopum, asserit majorum traditio, ecclesiæ contextum dudum. . . virgeæ *ligneo* induisse tabulatu."—Ibid. p. 40. St. Aldhelm died A.D. 709, according to William of Malmesbury ("Gesta Pontificum," ed. Hamilton, p. 382), in the old *wooden* church at Dulting or Doulting, in Somersetshire. A stone church was afterwards erected in its place, before A.D. 1125. King Edgar's charter to Ramsey Abbey in A.D. 974 mentions the first chapel, "built of *wooden logs* in fine work."—"Ramsey Chartulary," Rolls edit., f. 136.

Compare also Greensted Church, near Ongar, Essex, the only old wooden church now extant, the nave being built of oak. The body of St. Edmund, martyred by the Danes in A.D. 870, rested in this church one night. It is now in want of repair.

of the Druids may account for some of this peculiarity of church art. One instance, indeed, of a
wooden church occurs in the Yorkshire Domesday
Book, at Begeland, where we find a priest and a
wooden church—"*ibi presbyter et ecclesia lignea.*"
Thick walls, without the adjunct of buttresses; arches
of doors and windows rounded at the top of openings,
flat or triangular; jambs with rude imposts, or capitals
with square abaci, and furnished at times with
ponderous mouldings running round the arches;
arches joined occasionally in pairs, divided by short
and heavy shafts; thick external walls, deeply and
equally splayed with the actual opening in the middle
of the thickness; and, above all, extreme simplicity of
ground plan, not unfrequently inspired from a parallelo-
gram of two squares' length, with a smaller square
chancel, and seldom a porch; all these are indications
of the Anglo-Saxon style of church which was extant
at the time of the formation of the Domesday Book.
Bloxam[1] enumerates less than fifty extant churches,
containing vestiges of presumed Anglo-Saxon architecture. Recent discoveries have added but a very
few to this list, which includes Hexham, Jarrow, and
Monkswearmouth, co. Durham; Ripon, and Witting-
ham, Yorkshire; Dorchester, Oxon; Faversham,
Kent; Trinity Church, Colchester, Essex; Stoke
D'Abernon, Surrey; the larger church at Deerhurst,
Stretton, and Daglingworth, Gloucestershire; besides
those previously mentioned. Mr. J. H. Parker,[2]

[1] "Principles," pp. 57, 58.
[2] "Introduction to the Study of Gothic Archtecture," 4th ed.

following very much the same lines as Mr. Bloxam,
points out the distinctive Anglo-Saxon features of
Corhampton Church, Hampshire; Wickham, Berkshire; St. Mary's, Bishop's Hill Junior, York;
Caversfield, Buckinghamshire, and many others.

It must be understood that, limited as to area and
cubic contents as Saxon churches and chapels were,
as a rule, churches of larger scale were, no doubt,
occasionally erected. St. Aldhelm's Cathedral, at
Sherborne, Wiltshire, is an example of this. Here
the Saxon western doorway of the north aisle exists
entire[1] as regards its jambs and imposts; and part of
the arch, with the projecting moulding, so frequently
found all round arches or doorways of this date, still
remains. On the south side still stand the southern
jambs of the Saxon arch or doorway, with a simpler
projecting moulding; the corresponding northern
jamb was removed by the Normans, under bishop
Roger, who retained the southern jamb for the wider
archway. In the centre of the nave was a great
porch of contemporary date, of which the moulded
plinths still remain on the south side. These details
show that the width of this cathedral church was
between 55 feet and 60 feet. The length of the
edifice is shown by the finding of the bones of the
brothers of King Alfred in the eastern ambulatory,
where they are known to have been interred. This
gives nearly 200 feet for the Anglo-Saxon cathedral
in length, exclusive of the western porch, by nearly

1874, contains numerous woodcuts of great excellence and
utility, pp. 22 *et seq.*
[1] *Builder*, 1886, ii., p. 717.

60 feet wide. The western wall of the nave is only
2 feet 6 inches thick, and is composed of rough
rubble masonry.

The political condition and territorial influence of
the Church in the Domesday period has recently been
illustrated in a very exhaustive manner by Mr. James
Parker (before the Domesday Commemoration),
who has also closely investigated the circumstances
which attended the transfer of the seats of bishoprics
from towns to cities about eleven years before the
survey of Domesday was taken in hand. A formidable
mass of statistics has in this way been gathered up
concerning the number of manors held by the
bishops in the various counties. Some of the
property was held for the Church, other in military
fee, on condition, that is, of supplying contingents of
a specified number of men to swell the royal army when
need arose for its mobilisation. The episcopal body
in the Norman period (as also before it) wielded the
sword and lance, the mace and the battle-axe, as
deftly as the cross and the pen, the pastoral staff and
the thurible. No doubt the greater part of the
landed property which was held in one way or other
by the dignitaries of the Church, regular or secular,
consisted, as Mr. Parker points out, of the endowments of the ancient English Church, which the new
form of government did not endeavour to alienate
from it. Some of this was represented by manors
belonging to the two archbishops and the bishops
of the several dioceses, who appear in the schedules
and titles of Domesday as tenants *in capite;* a still
larger proportion was represented by manors belong-

ing to the various monasteries of the Benedictine
Order, and ecclesiastical corporations, who also
take a place in those lists. In the former case,
the endowments of the hierarchy of the Church, in
the necessarily imperfect ecclesiastical census of
Domesday Book, are placed (if Mr. Parker's calculations are taken as a basis) at 1,700 manors.
To the latter class, representing ecclesiastical
communities, no fewer than 1,700 manors are
apportioned. Besides all this, there are the endowments of the numerous manorial churches and
priests, new parish churches and parish clergy—
presbyters, *capellani*, or by whatever name they were
known, of which and of whom no satisfactory
estimate could be formed, for the value and nature
of the endowment was very rarely separated from the
total value and the territorial *descriptio* of the manor
to which it belonged or in which it was situate.
There were four bishops[1] of Norman dioceses, as
well as an appreciable number of monasteries and
other ecclesiastical foundations also in Normandy
holding lands in England. Mr. Parker sees in the
endowments of the Norman bishops a mere device
of a political nature for strengthening William's power.
This curious fact also he points out, that the two
principal political supporters of the king, Odo,
bishop of Bayeux, and Geoffrey, bishop of Coutances,
possessed preponderating and yet possible neutralis-
ing influence, the former in Kent and the south-
east, the latter in the west—a special plan of the

---

[1] Gislebert, bishop of Lisieux ; Geoffrey de Montbray, bishop
of Coutances ; Odo, of Bayeux ; and Gilbert, bishop of Evreux.

king, who wished to be able to fall back on the one,
if the other (as eventually happened) should fail in
his fidelity and allegiance. There were 840 manors in
the hands of these four foreign prelates. To Odo
belonged 220 manors in Kent, held in succession to
earl Godwine, and 340 as well in seventeen different
counties. Lanfranc, who had stepped from the
abbacy of Caen to the archbishopric of Canterbury,
held 75 manors, more than half the number being
in Kent, the other distributed through seven counties.

To the archbishop of York belonged 173 manors,
a still larger number, in six counties, including
thirteen in Gloucestershire, and one in Hampshire.
The bishops of the thirteen dioceses held manors in
different counties, not necessarily adjacent to their
cathedral cities. Two of these, the bishops of
Lincoln and Thetford (afterwards Norwich), held
over 100 manors each. London, under 80; Durham, Chester, and Winchester, over 50 each; Exeter,
about 45; Salisbury, Rochester, and Wales, about
20 each; Chichester, 10; Worcester, 7; Hereford,
6. As for distribution there are several anomalies.
For example, the bishop of London's manors amount
to about 32 in Essex, 25 in Middlesex, 21 in
Hertfordshire, 13 in Somersetshire, and 1 in Dorsetshire. The bishop of Winchester held as tenant-in-
chief in nine counties, although the bulk lay in
Hampshire. All the manors recorded in Domesday
Book as belonging to the bishop of Worcester
lay in Warwickshire. Mr. Parker thus attributes 700
manors to the English archbishops and bishops in all.

Ellis rightly rejects the highly-exaggerated statement of Spelman that at the time of the Domesday there were 45,011 churches in England. At the same time he admits that the whole number of recorded churches falls considerably under what there are grounds for concluding they must have amounted to about or soon after the time of the Conquest. Churches, which historical and literary notice, and archæological evidence, as has been shown, demonstrate to have existed, find no reference in the Survey, and the history of Canute and Edward the Confessor makes it clear that there was, in the early years of the eleventh century, a large increase in the number of sacred edifices. The common report that thirty-six[1] churches were destroyed by William, without compensation, when he enlarged the circuit of the New Forest, in Hampshire, also favours this view.[2] Perhaps the absence of glebe land attached to the churches has something to do with the silence of the Domesday concerning them.

Tithes also only enter incidentally into the record, so that we cannot say how far the Church was supported by voluntary oblations, dues, or masses. But there

[1] Or between twenty-two and fifty-two, according to the account given by Knyghton.

[2] This is one of the principal accusations of the chroniclers against the Conqueror's character. There is no doubt that some churches were destroyed, for traces still remain of them; but how far the ecclesiastical power—a very strong element— allowed this to be done without compensation, is doubtful. William's dread of rousing the anger of the Church would hardly have allowed him to offend it unnecessarily; as we see in his arrest of Odo, his half brother, not as "bishop of Bayeux,"—for the Church would have been up in resentment in a moment,—but as "earl of Kent," and, therefore, a lay vassal.

is no mention of tithes in Somersetshire, Devonshire, Cornwall, Middlesex, Hertfordshire, and Leicestershire. The dedication of tithes at this time seems to have been at the owner's choice, and not necessarily to have followed the parochial system. Thus, among other examples which might be easily mentioned, in the county of Hereford, even a foreign monastery, St. Mary de Cormeliis, had churches, priests, and tithe-revenues in several places. This arbitrary consecration and alienation of tithes at the will of the donors was not abolished until the end of the twelfth century. Sometimes the tithe of a wasted or ruined church was transferred to the priest of another parish. Church endowments are occasionally met with. Perhaps that of Boseham, in Sussex, was one of the richest examples, being possessed of land to the extent of not fewer than 112 hides in the time of King Edward the Confessor, and sixty-five at the time of the survey. This church is represented in the Bayeaux tapestry (ed. Fowke). If we may trust the artist, it was a structure of consequence. Of its connexion with the history of Harold, want of space prevents our saying anything in this place. Generally, however, a hide, half a hide, or a few acres, formed the usual area of endowments; but many larger instances occur, as at Barsham, Norfolk, 100 acres; Wellingovre (Wellingore), Lincolnshire, 143 acres; Berchingas, Suffolk, 83 acres. The Norfolk Survey is of value in this respect, as it records the amounts of Church lands. Ellis considers the *ecclesiola* and *capella* as subordinate to the *ecclesia*, and of sometimes separate endowment. There were

two of these "little churches" at Postinges in Kent,
but no church is recorded.   At Wallope, in Hampshire, both *ecclesia* and *ecclesiola* occur ; the one had
a hide and other tithe-income ; the other, eight
acres of tithe.

Perhaps the city or town of Norwich is the best
surveyed of all English places in respect of the
Church's condition there.   Stigand, the ex-bishop of
Elmham, who, after ejection, occupied successively
the sees of Winchester and Canterbury, but was
deposed and imprisoned, in A.D. 1070, by the
council at Winchester,[1] on April 4,. held here
in Norwich the two churches of St. Martin and
St. Michael, which together enjoyed an endowment
of 130 acres of land.   The burgesses held other
fifteen churches, endowed with 181 acres ; the
Abbey of Bury St. Edmund the moiety of another
church, dedicated to St. Laurence.   Notices also
occur of the churches of All Saints and St.
Simon and St. Jude.   There were no less than
forty-three chapels belonging to the burgesses,
not noticed as extant before the advent of the
Normans.   Winchester was also well provided with
churches.   Two churches out of the three in Dunwich, co. Suffolk, were added in Norman times ;
and at Sudbury, in the same county, the church of
St. Gregory possessed fifty acres of free land, and half
as many of meadow.   Ipswich contained ten churches,

---

[1] Where he died seventen years afterwards in the condition
of a miser, with a little key hanging round his neck, which
fitted a box or *scrinium*, where he kept a list of his money-
bags, hidden in secret places underground.

severally dedicated to the Holy Trinity; St. Mary (two, one belonging to a burgess named Culling); St. Michael; St. Botulph; St. Laurence, claimed by earl Alan from its possessor, Leffled, a free woman; St. Peter (owning five burgesses); St. Stephen, St. George (held by Roger de Ramis with burgesses and wasted mansions); and St. Julian, also in possession of a burgess, Alured filius Rolf. At Shrewsbury were six churches, each one entered in the Domesday as holding lands *in capite*. They were dedicated to St. Almundus, or Alchmund; St. Cedda, or Chad; St. Juliana; St. Mary; St. Michael; and St. Milburga. That of St. Mary held land in Herefordshire as well as in Shropshire. In Chester the church of St. Wareburg, or Werburgh, is mentioned as a tenant *in capite*. The church of Cirecestre, or Cirencester, held land in chief in Gloucestershire; that of Cranbourne, "Creneburnensis ecclesia," in Wiltshire, Dorsetshire, and Devonshire.

Among the English monastic institutions holding lands as tenants in chief (calculated by Mr. Parker as amounting to about 1,700 manors) at the time of the formation of the survey, the following are the most important:—

Abbotsbury Abbey held lands in Dorsetshire.

Abingdon, The Benedictine Abbey of St. Mary held lands in Berkshire, Oxon, Gloucestershire, and Warwickshire.

The Canons of St. Achebrannus, or St. Keverne, in Cornwall.

St. Alban's Abbey, in Berkshire, Hertfordshire, and Buckinghamshire.

St. Alcmund's Collegiate Church in Shrewsbury, in Shropshire.

Ambresberie Abbey for Nuns, in Wiltshire and Berkshire.

Batailge, or Battle Abbey, in Sussex, Kent, Surrey, Berkshire, Devonshire, Oxfordshire, and Essex.

Bedford, the Canons of St. Paul, in Bedfordshire.

Berchinges, or Barking Nunnery, in Essex, Surrey, Middlesex, Hertfordshire, and Bedfordshire.

St. Berriana, or Burian Collegiate Church, in Cornwall.

St. John of Beverley's Collegiate Church, in Yorkshire.

Bucfestre, or Buckfastleigh, held land in Devonshire.

Burgus S. Petri, or Peterborough Abbey, in several counties, Huntingdon, Bedford, Northampton, Leicester, Nottingham, and Lincoln.

In Canterbury, the Monastery of the Holy Trinity held land in Essex; the Abbey of St. Augustine in Kent.

St. Carentcck, or Crantoc, Collegiate Church of Canons, in Cornwall.

Certesyg, or Chertsey, an important Benedictine Abbey of ancient date, held in Surrey, Hants, and Berkshire.

Cetrez, Ceterith, or Chatteris Abbey, held in the counties of Cambridge and Hertford.

Coventrea, or Coventry, St. Mary's Abbey held in the shires of Gloucester, Worcester, Northampton, Leicester, and Warwick.

Croiland, or Cruiland, St. Guthlac's Benedictine

Abbey, of ancient foundation, held in the counties of Cambridge, Huntingdon, Northampton, Leicester, and Lincoln.

Dover, the Canons of St. Martin, in Kent.

St. Edmund's Bury, another important abbey of old foundation, in Suffolk, Oxford, Cambridge, Bedford, Northampton, Essex, and Norfolk.

Eglesham, or Eynesham Abbey, in Oxfordshire and Gloucestershire.

Glastonbury Abbey, the oldest monastery in England, held in the shires of Somerset, Hants, Berks, Wilts, Dorset, Devon, and Gloucester.

Gloucester, St. Peter's Church or Abbey, held lands in Gloucestershire, Hants, Worcester, and Hereford.

Handone, or Wolverhampton, at first a nunnery, afterwards, at the Conquest, a house of Secular Canons, in Staffordshire.

Hereford, St. Guthlac's, in the counties of Hereford and Worcester. St. Peter's Benedictine Priory, in this city, is referred to by Ellis in a valuable note.[1]

Holme or Hulme, St. Benedict's, in Norfolk.

Hortone, or Hortune Abbey, in Dorsetshire and Devonshire.

Leominster Abbey, in Herefordshire.

London, St. Martin's-le-Grand Collegiate Church, with a dean and priests.

Micelenie, or Muchelney Abbey, in Somersetshire.

St. Michael's Church, or Priory, in Cornwall, called St. Michael's Mount.

[1] Vol. i. p. 431.

St. Neot's Collegiate Church, in Cornwall.

Oxford, a Church of Canons, in Oxfordshire' and Buckinghamshire.

Pershore, the Benedictine Abbey of St. Mary, of which the early history is uncertain, held lands in Worcestershire and Gloucestershire.

St. Petroc's, or Bodmin, in Cornwall.

Ramesyg, or Ramsey, the Benedictine Abbey (of St. Benedict), an ancient foundation, held lands in many counties, in Cambridge, Huntingdon, Bedford, Northampton, Lincoln, Norfolk, and Suffolk.

Sceptesberiensis ecclesia, or Shaftesbury, an Abbey for Nuns, of great antiquity, held in Dorsetshire, Somersetshire, Wiltshire, and Sussex.

In Shrewsbury, the monastery of St. Peter held land.

Statford or Stafford, the Prebendal Canons held land.

Thvinam, Twinham, or Christchurch Priory for a Dean and Secular Canons, held land in Hampshire.

Tornyg, or Thorney, Benedictine Abbey, held lands in Cambridgeshire, Bedfordshire, Huntingdonshire, and Northamptonshire.

Waltham, the Abbey or College of Secular Canons of the Holy Cross, held in Essex and Hertfordshire.

Westminster Abbey of St. Peter, held in sixteen counties, among others Stafford, Lincoln, and Gloucestershire.

Wiltune, or Wilton, the Abbey of St. Mary for Nuns, held in Wiltshire, Dorsetshire, and Hants.

Wincelcumbe, or Winchelcombe Abbey, of great age and royal foundation, held in Gloucestershire, Oxfordshire, and Warwickshire.

Winchester, St. Mary's Nunnery, in Hants, Berks, and Wiltshire.

York, St. Peter's Abbey.

Among the officers of the Church and clerical dignitaries, as we have already noticed, archbishops, bishops, *presbyters* or priests; *capellani*, chaplains, or domestic priests; *clerici*, clerks; *diaconi*, or deacons; and *sacerdos*, occur. The terms for the body of the clergy were, no doubt, used in a general manner, and not with any very great amount of precision. The dignity of dean, archdeacon, and capitular membership seems to be unnoticed.

Church dues, called in Anglo-Saxon *Cyric sceat*, and in the Domesday Book *Circesset, circet, cirsette, circieti, circset*, was a *shot* or payment, or contribution, due to the Church in certain places, not apparently very frequent of occurrence. The amount varies considerably, and is sometimes expressed as a money payment; at others, as on the lands of Pershore Abbey, a *summa*, seam, or load of corn, as first fruits of the harvest, was due at Martinmas for each hide held by a *homo francus*.

The lands belonging to Worcester Cathedral, in the same way, paid the same amount of grain for each hide. Kennett considers that the word was a general term, not confined to corn, but including poultry, or any other kind of provisions, paid to the religious body. How far the Church dues were connected with tithes has not been determined.

CHAPTER XIII.

METALS—MONEY—PRODUCE—MISCELLANEOUS TERMS AND WORDS.

THE Domesday Book mentions·the following metals and products of the earth :—

1. Argentum.   4. Plumbum.
2. Aurum.   5. Lapides.
3. Ferrum.   6. Sal.

(1.) *Argentum*, or silver, is found in the phrase "argentum album," which will be noticed in the account of the *Libra*, or pound. The "pundus argenti" is found in a very old text.[1]

(2.) *Aurum*, gold, is of frequent occurrence. There is, for example, the *aurum Regina*, or "Queen Gold," which is found in three places. A treatise on this was written by Prynne,[2] somewhat ridiculed by Lord Coke. It appears to have been a royal due or revenue appertaining to the Queen Consort during her marriage to the King of England, payable by every one within the realms of England and Ireland who has paid a voluntary fine to the king of ten marks, or upwards, for any privileges, pardons, or other royal favours conferred on him by the king, and amounting to a tenth over and above the fine so paid. The duty was suspended from the death of

[1] Birch, "Cartularium Saxonicum," No. 436, A.D. 841.
[2] "Aurum Reginæ," 4to., London, 1668.

T

Henry VIII. to the accession of James I., and in the fourth year of his reign, on reference to the judges, it was determined to be the right of his queen, Anne. I am unable to say whether the Queens Consort of the House of Brunswick enjoyed this revenue. The Mark of Gold has been already noticed. There is also the *uncia auri*, which occurs in several passages, sometimes in connexion with the *aurum Reginæ.* It seems to have been a sub-division of the Mark sometimes,[1] at others of the Pound.[2]

The workers in gold, the *aurifabri*, have been mentioned in the place devoted to titular designations. Earl Hugh had a goldsmith, by name Nicholaus, who is specially mentioned. The art of making aurifrisium, or orphreys, was considered worthy of special encouragement.[3]

(3.) *Ferrum*, iron, or perhaps occasionally steel, was then, as now, of universal practical utility. Special words, *bloma*, or bloom, *massa* and *plumba*, were used to denote its weight or quality. There were *ferrariæ*, and *minariæ*, or iron-mines; *ferri fabricæ*, iron manufactories; *ferrarii*, or iron-workers, who prepared "ferrum cãr,' or "ferrum carrucis," the ironwork for the ploughs. In the city of Hereford there were six smiths, each of whom paid a penny rent for his forge, and was required to make a hundred and twenty ferra (? horse-shoes) with the king's stuff, and for this he received threepence.

(4.) *Plumbum*, or lead, like iron, had especial words with regard to its weight, but we are unable

---

[1] Chipeham, in Cambridgeshire "Inq. Com. Cantab.," p. 3.
[2] *Ibid.*, Westone, pp. 21, 22, 104.   [3] *See* p. 253.

to determine with any degree of accuracy the relative values of these terms. The Domesday Book of Derbyshire contains a passage indicating that—

5 plaustratæ (waggon-loads) = 50 *tabulæ*, or sheets, or that each *plaustrata* was composed of fifty *tabulæ*, for the sentence is ambiguous "V. plaustratas plumbi de L. tabulis," but this latter may be too ponderous.

The "Inqusitio Eliensis"[1] furnishes us with further light on the method of calculating the weight of lead. It is remarkable that it escaped the notice of Ellis:—

"*Carreta* plumbi del Pec continet .xxiiii. *fotineles.*

"Quodlibet *fotinel* de .lx. x. libris. et hoc est .xiiii. *cutti.*

"Quilibet *cuttus* de v. *libris.*

"Carreta de Lund (? Lundonia) est major illa de. cccc. libris. et xx libræ per minus centum."

Hence the following table may be constructed, if we assume that *plaustrata* is synonymous with *carreta.*

> 5 lb. = 1 *cuttus.*
> 14 *cutti* = 1 *fotinel* = 70 lb.
> 24 *fotinels* = 1 *carreta* of the Peak of Derby-shire = 1,680 lb. = 1 *plaus-trata* = 10 *tabulæ.*
> „ = 1 *carreta* of London = 2,100 lb. by the small hundred.

But as the small hundred was eighty, twenty-one small hundreds = 21 × 80 = 1,680 lb. So that, in fact, the Derbyshire and London waggon-load of lead was the same. It is noteworthy that 1,680 lb.

[1] Page 191.

is equivalent to fifteen modern hundredweights of 112 lb. each.

The lead mines are distinguished by the name of. *plumbariæ.*

. (5.) While discussing metals, it will, perhaps, be convenient to mention the stone *fossæ lapidum*, and. stone .pits or quarries, *quadrariæ*, which are also found in Domesday. There was also a *fossarius.*

(6.) Salt, *Sal;* this universal and indispensable commodity has been mentioned in many very ancient documents and literary records. Among the earliest. notice of a brine-work, perhaps, is a charter in the well-known chartulary of Worcester Cathedral, compiled by the Monk Heming (Cotton. MS. Tiberius. A. xiii. f. 196 *b*), whereby Ædilbald, king of the Mercians, grants to the Christian family (of monks) at Wigranceastre, or Worcester, a piece of land used for saltworks on the south bank of the river Salūuearpe, called Lootwic and Coolbeorg, suitable for three *casuli*, and six chimneys (*camini*), in exchange for. others on the opposite bank.[1] The date is between A.D. 716 and 717. The importance of salt in the economy of domestic life during the early period of our history may be illustrated also by notice of a salt-pan granted in A.D. 774 for 778 (?) by King Cynewulf, to Æthelmod, bishop, and the monks of Sherborne on the western bank of the river Lim, or Lyme, co. Dorset, "haut procul a loco ubi meatus sui cursum in mare mergit, quatinus illic præfatæ ecclesiæ sal· conqueretur ad sustentationem multiformæ necessi-:

---

[1] Birch, "Cartularium Saxonicum," No. 137.

tatis, sive in condimentum ciborum, sive etiam ut in divinis officiorum usibus haberetur et quibus cotidie Christianæ religionis causa multipliciter indigemus."[1]

In a Kentish charter,[2] dated A.D. 863, the use of the phrase "una salis coquinaria hoc est . 1. *sealtern steall*," shows the Saxon equivalent for the Latin term.

Many other notices might be recorded. At the period of the Domesday, salt was in great request,. and then, as it has been shown to be in the eighth century, prepared by two distinct methods.

In the parts bordering on the sea-coast, salt-pans, where evaporation could be carried out, afforded the most economical means of obtaining the needed supply. In the inland counties the brine springs were found to yield, by boiling the water, a valuable salt, for which Droitwich, originally called Wich, or Saltwich, and the other Wiches in the West of England, were the most celebrated. Rock salt, as far as England is concerned, was not worked until the year 1670. Ellis enumerates most of the salt-yielding places which find mention in the Domesday Book. Kent and Sussex were rich in salinæ, or salt-pans; Surrey, Hants, Dorset, and Devon, not so well supplied with them. Among inland counties, Buckingham, Glou-cester, Hereford, Warwick, Salop, were sparsely furnished with salinæ, and Berks, Middlesex, Herts, Oxford, Cambridge,[3] Huntingdon, Northampton, Leicester, Stafford, Derby, and York, almost, or

---

[1] Birch, "Cartularium Saxonicum," No. 224.

[2] *Ibid.*, No. 507.

[3] Only two, at Isingatona, in the "Inquisitio Eliensis," p. 131.

entirely, without them. At Sopeberie, in Gloucestershire, which had a boilery in Wiche, *i.e.* Droitwich, yielding twenty-five sextaries of salt, Urso d'Abitot so wasted the men who made it, that at the time of the survey they could deliver no salt. Worcestershire and Cheshire (the site of the Wiches or brine-yielding areas) were the two principal salt-producing counties in the Domesday; after them, Essex, Norfolk, and Suffolk. The salines, salinæ, or *salis putei*, were worked by the *salinarii*, or saltmakers, in a *domus ad sal faciendum*, a boilery. Salina has been conjectured also to signify the brine itself, or the "seal" or furnace in which the brine was boiled. The manufacture was carried on in leaden vats, *plumbi*, and in *hocci*, smaller pits or reservoirs (and *casuli*).[1] The method of computing the measures of salt involves special terms:—*Ambra, Bullio, Mensura, Mitta, Sextaria, Summa.* Of these the *Ambra, ombra,* or amphora, was equivalent to four bushels, or half a quarter, London measure.

Bullio was a fifteenth part of a *Summa*, or horse-load, *i.e.*, pack-load, used for other goods also—perhaps eight London bushels.

Mitta, or *Mita*, is reckoned to have amounted to eight or ten bushels. It was also used among the Saxons as a measure of wheat [2] and ale.[3] Two *ombras* went to the *mitta.*[4]

Sextaria, used also for other commodities,[5] was of uncertain amount.

---

[1] *See* page 276.   [2] Smith's "Beda," p. 771.
[3] Birch, "Cartularium Saxonicum," No. 464.
[4] *Ibid.*, No. 330.
[5] *Ibid.*, a liquid measure.

The term *vasculum*, though not appearing in the Domesday, was used in connexion with salt manufacture in the year 884, when Æthelred of the Mercians granted to a certain Æthulwulf certain land, "cum . . . pertinentibus . id est . . . salisque coctionibus id est vi. vascula possint præparari."[1] .

MONEY.

The varieties of money which are mentioned in the Domesday are not very great. They consist of—

1. Libra.
2. Marca.
3. Ora.
4. Solidus.
5. Denarius.
6. Obolus.
7. Quadrans.
8. Minuta.

(1.) The Libra, or Pound,[2] was of three kinds :—

(*a.*) The *Libra ad numerum*, the cash or ready money pound, composed of about 15 or 16 *oræ* at 15, 16, or 20 pence to each *ora*.[3] Other synonymous terms for the pound were :—

Libræ albæ, or white pounds.

    „ de albo argento. Pounds of white money or silver.

    „ blancæ, blanched pounds.

    „ candidæ, white pounds.

---

[1] Birch, "Cartularium Saxonicum," No. 552.

[2] *Ibid.*, No. 430, A.D. 840. The *libra* and *pund* are mentioned in an ancient charter under circumstances which seem to show that they were not identical.

[3] See C. F. Keary, F.S.A., "Catal. of Engl. Coins in the Brit. Mus., Anglo-Sax. Series," Vol. I. £1 = 15 or 16 *oies* = 40 *oa*. This ore would, therefore, be equal to 16 or 15 pence.

Pounds of White Money.

Libræ de albis denariis.

"„ denariorum candidorum.

"„ alborum nummorum.

"„ candidorum nummorum.

(*b.*) The *Libræ ad pensum,* or *Libræ ad peis,* or *Libræ ad pondus,* were pounds by weight of bullion, and not by numbers. Gold payments to the State are still made by this method, and not by tale or number. Other terms of similar import were :—

Pounds by Weight and Assay.

Libræ ad ignem et ad pensam.

Libræ arsæ et pensatæ.

Libræ ad pensam et arsuram[1].

The Receivers at the Exchequer examined the coins offered in payment, and when defective in weight and assay, made trial of a sample; or charged sixpence or a shilling (and even more, if the base condition of the coin so offered demanded it) in every twenty, instead of the actual trial by firing. When the coin had been melted, or had the percentage charged added to it, one author[2] declares that at the time of the Domesday the coin that was suspected was burnt in a fire always ready in the Exchequer for this purpose (presumably in a crucible), and then weighed. No doubt some payments in the Exchequer were accepted by tale, according to custom or privilege, for Kelham records that there were proper officers for weighing, counting, or telling,

---

[1] And in the Exeter Domesday Book "Libræ ad pondus et combustionem." [2] Brady.

assaying and laying up the money: a *pesour*, or weigher, a *fusor*, or melter, goldsmiths, and so forth. This trial of coinage was the only safeguard of the day against fabricators of base money, who flourished in the Domesday period as universally in England as they did in the waning days of the Roman Empire, if we may judge from the frequent occurrence of base moulds, false coins, and other relics which archæology has from time to time placed on record. If analogy of one or two cases may be taken as indicative of the general debasement of money in the time of Domesday, the difference of value between the apparent value by tale and the true value after the trial was very great. Ellis cites the instance of the Manor of Bosham, in Sussex, which was worth forty pounds in the time of King Edward and afterwards, and yielded a similar rent at the time of compiling the Domesday, yet it paid fifty pounds "ad arsuram et pensum," which are worth sixty-five pounds— that is, sixty-five pounds of current cash were found, after the crucial test to which they were submitted at the Exchequer, to be required to make the due sum of fifty pounds. This is equivalent to a debasement of nearly twenty-three per cent. of current money. So great and universal had the corruption of money become, that in A.D. 1125, thirty-one years after the completion of the Domesday Survey, the king took steps, which resulted, for the time at least, in the abatement of an evil which had made itself dangerous to the very existence of the people, for the owner of a pound could buy nothing with it, in any market.

"For se man þe hafde an pund he ne mihte cysten ænne

William of Malmesbury, who lived at this time, records, among a few other events for which he thought the year 1125 notable, this :—" Falsario- rum, qui monetam corruperant per totam Angliam, detruncatione notabilis. Propter eandem perinde falsitatem annonæ karitate, et edaci fame, tum præ- terea indiscreta vulgi clade infamis !" " The year was notable for the maiming of the false coiners, who had debased the money throughout all England, and infamous for the dearness of harvest, because of this corruption of the coinage, and for the bitter famine, and especially for the indiscriminate death of the people which it caused."[1] The " Anglo-Saxon Chronicle " details the horrid ceremony here referred to at length,[2] which was enacted at Winchester during the Christmas season.

(2.) Next in order of value to the *Libra* is the *Marka* or *marca*, a word derived from *Marc*, an Anglo-Saxon word, signifying a sign, or mark, probably so called from the devices which it bore. This consisted of—

(a.) The *Marka auri*, or golden Mark, which is mentioned in several places.[3] It appears to have been worth at a later period ten silver marks, and was only used as an expression.[4]

peni at anne market." — "Anglo-Saxon Chronicle" *ad an.* MCXXV. ; and again the year before, " Ꝥ se man þa hæfde at an market an pund he ne mihte cysten þær of for nan þing tƿelfe penegas," *ibid.*, *ad an.* MCXXIV.

[1] Ed. Hamilton (Rolles Series), p. 442.　[2] *Ad an.*, MCXXV.
[3] Salletone, Sussex, Chipeham, Cambridge, &c.
[4] From a passage in the Pipe-Roll of 1 Henry II.; Wickins argues that the Mark was worth six pounds of silver.

(*b.*) The *Marka argenti*, or silver mark, of which Ellis mentions a few instances.[1]

The half mark of gold and silver were money computations.

(3.) The *hora*, *ora*, or *ore* (a word originally perhaps signifying ore, or native metal, but Vigfusson and Cleasby derive the word from *aurum*), was also an expression, and not a coin. Ellis declares, on the authority of Hickes, that it is used for the ounce or twelfth part of the nummulary pound; that is, twenty pence.[2] But there must have been an *ora* of other values, for Ellis finds that in times earlier than Domesday an *ora* of sixteen pence[3] had been used, and that this very value was current in Domesday times is evident from a passage in the *Inquisitio Comitatus Cantabrigiensis*, which, as we have shown in the notice of the text, escaped Ellis, and all other Domesday students. In the Manor of Clinton, called Inchelintone in the corresponding part of Domesday Book,[4] we read "Hæc terra valet .ii. horas et quando recepit. .xii. denarios." The Domesday Commissioners, or their scribe, convert this into "Valet .xxxii. denarios. Quando recepit. .xii. denarios." The Danes[5] are asserted to have introduced the *ora* into England.

(4.) The *solidus*,[6] or shilling, was not a coin, but a

---

[1] Bertune, Gloucestershire ; and some Dorsetshire places.

[2] This is borne out by two passages, at least, in Domesday. Lye calls this the greater ora.

[3] Lye calls this the lesser ora.

[4] Vol. i. p. 198a, col. 1.

Lye, *ad verbum*.

[6] The classical *solidus* was a gold coin, at first called *aureus*,

sub-division of account, and in this respect resembled
the moneys already discussed. It is worthy of notice
that while the Saxon shilling was sub-divided into
five pennies, that of Domesday is like the shilling of
to-day, equivalent to twelve pence.

(5.) It is not until we descend down the scale to the
denarius[1] or penny,[2] sometimes *nummus*,[3] that we
arrive at the visible coinage, and this was the only coin
known for long before and after the Domesday Survey.
It was, in fact, the unit of value, and it is by this that
the true understanding of such terms as *Wardepeni,
Warpenna*,[4] payment to the Sheriffs and others for
Castle wards or custody ; *denarii Sancti Petri*, or
St. Peter's pence, a Church rate due to the pope ;
and the *third penny of the shire*, due to the earl.

The Penny of Rouen, or *Denarius Rodmensium*, or
Rothomagensium, occurs in the account of two Devonshire manors, belonging to St. Mary's Church, at Rouen.

and equivalent to twenty-five silver *denarii*, at first ; afterwards
reduced.

[1] The word itself is derived from *deni, ten each*, or *by tens*,
and thus the Roman denarius, a silver coin, originally contained ten *asses*.

[2] The *penny* in its earliest form, *peñd* or *pending*, which
occurs in a charter dated between A.D. 616 and 618 (Birch,
"Cart. Sax.," vol. II., No. 837, and twice in the text of the will
of Abba the Reeve, about A.D. 833, *ibid*, vol. I, pp. 575,
576, is evidently connected with words for weight, pund,
pondus, pendere, and so on. The *d* appears to have been
eliminated eventually, and the most common forms are *Peneg,
penig, peninc, pening*, and *penincg*.

[3] As in Hamilton's "Inq. Com. Cantab." p. 2 ; Manor of
Kenet.

[4] *Warpennos* is the original word in the "Inq. Com. Cantab."
p. 59.

(6.) The *obolus*,[1] or halfpenny, and—

(7.) The *Quadrans, Ferdinc, Ferding, Ferting,* or farthing,[2] which also occurs in several instances throughout the Domesday Book, were the half and fourth part respectively of the denarius. It has been thought that the cross, which is almost always the symbol employed on the reverse of the early coinage of England, was purposely employed to facilitate the breaking of the silver penny if it were required, and hoards of coin which have been found containing money ranging from Saxon times to the end of the fourteenth century generally includes some pieces which have been thus broken. But it is more reasonable to assume that the cross was employed on coins at first in its higher and more universal significa-tion, as also in the signatures and attestations of witnesses at a period which reaches back almost, if not quite, to the commencement of the Christian era, —and that the utility of following the grooves or de-pressions in the metal made by the limbs of the cross was an after-thought, and merely an accidental coinci-dence. Among the early coins thus halved and quartered in the national collections in the British Museum are several, found at Cuerdale, of the Danish kings of Northumbria. They are not un-common after the time of Alfred, but rare before that period. Farthings—that is, quarter pieces—do not occur much before the era of Edward the Con-fessor.

[1] A word derived, like many Saxon words, from the Greek. The small Greek coin so called was the sixth part of a drachma; and had little or no real connexion with the Saxon *obolus.*

[2] *i.e.,* fourth part.

(8.) The *Minuta,* or mite, occurs but once in the
Domesday. The preponderance of opinion appears to
be that this is the equivalent of the Saxon *styca,*[1] eight
of which went to the penny, and hence the minuta
was half a farthing. It was used, if at all, as common
change. They were of brass or copper, washed.
The *styca* of Northumbrian royal dynasties, and of
the archbishops of York, are the only ones we are
now acquainted with. Their devices are various, and
many of them have been figured and described by
writers on the early coinage of England. A very
remarkable hoard of several thousands of these small
coins in a mass, found in the parish of Hornington,
West Riding, Yorkshire, is described by Mr. William
Fennell in the Journal of the British Archæological
Association for 1849, vol. iv. p. 127. Another find
of about ten thousand, in a pot, also much corroded,
was found in 1842, not far from Bootham Bar, in
the city of York.[2] They appear to have belonged in
the main to the ninth century. The *styca* stops
about A.D. 867.

Among the produce of which Domesday takes
notice are the *animalia,* or *animalia ociosa,* plough or
store cattle; fisheries, *piscariæ;* of eels, *anguillæ;*
herrings, of which large quantities were paid as rent

[1] Lye derives the styca, from *sticce,* steak, or portion,
frustrum, offa, minuta pars. He refers to the passage in
Mark, xii 42, "tpegen stycas, þet is feorðung peninges—two
mites, which make a farthing." But cf. *stück,* Germ., a piece.

[2] Journal Brit. Arch. Assoc., vol. ii. p. 230. The following
vol. iii. p. 119, records another discovery of a large quantity of
stycas found during excavations at York.

by the various manors on the coast, indicating the
value of this fish as an article of diet; salmon rarely
occur, they appear as coming from the Severn and
the Wye; *piscinæ*, or *vivaria*, fish-ponds. The
heiemaris, sea-net or a sea-hedge, no doubt an inclo-
sure, with artificial adjuncts for catching sea fish, was
used in fisheries. Bread, butter, cheese, honey, corn,
flour, malt, pease, beer, and cakes for dogs, appear
among the miscellaneous objects of food produce.

Miscellaneous terms and words include Burgheristh,
probably the same as *Burghbrech* or *Borhbrece*,
breaking the peace of the borough. *Forestel*, or for-
stalling, that is, rushing out unexpectedly and assault-
ing an enemy or traveller. *Gribrige*, or *Grithbryce*,
breaking the peace. *Hainfare*, or *heinfare*, flight after
committing murder. *Handsoca*, or *hamsocna*, entering
or injuring any one's house or home, *ham*. *Raptum*
or rape, punished with mutilation. *Revelach* (*i.e*,
rcaflac), any traitorous act or insurrection according
to Kelham, robbery or rapine, forfeiture of blood,
i.e., bloodshed, paid a money fine, but a murderer
forfeited body (by death) and property to the king.
Blodewita and *homicidium*, the fine for bloodshed.
Hangewita, penalty for hanging a thief or letting him
go, without judgment. *Latrocinium*, penalty for
robbery. *Legrewita*, or *lairwita*, penalty for inconti-
nence or violence; in Kent (except in a few places)
the king took the man, and the archbishop of
Canterbury the woman, found guilty; a curious example of the connexion of the ecclesiastical with the
secular law.

CHAPTER XIV.

HISTORICAL EVENTS—THE PENENDEN SUIT—THE ELY
SUIT—THE WORCESTER SUITS—FOREIGN TENANTS
AND MONASTERIES.

THE Domesday Book does not present very many
notices of historical events. Hence Sir Thomas
Duffus Hardy, in his Catalogue of MS. relating to
English History, does not speak very highly of the
historical value of the book. But we should hardly
expect to find many references of the national character in a manuscript devoted simply to an examination
of the condition of the taxable parts of the country.
Notices of the condition of this area in the time
of Edward the Confessor abound, for the Commissioners had it under royal command to record the
state of their several properties at that time. This
they must have taken from the account furnished by
the tenants, who may or may not have produced
contemporary documents to support their statements.
Hence, in some measure, by the acceptance of the
statements and declarations—taken, of course, on
oath—made by the occupiers of the land, the people
of England may be said to have taxed themselves,
for although in many cases the Commissioners declare
the present worth of certain manors to be in excess
of the sum at which it has been declared to stand
assessed, there is no evidence to show that the Crown

raised the rate or the assessment, in accordance with the statements made by the Commissioners as to value.

The earlier King Canute, or Cnut, sometimes Gnut; Imma, or Emma, his queen; and Æthelred, her first husband, the father of King Edward the Confessor, are mentioned.

The Confessor's benevolence to monasteries and the Church is well displayed by many examples cited by Ellis, and for this he appears to have been held in great respect. The term "glorious" is applied to him on two occasions. Eddid, or -Editha Regina, queen of Edward the Confessor, occurs as a donor of land to a certain Alsi. She retained her landed estates until her death in A.D. 1075, when they fell into the king's possession.

Goda, the countess, sister of Edward the Confessor, held the manor of Lambeth. She appears to have led a religious life, if we may judge from the inventory of things found at Lambeth and taken to St. Andrew's Cathedral, Rochester, on which King William Rufus had bestowed the manor by a charter, signed with his mark, still extant among Lord Frederick Campbell's Charters in the British Musuem, vii. 1. They consisted of a gold and silver pix, copies of the Gospels adorned with silver and precious stones, and a variety of church ornaments. Notices of illustrious persons include Siuuard, earl of Northumberland; Godeva, countess of Mercia; Hereward the Wake; the exiled Harold, called *liber homo*, and his holdings looked on in some cases as *invasions;* the exiled Godwine, who in 1050 sailed away to Flanders from Boseham,

U

a place belonging to Harold, and from which, too, in A.D. 1059 he was forced by a storm, when fishing, to the opposite coast—an event of consequence as resulting in the Norman Conquest of England.

· The decision of the great suit which was held at Pinnenden or Penenden in Kent is alluded to in the Survey of that county. Ellis only takes a passing notice of this event, and dates it "about the year 1072." The recent discovery of a document bearing upon this important event in the history of the English Church, which had hitherto escaped the notice of all historians and writers on Domesday subjects, not excepting Sir Henry Ellis himself, who had many opportunities of noticing the document when it was under his charge as Keeper of the Manuscripts in the British Museum, where it is pre-served among the Cottonian Manuscripts (Augustus, ii. 36), enables me to print here for the first time a new light illustrating Domesday historical events.

· Rev. L. B. Larking, the learned expounder of the Kent Domesday, writing of the possessions[1] which had been subjected to the spoliation of Odo, bishop of Bayeux,— which perhaps for that very reason had been first separately and distinctly noticed by the Commis-sioners,—enters into a long account of this celebrated controversy, deeming it advisable, in order to illustrate the character and usurpations of Odo, to transcribe from Eadmer and Selden the accounts which they give of the affair, in which the spoliations of this grasping ecclesiastic and his men are fully detailed. Eadmer's

---

[1] "Domesday Book of Kent," p. 188.

account shows the details of the circumstances which led to the trial very succinctly.

The trustworthy historian, Eadmer, in a passage where he relates the invasions which Odo, bishop of Bayeux, had committed on the lands of Christchurch, Canterbury, writes as follows :—"Odo[1] siquidem episcopus Baiocensis, ut de aliis taceam, frater prædicti regis Willelmi, et Cantiæ comes, priusquam Lanfrancus Angliam intrasset magnus et præpotens per totum regnum habebatur. Hic, dominatione qua in immensum sustollebatur, non modo terras, sed et libertatem nominatæ ecclesiæ, nullo ei resistente, multipliciter invaserat, oppresserat, tenebat. Quæ ubi Lanfrancus ut erant didicit, apud regem de illis egit sicut oportere sciebat. Unde præcepit rex quatinus, adunatis primoribus et probis viris non solum de comitatu Cantiæ, sed et de aliis comitatibus Angliæ querelæ Lanfranci in medium ducerentur, examinarentur, determinarentur. Disposito itaque apud Pinnedene principum conventu, Goffridus episcopus Constantiensis vir ea tempestate prædives in Anglia, vice regis Lanfranco justitiam de suis querelis facere jussus, strenuissime fecit. Lanfrancus enim valida ratione subnixus ex communi omnium astipulatione et judicio ibi cuncta recuperavit quæ ostensa sunt antiquitus ad jura ecclesiæ Christi Cantuariensis pertinuisse, tam in terris quam in diversis consuetudinibus."

The date of the suit or enquiry is supplied by the appendix[2] to the Anglo-Saxon Chronicle for the year 1074.

[1] "Eadmeri Historia," ed. Rule (Rolls ser.), p. 17.

[2] MS. Corp. Chr. Coll. Cantab. No. clxxiii., *ad an.* "Hoc ·

The gist of the entry is as follows :—In this year also was held the great plea in the place called Pinenden, wherein Lanfranc recovered, by process of land for himself and his church, all his lands and customs as freely, in land and in sea, as the king holds his own, except three, viz., if the king's highway be dug open by one of the archbishop's men, if a tree fall on it when being felled, if homicide or bloodshed be on it, the offenders in these points to be delivered to the king's ministers. Selden, founding his account on that given in a Rochester MS. (collated by Larking with the Cotton. MS. Vespasian A. xxii., f. 120) shows that Odo, who had settled in Kent with great pomp, seized lands belonging to the Cathedral of Canterbury before Lanfranc arrived. On Lanfranc's appointment to be archbishop, he found the lands in disorder, and obtained the king's permission to have a meeting of the whole county and men of the county, all the Franks, and especially English learned *in the ancient laws* and customs. This took place at Pinendena, or Penenden Heath, where the suit occupied three days, and appears to have been chiefly occupied with the invasions of Odo. But the archbishop, during this time, successfully wrested the lands of the Church from Herbert filius Ivonis, Turoldus de Rouecestria, Radulfus de Curva Spina, and Hugo de Monteforti, in Raculf, Sandevic, Rateburg, Medetune, " Saltvude cum Burgo Hethe ad Saltvude pertinente," and many other places in Kent; in London the Monastery of St. Mary, with the lands

quoque anno." See Thorpe, " Anglo-Sax. Chron." (Rolls series), vol. i. appx.

and houses held by Livingus the priest and his wife; and other persons in Middlesex, Buckinghamshire, Oxfordshire, Essex, and Suffolk. Not only did Lanfranc succeed in regaining the lands belonging to his church, thus wrongfully alienated by the powerful bishop of Bayeux, but he also established his right to the important privileges of Soca, Saca, Tol, Team, Flymenafyrmthe, Grithbrece, Foresteal, Haimfare, Infangenetheof, and other customs. This was decreed by the whole Assembly, among whom were Goisfridus, bishop of Coutance, who represented the king and exercised the office of chief justice; Lanfranc, who gained all his points; Odo, as earl of Kent; Ernostus, bishop of Rochester; Ægelric, bishop of Chichester, a very old man, and very learned in the land laws, who by the king's special command was taken thither in a *quadriga*, or four-horsed carriage, to discuss and expound those same ancient customs of the laws; Richard de Tunebregge; Hugo de Monte forti; William de Arces; Haimo, sheriff of Kent, and others.

The newly-discovered manuscript leaf in the British Museum is a digest or minute of the points moved by Lanfranc, and discussed at the county court, and of the decision at which the judges arrived. This probably came, with many other Canterbury charters, into the possession of Sir Robert Cotton, the founder of the Cottonian Library.

Fulchestan . de beneficio regis est.

Ratebourc de archiepiscopatu est . & edzinus dedit goduino.

Stepeberga de archiepiscopatu est . & ecclesia .

Christi erat inde saisita quando rex mare transivit . modo episcopus baiocensis habet.

In tilemanestun quando rex mare transivit erat ecclesia Christi saisita de ducentis jugeribus terrae . & in fenglesham de centum jugeribus . &. in elme de viginti quinque jugeribus . & modo ea osbernus ab episcopo[1] tenet.

Totesham alnod child de monachis tenebat quando rex mare transivit . & firmam inde reddebat . & modo episcopus[1] habet.

Torentun viginti quinque jugera habet & ecclesia habebat quando rex mare transivit . & modo episcopus[1] habebat sed dimisit.

Witriscesham ecclesia Christi habebat quando rex mare transivit . & modo osbernus paisforere ab episcopo[1] habet.

Auuentiugesherst . & edruneland . & aduuoluuinden . ecclesia tenebat quando rex mare transivit . & firmam inde habebat . & modo Robertus de romenel ab episcopo[1] habet.

Prestitun alnod child ab archiepiscopo tenebat quando rex mare transivit . & firmam reddebat . & modo turoldus ab episcopo[1] habet.

Godricus decanus dedit fratri suo quartam partem solingi quod pertinebat ad clivam . & modo robertus uuillelmus ab episcopo[1] habet.

Sunderhirsc de archiepiscopatu est . & archiepiscopus dedit goduino . & episcopus[1] modo habet.

Langport & neuuenden de archiepiscopatu est . & archiepiscopus dedit goduino . & episcopus[1] statim in placito cognovit esse de ecclesia.

[1] Odo here is intended.

. Saltoda de archiepiscopatu est . & archiepiscopus. dedit goduino . & modo hugo de dono regis habet. .

. Fecit archiepiscopus Lanfranchus alios . clamores super episcopum[1] et super hugonem . sed in hundretis debent diffiniri.

Pimpe et chintun .. & uuestaldingis adalredus de archiepiscopo tenebat . & modo Richardus habet.

Penesherst de archiepiscopatu est . & archiepiscopus tenebat quando rex mare transivit . & censum & firmam inde habebat.

Tertium-denarium[2] de comitatu archiepiscopus qui ante edzinum[3] fuit ' habuit. Tempore edzini rex eduuardus dedit goduino. Terras omnes quæ pertinent ad archiepiscopatum & ad abbatiam sancti Augustini . & terras comitis Goduini . testati sunt esse liberas ab omni consuetudine regia . præter antiquas vias quæ vadunt de civitate ad civitatem . & de mercato ad mercatum . & de portu maris ad alium portum.

. De illa calumnia quam episcopus odo fecit de pratis archiepiscopi & sancti Augustini . judicaverunt omnes quod in justicia haberet . & prata utriusque ecclesiæ sicut ceteræ terræ libera esse deberent.

Terra Goduini damæ ad ecclesiam sancti Augustini pertinet . & quando rex mare transivit ecclesia de

---

[1] Odo here is intended.

[2] The third penny of the County of Kent would, of course, fall to Odo, as earl of the County. It does not appear that Lanfranc made good his claim to this.

[3] Edzinus, or Eadsige, succeeded to the archiepiscopal dignity in A.D. 1038, on the death of Ethelnoth, 29th Oct. of that year. He was consecrated 13th Nov., 1020. Eadsige died 29th Oct., 1050.

terra illa servicium habebat . & modo hugo ·de dono regis habet.

The endorsement, in another handwriting, is :—

Quod archiepiscopus antiquitus habebat tercium denarium de comitatu cantie . 7 hoc jure ipsius esse debet. Scriptum de terris quas antiquitus habuit Cantuariensis ecclesia.

The Ely suit is only known by the entry in the Cambridge University manuscript O. 2. I. f. 210 *b*, printed in Hamilton's *Inquisitio Comitatus Cantabrigiensis*. This appears to be in many respects, similar to the newly-found document relating to the Penenden suit. It seems that bishops Gosfrid, of Coutance, and Remigius, of Lincoln, "Walthews the Consul," *i.e.*, the earl Waltheof, Picot, the sheriff of Cambridgeshire, and Ilbert, perhaps Ilbert de Hertford (Hereforda), who is mentioned in another part of the county record, sat as royal commissioners in a county court, to determine claims brought by the Church of St. Mary, St. Peter, and St. Æthelrytha, of Ely (as possessing in the time of King Edward the Confessor), against sundry possessors of manors and other properties in the counties of Cambridge, Essex, Suffolk, and Norfolk. The opening paragraph of the document explains itself.

"Ad[1] illud placitum quo pontifices Gosfridus . et Remigius . consul vero Walthews necnon vicecomes . Picotus . atque Ilbertus jussu Willelmi Dei dispositione Auglorum regis cum omni vicecomitatu sicut rex preceperat convenerunt . testimonio hominum rei

---

[1] The words have been extended.

veritatem cognoscentium determinaverunt tèrras quæ
injuste fuerant ablatæ ab æcclesia Sanctæ Dei geni-
tricis Marie de insula Ely . et Sancti Petri apostolorum
principis . Sanctæque Æthelrythe virginis . quatinus
de dominio fuerant tempore videlicet regis Ædwardi .
ad dominium sine ·alicujus suorum contradictione
redirent quicūnque eas possideret . Nomina quarum
cum eorum quibusdam qui eas adhuc injuste retinent
subscribuntur." Then follows the list of names of
lands and of services, and of those who hold them
from the Abbey. Curiously enough the king,
William himself, is entered as unjustly withholding
"Metheluuald and Crokestune (Norf.), and Snegel-
uuelle and Dictun" (Cambr.); and Picot the sheriff as
withholding the fourth penny "rei puplice de Grante-
brice," which the abbot of Ely had enjoyed since the
time of King Edgar and St. Æthelwold the bishop.

The Domesday Book for Worcestershire is illustrated in an interesting manner by the Chartulary
prepared by the Monk Heming, in obedience to the
directions of Wlstan, bishop of Worcester, to which
several references have already been made. Although
composed for the greater part from transcripts of
Anglo-Saxon charters which the bishop had gathered
together during the progress of his inquiry into the
possessions of his church, there are copies of other
documents, which bear upon the history of Domesday,
the manner of its compilation, and the phraseology
of its text.

One of these is a letter[1] of bishop Oswald, who occu-

[1] At f. 134.

pied the see from A.D. 961 to 992, to King Eadgar, describing in detail the manner, whether by lease for three lives or otherwise, in which the lands of the bishop and the monks of Worcester Cathedral Priory were held. At the end is a paragraph indicating that three copies were made of the letter, which was evidently looked upon as a formal report to the Crown, one of which was preserved at Worcester, a second in the keeping of Archbishop Dunstan[1] at Canterbury (probably as chief protector of the liberties and possessions of the Church), and the third in the charge of Bishop Athelwold[2] (among the Crown documents) in Winchester city. "Harum textus . . . epistolarum tres sunt ad pretitulationem et ad signum . una in ipsa civitate quæ vocatur. Uuigraceaster . altera cum venerabili Dunstano archiepiscopo in Cantuaria . tertia cum Atheluuoldo episcopo in Uuintonia civitate."

The history of bishop Wlstan is of interest. He assisted King Edward the Confessor at the dedication of St. Peter's Abbey at Westminster; but on the change of government made early submission to the Conqueror at Berkhampstead. He also assisted at the coronation of William by Aldred, archbishop of York. In return, we find a deed in Heming's Chartulary,[3] dated in A.D. 1067, in which the king grants to the Church of Worcester two hides of land at Cullaclife, on condition that the Church should intercede, in their prayers to God, for himself and his

---

[1] A.D. 960-988.   [2] A.D. 964-984.
[3] Dugd. "Mon. Angl." vol. i. p. 57.

companions, "quos' secum adjutores habuit cum dominatum terræ istius adquisierat."

In the search and the spoil of monasteries which took place in A.D. 1069, Worcester was not spared, as we gather from another passage in the same manuscript.[1]

On the death of archbishop Aldred in the same year, bishop Wlstan instituted a suit for the recovery of twelve manors, which had been taken from the see and annexed to that of York. This was brought before the council at Winchester in A.D. 1070, and, after delays, he recovered the property for his see, and obtained a complete confirmation of its ancient privileges to their fullest extent.

Ageluui, or Egilwin, abbot of Evesham, called in the Domesday Book Eluui, and Aluuinus, took from the see of Worcester lands at Actun, Earesbyri, and Beningwurthe, many houses in the city of Worcester, lands at Mylecota and Westun in Warwickshire, and at Eownilad and Dæiglesford (Evenlode and Daylesford), in Worcestershire. He was much favoured by Harold, and also enjoyed the esteem of William the Conqueror, who entrusted him with the charge of the counties of Worcester, Gloucester, Oxford, Warwick, Hereford, Stafford, and Salop.

The Chartulary above-mentioned contains a report entitled "De conflictu Wlstani episcopi et Agelvvii abbatis," who is there stated to have much increased in secular power, so that by reason of his ingenuity, craftiness, and knowledge of secular laws, which he exclusively studied, he surpassed all others, espe-

---

[1] P. 393 (Hearne's edition).

cially Wlstan, who devoted his time chiefly to
religious matters, at a time when their country had
been conquered by the Normans, and all the better
sort of the barons of the county of Worcester destroyed. The altercation between Wlstan and
Ageluui continued till the abbot's death, 14 Kal.
March (16th February), A.D. 1077, which resulted
from gout. But, according to · Dugdale,[1] he had
improved the condition of his own monastery.
Bishop Wlstan, on hearing of the abbot's death,
instituted, according to the custom of the time,
certain religious services in commemoration of the
deceased man, but was speedily attacked himself with
gout, and was warned in a dream to cease his inter-
cessions on behalf of Ageluui. He does so, and
recovers. Here a reflective passage is introduced,
showing how heinous is the crime of invading property belonging to monasteries, when God is averse
even to our interceding with Him on behalf of the
trespassers !

Walter de Cerasia, who succeeded to the abbacy
of Evesham, received his appointment from King
William. During his rule the controversy with bishop
Wlstan arose again, for he kept possession of the
lands in dispute. The Survey of the abbey, which
was taken in this abbot's time, shows that the gross
number of hides held by this abbey in the counties
of Gloucester, Worcester, Northampton, and Warwick
amounted to 218½ and 12 acres, producing rental of
£129. 10s. He increased the number of monks,

---

[1] "Mon. Angl." new ed., vol. ii. p. 3.

notwithstanding the depredations committed on the
monastic possessions by bishop Odo, who had begged
them of William, and obtained them for himself.
Thus, says the writer of the Report, "de conflictu,"
we lost them, "for the bishop of Worcester scarcely
obtained the services of any of them; and he who
first robbed us had nought but sin." Hearne prints
from Heming's Cartulary the "COMMEMORATIO
PLACITI," between this abbot and bishop Wlstan,
wherein the bishop claimed from the abbot "sac and
soc, and sepulture, and cirsceat, and requisitions,
and all the customs to be performed to the church of
Worcester in Oswaldeslawe Hundred, and the king's
geld, and service, and expeditions on land and on sea,
for the fifteen hides of Hantona and the four hides
of Benningcwrde, which the abbot ought to hold of
the bishop like as other feoffees of the Church hold
freely, for all due service of king and bishop."

After several delays, finally the cause was *ventilata*,
moved, and argued, by the justice, writ, and precept
of King William the Elder, sent from Normandy, in
presence of Gosfrid, bishop of Coutance, whom the
king had specially commissioned to see that right was
done between the two litigants. Bishop Gosfrid held
at Worcester a "*magnus conventus*," a great gathering
of the neighbouring counties and barons. After the
opening of the case, the bishop of Worcester sets
out his claim against the abbot. The abbot replies
in defence. Bishop Wlstan produces his list of
witnesses who had cognisance of the matters in the
time of King Edward, and had undertaken the
services above-mentioned for the benefit of the

bishop. Then by precept of the king's justice and decree of the barons, judgment was about to be delivered, but because the abbot had stated that he had no witnesses against the bishop, the court (*optimates*) decreed a day on which the bishop's witnesses should prove on oath the statements which he had made, and the abbot should produce whatever reliques he should think fit (with the object of taking an oath on them that what he alleged was true). This was agreed on both sides.

The day appointed arrived. The bishop and the abbot put in their appearance before the barons who had taken part in the previous hearing of the plea and appointment. Abbot Walter brings the sacred remains of Saint Ecguuine, the founder of his monastery. On the bishop's side appear lawfully competent persons ready to take the required oath. Among them came Edric, who had been, in the time of King Edward the Confessor, the *stermannus*, or pilot of the bishop's ship, and had led the bishop's army in the king's service; now he was *homo* of Rodbert, bishop of Hereford, at the time he took this oath, and held nothing of the bishop of Worcester (therefore he was not an interested or biassed witness). "There was also Kinewardus, sheriff of Worcester, an eyewitness; and Siwardus, a rich lord of Shropshire, and Osbern, son of Richard, and Turchil of Warwickshire, and many others, old men and noble, of whom the greater part now sleep." But many are still alive, the record continues, who heard them, and still many of the time of William the king, testifying the same. "The abbot, when he saw the oath and the proof was all ready, took the advice of his friends, and withdrew his defence, admitted the claim, and came to terms, and made a compact with the bishop; and the knights, *homines*, of St. Mary (of Worcester) and of the bishop, are ready to prove by oath and battle against Rannulf, brother of abbot Walter, who joined his brother in this plea against the bishop, if they wish to deny the compact between the bishop and the abbot."

To this naturally follows in the Worcester Chartulary, the royal charter of King William to V.[1] the sheriff, Osbern, son of Escrop, and all the French and English of Worcestershire, that bishop Wlstan is to have sac and the other privileges, which he successfully claimed (diratiocinavit) against the abbot of Evesham, and if the abbot desired to hold them, he must hold them like others holding of the bishop in fee. This charter is attested by Gosfrid, the bishop who had conducted the trial, and R. de Ivereio.

In another page[2] of this manuscript the text of the above-mentioned compact between bishop Wlstan and abbot Walterius is given at length. From it we gather that "This is the confirmation of the compact made between bishop Wlstan and Walterius, abbot of Evesham, concerning the fifteen hides in Heamtone and four in Bennincuuyrthe: That is, that the abbot admitted, by attestation of all the convent of the church of Worcester, and many of the brethren of Evesham, and Remigius, bishop of Lincoln, and Henry de Fereris, and Walter Giffardus, and Adam, the king's princes, who had come to enquire into the lands of the county

[1] Vrso d' Abitot.   [2] f. 135 b.

, (*i.e.* the commissioners for the Domesday Survey), that these fifteen hides rightly belong to the bishop's hundred of· Osuualdes lauue, and ought, with the bishop himself, to pay the king's *census*, and all other sérvices belonging to the king, &c. And the said four hides in Bennincuuyrthe likewise. But the bishop claimed more than that here, for he claimed the whole land in demesne; yet, because the abbot humbly admitted this, the bishop, at the request of those present, allowed the abbot and brethren of Evesham to hold the land on condition of their making therefor such honourable recognition and service as he himself would if demanded." Of this document the princes above-mentioned are witnesses, and also:—Serlo, abbot of St. Peter's, Gloucester; Nigellus, clerk of bishop Remigius; Ulf, and Rannulf and Alfuuinus, monks of the same; Wlfi, presbyter; Edric de Hindelep; Godric de Piria; Ailric[1] or Algeric, archdeacon of Worcester, and others.

This valuable Cottonian Manuscript also contains an account of the survey of the Liberty of the Hundred of Oswaldslow, taken during the reign of William the Conqueror, upon the oath of the whole shreivalty of Worcester. This proceeding took place before the same four princely Commissioners who conducted the formation of the Domesday Book:—"Remigio scilicet Lincolniense episcopo, et comite Walterio Giffardo, et Henrico de. Fereris, et Adam fratre Eudonis dapiferi regis, qui ad inquirendas et describendas possessiones et consuetudines tam regis quam principum suorum, in hoc provincia et in pluribus aliis ab ipso

[1] Occurs A.D. 1089, 1094. Hardy's Le Neve's "Fasti."

rege destinati sunt, eo tempore quo totam Angliam idem rex describi fecit."

This deed was copied in duplicate, and a copy preserved, *along with the Domesday itself*, in a royal charter:—"In authentica regis cartula . . . . quæ in thesaura regali *cum totius Angliæ descriptionibus* conservatur." The names of the jurors on the bishop's behalf include Reoland, Trokemardtune, Adam de Lent, and Normannus the pincerna, or steward of the bishop; on behalf of the prior, William de Rupe, Rodbert le Parler, Richard de Grimelei. A large number of important witnesses attest the deed.

The copy which this MS. contains of the Domesday for the lands belonging to the See of Worcester:— "Descriptio Terræ Episcopatus Wigornensis ecclesie secundum cartam regis quæ est in Thesauro Re[gis]," differs in diction, phraseology, and other particulars from that in the Domesday Book itself. It should be collated for any future edition of the Domesday of Worcestershire. It is preceded by a copy of King Henry I.'s charter to Walter de Bellocampo and "Coll Wirecestresire" to charge the Worcestershire lands of the bishop of Worcester with geld only for three hundred four score and seven and a half hides.

Among smaller miscellaneous notes of historical interest found in the Domesday Book are the journey of William the Conqueror into Wales in A.D. 1079; William Rufus is noticed as having usurped land at Staplebrige, county Dorset, from the See of Salisbury. The manor of Teuuinge, or Tewyn, county Hertford, was given by William to Aldene and his

x

mother for the soul of his son, Prince Richard·;[1] and Gosfridus, the chamberlain of Mathildis, or Maud, his ·daughter, held land·at·Heche in Hampshire,·for which he did service to·that·princess. .Ellis notices also the .royal purchase of a ship from Vlchel for a carucate of .land in Lincolnshire, "but he who 'sold the ship is dead,·and no one has the land except by 'the king's ,grant." The land had evidently reverted to thè Crown.

. The valuable MS. preserved in the Library of the Dean and Chapter of Rochester, known ·as the "Textus Roffensis" contains[2] a survey .of the possession of the bishop and see which may be com- pared·with the entries·relating to the same property in the Domesday Book. .William the Conqueror was a considerable benefactor to this cathedral. ' At the point of death[3] he bestowed on it a hundred pounds, a·royal tunic, his own ivory horn, a *dorsale*, and a *feretrum* or pix, of silvered work. His grant of the Manor of Lamhytha, or Lambeth (afterwards acquired in exchange from the See of Rochester by the arch- bishop of Canterbury,·formerly held by Goda the countess), was made "·pro salute animæ meæ patris mei et omnium parentum meorum et pro restauratione damni quod eidem ecclesiæ licet invitus intuli, pro· conquirendis inimicis·meis qui intra jam·dictam civitatem contra me et contra regnum meum injuste congregati· erant, de quibus omnipotens Deus sui gracia victoriam michi contulit." " For the safety of my soul, and of my father's and of all my relations',

---

[1] " And Aldene showed the King's Charter " to the Commis- sioners, by which it is clear that titles; at·least in some in- stances, were inquired into.

[2] Edited by Hearne, 1720, p. 209.   [3] Ibid. p. 211.

and as a recompense for the loss which, although unwilling, I inflicted on that same church, in order to overcome my enemies who were unlawfully gathered together within the said city against me and against my realm, over whom God Almighty by His grace conferred on me the victory."

The tenures of the Norman companions of the Conqueror were naturally of immense proportions throughout the realm, and they sufficiently indicate the liberality with which the king had rewarded the co-operation with him in his successful endeavour to obtain possession of the kingdom. Some of the principal Norman personages have been mentioned in the following list, derived from Ellis's "Index of Tenants in Capite," and Dugdale's "Baronage." This I have supplemented with an account of the chief foreign monasteries holding possession in England, generally also gifts from William or his nobles. It is curious that some of the largest and most splendid French monasteries were erected at the cost of the Norman barons, within a very short time after the Conquest. These large landed donations to foreign religious houses created great discontent in England. They were managed by a system established in England of "cells," subordinate houses, or "alien priories," under command of the chief house abroad; their produce was popularly exaggerated; and after frequent seizure into the hands of the Crown when war was declared between the two countries, they were finally suppressed, and this, perhaps, as Ellis conjectures, formed a precedent for the dissolution of all monasteries by Henry VIII.

. As a large instance of a foreign tenant-in-chief, we may select the case of Robert, earl of Moretaine, half-brother to King William, who held the following manors :—

Sussex ...	... 54	and Pevensey Borough.
Devonshire	... 75	and a church and house in Exeter.
Yorkshire...	 196	
Wiltshire ...	... 5	
Dorsetshire	... 49	
Suffolk ...	... 10	
Hampshire	... 1	
Middlesex	... 5	
Oxfordshire	... 1	
Cambridgeshire ...	5	
Hertfordshire	... 13	
Buckinghamshire	29	
Gloucestershire ...	1	
Northamptonshire	99	
Nottinghamshire ...	6	
Cornwall ...	... 248	and the castles of Dunhevet and Tremeton.

Among the principal foreign[1] companions of the Conqueror are the following :—

. Roger de Montgomery, earl of Arundel and Shrewsbury, held 157 manors, the city of Chichester, the castle of Arundel, nearly all the county of Salop, besides the city of Shrewsbury.

. Hugh de Abrincis, earl of Chester, A.D. 1070, held 124 manors, besides a large part of Cheshire.

[1] The four foreign bishops have been mentioned in the account of the Church. Chapter xii.

Alan, earl of Brittany and Richmond, who commanded the rear-guard of William the Conqueror's forces at Hastings, held 435 manors, chiefly in Richmondshire, North Riding of Yorkshire, and ten burgesses in Cambridge town.

Walter Giffard, earl of Buckingham, held 107 manors.

Odo, earl of Champaigne, and in the English peerage earl of Albemarle and Holderness, held a large number of manors in Suffolk.

William de Warren, earl of Warren in Normandy, and of Surrey[1] in England, held about 228 manors and lordships.

We find also :—

FOREIGN TENANTS OF LANDS IN CAPITE IN ENGLAND.

Urso de Abitot, sheriff of Worcestershire.
Adeliz, wife of Hugh de Grentemaisnil.
Norman de Adreci.
Walterius de Aincurt.
Adeliza, countess of Albemarle, half-sister of
   William the Conqueror.
Robert de Albemarle.
Earl Albericus.
Nigel de Albingi, or Albini.
Goisfred Alselin.
Alured of Spain.
David de Argentomago.
Azelina, wife of Ralph Tailgebosch.

---

[1] "Et qui (Will. I.) me Comitem Surreiæ fecit." Charter in Dugd. "Mon. Angl." vol. i., p. 616 (first edit).

Baldwin, the sheriff of Devonshire, son of Gilbert, earl of Brion, and one of the king's generals.

Hugh de Belcamp.

Ralph de Bellofago.

Drogo de Bevraria, a Fleming.

Herveus Bituricensis.

Hugo de Bolebec.

Ida, countess of Boulogne.

Roger de Boscnorman.

William de Braiosa.

Gislebert de Bretevile.

Rainer de Brimov.

Serlo de Burci.

Ernegis de Burun.

Roger de Busli.

William de Cahainges.

Gunfrid de Cioches.

Sigar de Cioches.

Roger de Corcelles, or Cvrcelles.

Ansfrid, and Gozelin de Cormeliis.

Richard de Curci.

William de Dalmari.

Robert Dispensator.

Drogo filius Ponz.

William, earl of Evreux.

Edward of Salisbury, sheriff of Wiltshire, son of the earl of Rosmar.

Eudo Dapifer, son of Hubert.

Eustace, earl of Boulogne.

William de Faleise.

Ralph de Felgeres.

Henry de Ferieres or Ferrariis.
Walter Flandrensis.
Gislebert de Gand.
Robert Gernon.
Osbern and Walter Gifard.
Hugh de Grentemaisnil.
Hugh de Gurnai.
Hamo Dapifer, sheriff of Kent.
Ernulf de Hesding.
Hunfrid the chamberlain.
Richard de Ingania.
Judita, the countess, wife of Waltheof.
Roger de Iveri.
Ilbert and Roger de Laci.
Hugo Lasne, or Asinus.
Ralph de Limesei.
William Loveth or Lovet.
Durand, and Robert Malet.
Gislebert Maminot.
Goisfrid de Mannevile.
The earl of Mellent.
William de Moion.
Hubert de Montecanisio, or Monchensy.
Hugh de Montfort.
Robert, earl of Moretaine.
Ralph de Mortemer.
Nigel Medicus.
William de Odburvile.
Robert de Oilgi.
Osbern, filius Ricardi.
Roger de Otburvilla.
Robert, earl of Ow, or Eu.

William de Ow, or Eu.
Ralph Pagenel.
William de Perci.
William and Rannulf Peverel.
Roger of Poictou, Pictaviensis.
Ralph de Pomerei.
Hugo de Porth.
Ralph, filius Huberti.
Rainald, filius Ivonis.
Rannulf, filius Ilgeri.
Wido de Reinbuedcurt.
Richard of Tonebrige, son of earl Gislebert.
Robert, filius Corbutionis.
Hugh de St. Quintin.
Galter de St. Walery.
Harduin de Scalers.
William de Scohies.
Richard de Surdeual.
Berengarius, and Ralph, and Robert de Todenci.
Turstin, filius Rolf.
Peter de Valognes.
Robert de Veci.
Alberic de Ver.
Bertrannus de Verdun.
The wife of Geri de Loges.
The wife of Hugh de Grentemaisnil.
The wife of Richard, filius Gisleberti.
Walter de S. Waleri.
William, filius Ansculfi.
Goisfridus de Wirce or Lawirce, and many others

Foreign Monasteries holding Lands in England.

The Abbey of St. Ouen in Caen.
The Canons of Bayeux.
The Abbey of Bec in Normandy.
The Abbey of Bernay.
The Abbey of St. Stephen, Caen.
The Nunnery of Holy Trinity, Caen.
The Canon of Coutance.
The Canon of Lisieux.
The Abbey of Cormeilles.
The Abbey of St. Denys, near Paris.
The Abbey of St. Evroul.
The Abbey of Fécamp.
The Abbey of St. Peter at Ghent.
The Abbey of Jumieges.
The Abbey of Grestain.
The Abbey of Holy Cross at St. Leufroy, in the
    diocese of Evreux.
The Canons of Lisieux.
The Abbey of Lyra, or Lira.
The Abbey of Monteburg.
The Abbey of Preaux, or de Pratellis.
The Cathedral Church of Rheims.
The Abbeys of Holy Trinity of St. Ouen and of
    St. Mary de Pre, Rouen.
The Monastery of St. Florence, Saumur.
The Abbey of St. Peter-sur-Dive.
The Abbey of Troarz, or Trouarn, in the diocese
    of Bayeux.

The Abbey of St. Vallery in Picardy.
The Abbey of Vaüdrille or Fontenelle.
The Monastery of Villarium.

Many of the original charters of the king and others granting English lands to these monasteries are still extant in the British Museum and other collections.

Ancient manners and customs may be richly illustrated from the casual entries which are found in the Domesday Book.. Among others, the gift by a man of his two daughters to Wilton Nunnery, along with his land; the grant by a tenant of his land to the Abbey of Malmesbury when he became a monk there; the continuation of the old Anglo-Saxon custom of granting land for the term of three lives; the *judicium*, ordeal, and the *bellum*, duel. Land appears to be held " in dower " occasionally, and " in marriage." The nuncupative will or death-bed bequest is found in the Worcester Survey; the method of giving seisin of land to the church by placing the charter or a copy of the Gospels on the altar; rent of liquor to be drunk at festivals; the sport of hawking; the maintenance of aeries, or breeding and training places of hawks, in Bucking-hamshire, Cheshire, and other western counties; the forfeiture of land by a widow if she remarried within a year after her husband's death; and evidences of the marriage of the clergy, are among the most noticeable of these miscellaneous references with which the text of the Domesday Book is replenished.

CHAPTER XV.

LITERATURE. — ILLUSTRATIVE MANUSCRIPTS AND PRINTED WORKS.

WE may begin the notice of the literature, which may be not inaptly termed the Domesday Cycle, with a short account of the publication of the Survey itself. In the year 1767 royal orders were given for the publication of this among other records. The next year specimens, one executed with type, the other by engraving, were prepared and submitted to the Society of Antiquaries for their opinion ; at first the engraved specimen found most favour, but ultimately it was decided to print the book with metal types cast in facsimile from the best style of handwriting in the manuscript ; the printing was sanctioned and the work commenced in the year 1770, and was finished in 1783, having been ten years passing through the press. The type was destroyed accidentally by fire in the year 1808. The work was published, under the editorship of A. Farley, in the form of two large folios, uniform with the other publications of the Record Commissioners. Vol. 3, containing a series of indexes of persons, places, and subjects, was printed in 1816, and in the same year the fourth volume of "Additamenta," embracing the "Exon Domesday," the "Inquisitio Eliensis," the "Boldon

Book," and the "Winton Domesday," with their proper indexes, was also issued. These two volumes were edited by Sir Henry Ellis.

The preparation of a full bibliography of Domesday Book, including notices of all the early MSS. which contain extracts or abstracts, printed works, separate papers, essays, Norman charters, and other notices, would be the first step towards the simplification of the critical study of the Survey. This will form one of the sections of the work to which some Domesday students are about to give their attention. A few, however, of these MSS. and books may be appropriately mentioned here in a popular and general work on the subject, such as this is.

Among the general literature of the subject are the following works :—

The "Photo-zincographed Facsimile of the Domesday Book," prepared by command of Her Majesty at the Ordnance Survey Office, Southampton, Colonel Sir Henry James, director, 35 parts, 1861–1863, folio and 4to.

Philip Carteret Webb: "A Short Account of some particulars concerning Domesday Book," London, 1756, 4to. This work contains a list of parts of Domesday already in print, &c.

P. C. Webb: "A Short Account of Danegeld," 1756.

R. Kelham: "Domesday Book Illustrated," London, 1788, 8vo.

J. Nichols: "Dissertation on Domesday Book" in the "History of the County of Leicester," vol. i. part I., page 33, 1795, folio.

E. A. Freeman: "History of the Norman Conquest," vol. v., 1876.

Rev. R. W. Eyton: "Notes on Domesday," in Transactions of the Shropshire Archæological Society, 1877, 8vo.

. W. de G. Birch: "The Domesday Book," in Journal British Archæological Association, vol. xli., 1885.

J. Burtt: "On a Reproduction of a Portion of the Domesday Book by the Photo-zincographic Process," Archæological Journal, vol. xviii., page 128. See also Archæological Journal, vol. vi. page 303; vii. 215.

Grose: "Antiquities of England and Wales," vol. i., page 78, 1773.

R. Brady: "An Introduction," &c., 1684, folio.

Léchaudé D'Anisy: "Recherches sur le Domesday," 1842, 4to.

Rev. S. Denne: In "Archæologia," vol..viii., 1787.

J. H. Walker: "Churches in the Domesday Book," in *Gentleman's Magazine*, vol. xix.

G. Hickes: "Thesaurus," vol. i., 1705. "Grammatica Anglo-Saxonica," page 144.

O. C. Pell, Papers in the Roy. Hist. Soc. Trans, 1887; and Cambridge Ant. Soc., 1887.

. Among the papers recently read before the Domesday Commemoration of the year 1886, inaugurated by the Royal Historical Society, or later, which will be published during the present year, are the following :—

Mr. Hubert Hall: "On the History of the Domesday Book."

Rev. Canon Isaac Taylor, M.A.: 1. A Popular

Lecture; 2. "Domesday Wapentakes and Land Measures."

Mr. S. A. Moore, F.S.A.: "The Statistics of Domesday Book."

Mr. J. H. Round, M.A.: "The Danegeld."

Mr. J. Parker, M.A.: "The Church in Domesday."

Mr. W. de G. Birch, F.S.A.: The Materials for Re-editing Domesday Book."

- Mr. H. E. Malden, M.A.: "The Surrey Domesday Book."

Mr. F. E. Sawyer, F.S.A.: "The Sussex Domesday Book."

Mr. H. J. Reid, F.S.A.; "The Parish Church in Domesday."

Mr. O. C. Pell, M.A.: "A New View of the Geldable Unit of Assessment of Domesday: the Libra, Hida, Carucata, &c."

The literature especially illustrative of single counties, or small groups of two or more counties, embraces, in addition to many extracts, translations, and notices contained in the histories of the respective counties, the following works, which the student of Domesday will find of use, and in many cases necessary to be consulted :—

1. KENT :—

The Canterbury Cathedral MS., E. 28, The Cottonain MS. "Vitellius," C. viii. "Domesday Monachorum."

The "Textus Roffensis," MS. of the Dean
and Chapter of Rochester, Ed. Hearne,
1720.

Rev. L. B. Larking: "The Domesday Book
of Kent," London, 1869, folio.

S. Henshall and J. Wilkinson: "Domesday,"
&c., London, 1769, 4to.

Elton: "Tenures of Kent."

2. SUSSEX :—

Rev. W. D. Parish: "Domesday Book in
relation to the County of Sussex," Lewes,
1886, folio.

S. Henshall, &c. (see above under KENT).

3. SURREY :—

H. Moody: "Extension."

S. Henshall, &c. (see above under KENT).

4. HAMPSHIRE :—

The Winton Domesday MS., Soc. Antiq., 154.
Surveys of A.D. 1107 and A.D. 1148.

R. Warner: "H. extracted from the Domesday Book," London, 1789, 4to.

H. Moody: "Extension."

5. BERKSHIRE:—Mr. H. J. Reid, F.S.A., is now
preparing the Domesday Book for this county.

6. WILTSHIRE :—

The "Exon Domesday," in vol. iv. of the
Record Edition of the Domesday Book;
edited by Sir H. Ellis.

H. P. Wyndham: "W. Extracted from the Domesday Book," Salisbury, 1788, 8vo.

Rev. W. H. Jones: "D. for Wiltshire," Bath, 1865, 4to (a work of considerable research).

7. DORSETSHIRE :—

The "Exon Domesday."

Rev. W. Eyton: "A Key to D.," &c., London, 1874, 4to.

J. Hutchins' "History of Dorset."

8. SOMERSETSHIRE :—

The "Exon Domesday."

Rev. R. W. Eyton: "Domesday Studies," &c., London, 1884, 4to.

9. DEVONSHIRE :—

The "Exon Domesday."

The "D. Domesday," published by the Devonshire Association for the Advancement of Science, Plymouth, 1884, 8vo. In progress.

10. CORNWALL :—

The "Exon Domesday."

"Extension" of the Domesday Book.

11. MIDDLESEX :—

'The "St. Paul's Domesday," MS. of the Dean and Chapter of St. Paul's. Liber L., A.D. 1181. Edit. W. H. Hale (Camden Society).

H. Moody: "Extension."

Rev. W. Bawdwen: "Domesday Boc," Doncaster, 1812, 4to.

Gen. P. Harrison, 1876, folio.

12. HERTFORDSHIRE :—

Rev. W. Bawdwen (see above under MIDDLE-SEX).

13. BUCKINGHAMSHIRE :—

Rev. W. Bawdwen (see above under MIDDLE-SEX).

14. OXFORDSHIRE :—

Rev. W. Bawdwen (see above under MIDDLE-SEX).

15. GLOUCESTERSHIRE :—

The "Gloucestershire Fragment," Domesday Commemoration.

Rev. W. Bawdwen (see above under MIDDLESEX).

Alf. S. Ellis, in "Transactions Bristol and Gloucester Archæological Society," 1880, vol. iv.

C. S. Taylor, "An Analysis of the Domesday Survey, *ibid.*, 1887.

16. WORCESTERSHIRE :—

The Cottonian MS. "Tiberius," A. XIII. (Heming). Edit. Hearne.

The Cottonian MS. "Vespasian," B. XXIV. (Evesham).

W. B. Sanders: "A Literal Extension," &c., Worcester, 1864, folio.

17. HEREFORDSHIRE :—

18. CAMBRIDGESHIRE :—

The Cottonian MS. "Tiberius," A. VI. Edited

by N. E. S. A. Hamilton as "Inquisitio Comitatus Cantabrigiensis."

Rev. B. Walker: "On the Measurements and Valuations of Domesday Book," Cambridge Antiquarian Society, 1881, 1884.

Rev. B. Walker: "On the Inquis. Com. Cantab.," *ibid.*, 1887.

19. HUNTINGDONSHIRE :—

Rob. Ellis: "Extension," 1864.

20. BEDFORDSHIRE :—

W. Airy: "Digest of the D. of Bedfordshire," Bedford, 1881, folio.

21. NORTHAMPTONSHIRE :—

The "Liber Niger" of Peterborough MS. Soc. Antiq. 60; A.D. 1125.

J. Morton: "The Natural History of Northamptonshire," London, 1712, folio.

S. A. Moore: "Extension."

22. LEICESTERSHIRE :—

J. Nichols: in "History of the County of Leicester," vol. i., part I., page 1, 1795, folio.

23. WARWICKSHIRE :—

W. Reader: "Domesday Book for the County of Warwickshire," Coventry, 1835, 4to.

E. P. Shirley: "Extension."

C. Twamley: "Archæological Journal," vol. xxi., page 373, 1864.

24. STAFFORDSHIRE :—

Rev. R. W. Eyton: "Domesday Studies,"
&c., 1861.

25. SHROPSHIRE :—

26. CHESHIRE (and LANCASHIRE) :—

Sir P. Leycester: "Historical Antiquities,"
London, 1673, folio.
W. Beamont: "Literal Extension," &c., 2nd
edition, Chester, 1882, folio.
Ormerod : "Miscellanea Palatina," 1851, 8vo.
See also "Archæological Journal," vol. xvii.,
page 104. .

27. DERBYSHIRE :—

Ll. Jewitt: "Extension."
Rev. W. Bawdwen (see below under YORK-
SHIRE).
J. P. Yeatman.

28. NOTTINGHAMSHIRE :—

Rev. W. Bawdwen (see below under YORK-
SHIRE).
W. H. Stevenson: "The Domesday Survey
of Nottinghamshire and Rutlandshire" (in
progress).

29. RUTLANDSHIRE :—

Rev. W. Bawdwen (see below under YORK-
SHIRE).
C. G. Smith (see below under LINCOLNSHIRE).

30. YORKSHIRE :—

"The Register of the Honour of Richmond,"
(1) MS. at Castle Howard belonging to
Mr. G. Howard; and (2) Cottonian MS.
"Faustina," B. VII.

"Transcripts from the Domesday Book,"
printed at London in 1722, folio.

Rev. W. Bawdwen: "Domesday Book," Doncaster, 1809, 4to.

31. LINCOLNSHIRE :—

"The Lincolnshire Survey," A.D. 1101–9;
Cottonian MS. "Claudius," C. v. Edit.
J. Greenstreet.

Rev. W. Bawdwen (see above under YORK
SHIRE).

C. Gowen Smith: "A Translation," &c.,
London, 1871, 8vo.

32. ESSEX :—

T. C. Chisenhale-Marsh : "Domesday Book
relating to Essex," Chelmsford, 1864, 4to.

33. NORFOLK :— -

Rev. G. Munford: "Analysis," &c., 1858, 8vo.

34. SUFFOLK :—

35. DURHAM :—

"The Boldon Book," British Museum, Stowe
M.S. 510.

"The Boldon Book," Edit. Ellis in Domesday
Book, vol. iv.

LIST OF DOMESDAY ABBREVIATIONS AND CONTRACTIONS. *p. 46 see Such*

The contractions used by the scribes who wrote out the fair copy of the Domesday Book are very numerous, but to those who are well acquainted with mediæval Latin they offer hardly any difficulty. By way of assisting those who desire to read the original contracted text, a few of the principal abbreviations and contractions most commonly occurring are here subjoined :—

teñ = tenet.

ep̄s, ep̄i, ep̄o, &c., = episcopus, and cases.

p̣ = per.

ꝑ = pro.

p̃ = præ—, as p̃dc̃o = prædicto

t̃ra, t̃re, &c., = terra, and cases.

7 or & = et.

ꝰ at end of a word = —us.

— a line over a vowel adds to it the letter *m*, as cū = cum.

m° = modo.

caŕ = caruca, sometimes carucata.

defđ = defendit.

dñium, &c., = dominium, &c.

ⁱ over or between letter adds *ui*, as qⁱdā = quidam, or *ri*, as pⁱmo = primo.

T. R. E. = tempore regis Edwardi.

tot̃ = totum.

sot̃ = solidi, &c. *(Shillings)*

ē = est.

s̃t = sunt.

lib̃ = libræ, &c.

uiłłi, &c., = villani, &c.

 ~ a curved line over or through letters adds *er*,
as osbn^9 = osbernus; or *ur*, as pasťa = pastura; or *mn*, as ões = omnes.

M̄ = Manerium.

borđ = bordarii, &c.

dim̃ = dimidius, &c.

deñ = denarii, &c.

^{a} over line adds *ra*, as ac^a = acra, &c.; p^{a}tū =
pratum.

fuer̃ = fuerunt, tenuer̃ = tenuerunt, &c.

ñ = non.

iđ, eađ, &c., = idem, eadem, &c.

s$_3$ = set, for sed; val$_3$ = valet, &c.; ten$_3$ =
tenet.

—b$_3$ at end of words = —bus.

—a$_3$, —o$_3$ at end of word = —arum, —orum.

socħi, &c., = sochemanni, &c.

qđ = quod.

dñs, dñi, &c., = dominus, domini, &c.

sēp = semper.

uirg̃ = virgata.

ħ = hida, &c.

o = ovis, oves, &c.

p. = porcus, &c.

c̃ = caruca.

abƀ = abbas, &c.

3 between letters adds —er, as manȝium, = manerium; tȝra = terra.

nicħ = nichil, nihil.

com̃ = comes.

dñ = denarii, &c.

nⁱ = nisi.

ħ = hic, hæc, hoc.

hō = homo; hōēs = homines.

—ƀ at end of words = —bat, —bant,

qđo, qñ = quando.

qᵒqȝ =quoque.

uᵒ = vero.

hñt = habent; hũit = habuit; ħt = habet.

q̃ = qui, quæ, &c.

reg̃ = regis, &c.

hunđ = hundretum, &c.

inueñ = inveniebat.

ł = vel.

posſ̃ = possunt.

ṽ = virgata, &c.

refic̃ = reficiendus, &c.

æccła, &c., = æcclesia, &c.

ſ̃ = sanctus, &c.

qᵃȝ = quarentena, quarum.

leṽ = leuga.

lg̃ = longitudo, &c.

lat̃ = latitudo, &c.

The diphthong æ is generally written as an e, with
a cedilla below it.

The other abbreviated and contracted words may

be easily read with a little practice. Full lists of contracted words may be consulted in the works of Walther, Chassant, Hardy's "Registrum Dunelmense" in the Rolls Series, and the "Introduction" to the Close Rolls, published by the Record Commissioners.

THE END.

WYMAN AND SONS, PRINTERS, GREAT QUEEN STREET, LONDON, W.C.

By the Rev. F. Bourdillon, M.A.

				s.	d.
BEDSIDE READINGS.	SERIES I. 12mo....	*Cloth boards*		1	4
Ditto	SERIES II.	ditto		1.	4
The two Series in a volume		ditto		2	0

THE WEEK OF MOURNING; or, SHORT AND SIMPLE
EXPOSITIONS OF SCRIPTURE, FOR THE USE OF THE
BEREAVED ... ... *Cloth* 0 10

ALONE WITH GOD; or, HELPS TO THOUGHT AND
PRAYER, FOR THE USE OF THE SICK; BASED ON
SHORT PASSAGES OF SCRIPTURE ... *Cloth boards* 1 0

LESSER LIGHTS.	SERIES I. Post 8vo.	*Cloth boards*	2	6
Ditto	SERIES II.	ditto	2	6

A QUIET VISITOR. A BOOK FOR LYING-IN WOMEN.
Post 8vo. ... ... *Cloth boards* 0 10

OUR OWN BOOK. VERY PLAIN READING FOR PEOPLE
IN HUMBLE LIFE. Post 8vo. ... *Cloth boards* 1 0

VOLUME OF TRACTS.	SERIES I. ...	*Cloth boards*	1	6
Ditto ditto··	SERIES II. ...	*(large type)*		
		Cloth boards	1	6

L

PUBLICATIONS

OF THE

Society for Promoting Christian Knowledge.

	s.	d.

Aids to Prayer.
By the Rev. DANIEL MOORE. Printed in red and black. Post 8vo. .... *Cloth boards* 1 6

Being of God, Six Addresses on the.
By C. J. ELLICOTT, D.D., Bishop of Gloucester and Bristol. Small post 8vo. .... *Cloth boards* 1 6

Bible Places; or, The Topography of the Holy Land.
By the Rev. Canon TRISTRAM. With Map and numerous Woodcuts. Crown 8vo. .... *Cloth boards* 4 0

Called to be Saints.
The Minor Festivals Devotionally Studied. By CHRSITINA G. ROSSETTI, Author of "Seek and Find." Post 8vo. .... *Cloth boards* 5 0

Case for "Establishment" stated (The).
By the Rev. T. MOORE, M.A. Post 8vo....*Paper boards* 0 6

Christians under the Crescent in Asia.
By the Rev. E. L. CUTTS, B.A., Author of "Turning-Points of Church History," &c. With numerous Illustrations. Crown 8vo. .... *Cloth boards* 5 0

Daily Readings for a Year.
By ELIZABETH SPOONER. Crown 8vo....*Cloth boards* 3 6

Devotional (A) Life of Our Lord.
By the Rev. E. L. CUTTS, B.A., author of "Pastoral Counsels," &c. Post 8vo. ....*Cloth boards* 5 0

s. d.

Gospels, The Four.

Arranged in the Form of an English Harmony, from the Text of the Authorised Version. By the Rev. J. M. FULLER, M.A. With Analytical Table of Contents and Four Maps. ....*Cloth boards* 1 6

Land of Israel, The.

A Journal of Travel in Palestine, undertaken with special reference to its Physical Character. By the Rev. Canon TRISTRAM. With two Maps and numerous Illustrations. Large post 8vo. .... *Cloth boards* 10 6

Lectures on the Historical and Dogmatical Position of the Church of England.

By the Rev. W. BAKER, D.D. Post 8vo. *Cloth boards* 1 6

Paley's Evidences.

A New Edition, with Notes, Appendix, and Preface. By the Rev. E. A. LITTON. Post 8vo. *Cloth boards* 4 0

Paley's Horæ Paulinæ.

A New Edition, with Notes, Appendix, and Preface. By the Rev. J. S. HOWSON, D.D., Dean of Chester. Post 8vo. ....*Cloth boards* 3 0

Peace with God.

A manual for the Sick. By the Rev. E. BURBIDGE, M.A. Post 8vo. 1 6

"Perfecting Holiness."

By the Rev. E. L. CUTTS, B.A. Post 8vo. *Cloth boards* 2 6

Plain Words for Christ.

Being a Series of Readings for Working Men. By the late Rev. R. G. DUTTON. Post 8vo. ......*Cloth boards* 1 0

Prayer Book (History of the).

By Miss PEARD, Author of "One Year." *Cloth boards* 1 0

Readings on the First Lessons for Sundays and Chief Holy Days.

According to the New Table. By the Rev. PETER YOUNG. Crown 8vo. ....*In two volumes* 6 0

Religion for Every Day.

Lectures for Men. By the Right Rev. A. BARRY, D.D., Bishop of Sydney. Fcap. 8vo..............*Cloth boards* 1 0

Scenes in the East.   *s. d.*
Consisting of Twelve Coloured Photographic Views of
Places mentioned in the Bible, beautifully executed,
with Descriptive Letterpress. By the Rev. Canon
TRISTRAM................*Cloth, bevelled boards, gilt edges*   6   0

Seek and Find.
A Double Series of Short Studies of the Benedicite.
By CHRISTINA G. ROSETTI. Post 8vo. *Cloth Boards*   2   6

Servants of Scripture, The.
By the Rev. JOHN W. BURGON, B.D. Post 8vo. *Cl. bds.*   1   6

Sinai and Jerusalem : or Scenes from Bible Lands.
Consisting of Coloured Photographic Views of Places
mentioned in the Bible, including a Panoramic View
of Jerusalem, with descriptive Letterpress. By the
Rev. F. W. HOLLAND, M.A. Demy 4to.
                  Cloth, bevelled boards, gilt edges   6   0

Some Chief Truths of Religion.
By the Rev. EDWARD L. CUTTS, B.A., Author of
"St. Cedd's Cross," &c. Crown 8vo. *Cloth boards*   2   6

Thoughts for Men and Women.
THE LORD'S PRAYER. By Emily C. ORR. Post 8vo.
.... *Limp cloth*   1   0

Thoughts for Working Days.
Original and Selected. By Emily C. ORR. Post 8vo.
                             Limp cloth   1   0

Time Flies ; a Reading Diary.
By CHRISTINA G. ROSETTI. Post 8vo. *Cloth boards*   2   6

True Vine (The).
By the author of " The Schönberg-Cotta Family." &c.
Printed in red and black   Post 8vo.......*Cloth boards.*   1   6

Turning-Points of English Church History.
By the Rev. EDWARD L. CUTTS, B.A., Vicar of Holy
Trinity, Haverstock Hill. Crown 8vo. *Cloth boards*   3   6

Turning-Points of General Church History.
By the Rev. E. L. CUTTS, B.A., Author of " Pastoral
Counsels," &c. Crown 8vo...................*Cloth boards*   5   0

LONDON:

NORTHUMBERLAND AVENUE, CHARING CROSS, W.C.
43, QUEEN VICTORIA STREET, E.C.
BRIGHTON: 135, NORTH STREET.

Lightning Source UK Ltd.
Milton Keynes UK
UKHW021829050519
342158UK00003B/50/P

9 781361 943045